Good Practice in Adult Mental Health

Good Practice Series

Edited by Jacki Pritchard

This series explores topics of current concern to professionals working in social work, health care and the probation service. Contributors are drawn from a wide variety of settings, in both the voluntary and statutory sectors.

of related interest

Good Practice with Vulnerable Adults
Edited by Jacki Pritchard
ISBN 1 85302 982 3
Good Practice Series 9

Good Practice in Risk Assessment and Risk Management 1
Edited by Hazel Kemshall and Jacki Pritchard
ISBN 1 85302 338 8
Good Practice Series 3

Good Practice in Risk Assessment and Risk Management 2
Protection, Rights and Responsibilities
Edited by Hazel Kemshall and Jacki Pritchard
ISBN 1 85302 441 4
Good Practice Series 5

Good Practice in Working with Violence
Edited by Hazel Kemshall and Jacki Pritchard
ISBN 1 85302 641 7
Good Practice Series 6

Good Practice in Working with Victims of Violence
Edited by Hazel Kemshall and Jacki Pritchard
ISBN 1 85302 768 5
Good Practice Series 8

Good Practice in Supervision
Statutory and Voluntary Organisations
Edited by Jacki Pritchard
ISBN 1 85302 279 9
Good Practice Series 2

Good Practice in Counselling People Who Have Been Abused
Edited by Zetta Bear
ISBN 1 85302 424 4
Good Practice Series 4

Good Practice in Social Work 10

Good Practice in Adult Mental Health

Edited by
Tony Ryan and Jacki Pritchard

Jessica Kingsley Publishers
London and Philadelphia

First published in 2004
by Jessica Kingsley Publishers
116 Pentonville Road
London N1 9JB, UK
and
400 Market Street, Suite 400
Philadelphia, PA 19106, USA

www.jkp.com

Library of Congress Cataloging in Publication Data
Good practice in adult mental health / edited by Tony Ryan and Jacki Pritchard.-- 1st
    American pbk. ed.
        p. cm. -- (Good practice in social work ; 10)
    Includes bibliographical references and index.
    ISBN 1-84310-217-X (pbk.)
    1. Mental health. 2. Mental illness--Prevention. 3. Mentally ill--Services for--Great
Britain. 4. Psychiatric social work--Great Britain. I. Ryan, Tony, 1958- II. Pritchard, Jacki. III.
Series.

    RA790.G59 2004
    362.2--dc22

                                                                      2004005660

British Library Cataloguing in Publication Data
A CIP catalogue record for this book is available from the British Library

ISBN-13: 978 1 84310 217 5
ISBN-10: 1 84310 217 X

Printed and Bound in Great Britain by
Athenaeum Press, Gateshead, Tyne and Wear

For our sons:
Kieran Ryan
Nathan Pritchard

CONTENTS

List of Figures

List of Tables

PREFACE

Mental illness affects one in three people in their lifetime and as such is a major area of health and social care provision. Given the prevalence, and the limited resources available to support people with mental health needs and their carers, a wide range of individuals, professionals and agencies come into contact and provide support to people from all strata of society. There is a variety of mental illnesses and disorders, some of which carry more stigma than others. Consequently, there is an array of interventions and responses available to effectively support people with mental health needs. Because of the complexity of the range of illnesses and their effects, the knowledge needed to support people may be varied. It is not just specialist mental health professionals who come into contact with people with mental health needs but also a wide range of other health and social care personnel, including employment support workers, housing workers, probation staff, care workers in residential homes, domiciliary care workers and staff working in street agencies.

It is for the above reasons that we decided to edit this book. It is intended to be read by mental health professionals with experience in the field through to workers across all sectors who may be required to recognise a mental health need or problem and to provide some form of support. The book is also intended to provide such readers with a better insight into the mental health system in order to help people they are working with access specialist services and support. It will also be beneficial to anyone who has little or no experience in mental health but who is considering a career in this area.

Our objective in bringing together this collection is to provide guidance on good practice in adult mental health. In order to do this a wide range of issues need to be understood; these include theory, practice, law, politics and the personal experiences of service users and carers. To achieve this we felt it was vital to demonstrate the human nature and impact of mental ill health. Contributors have achieved this by

11

using case studies based on their experiences of either working in the field or being a service user or carer.

The book is designed in such a way that the reader or trainer can dip in and out of sections as best meets their needs. A variety of materials are included: case studies, vignettes, questions for group discussion, good practice points and facts. Contributors have included further reading materials and useful organisations. A glossary is also provided at the end of the book, which although not exhaustive, covers all the key terms used in the book.

The field of mental health and illness has changed dramatically over the past fifty years; it is dynamic and constantly evolving as we learn more about how best to support people with mental health needs. The closure of old Victorian asylums and an emphasis on community-based support and treatment has brought a greater awareness and understanding of mental health and illness. Society's attitude is changing but still has some way to go. Attitudes have changed because people have become more enlightened through education, training and personal experience. This book is an attempt to continue that trend by educating people who are sympathetic to the issues surrounding mental health and who are in a position to then raise awareness amongst others – be that in their work role or their wider social role.

The book has been constructed in a way that takes the reader through the history and theory of mental illness, the legal and policy frameworks as applied to current practice, and then describes a number of interventions and methods of delivery across different groups of service users. Although mental health and illness is a very complex area, and we have by no means covered all aspects, this text brings together many of the current key issues that are relevant to professionals working in the field and to anyone else who has an interest.

We hope readers of this text will be enlightened and inspired in a way that helps them to work more effectively with those people with whom they come into contact who have mental health needs.

Tony Ryan and Jacki Pritchard

CHAPTER 1

WHAT IS MENTAL HEALTH, ILLNESS AND RECOVERY?

PIERS ALLOTT

INTRODUCTION

This chapter aims to provide an overview of definitions of mental health, illness, recovery and wellness. To aim to achieve any more within the space available is all but impossible given that the argument over this question has raged for at least the last thirty years with some referring to mental illness as a myth (Szasz 1960). Many people who have been diagnosed as 'mentally ill' also reject such classification and may argue that they have nothing to 'recover' from. It is without doubt that the life experiences of a significant number of people defined as mentally ill have often been extremely damaging. Hearing the narratives of many people in recovery, one is often struck with a sense of awe that they have survived at all. This includes the experiences of people from black and ethnic minority communities, from whose cultures there is a great deal to learn. Many people have not only managed to survive their difficult life experiences but also to survive their 'mental illness' and the consequences of an often less than supportive mental health system in which their life experiences were cast aside because they were perceived to be disturbed in their feeling, thinking and perceptions of the world. Many people have thrived as a result of their experiences, demonstrating that adversity can often be overcome and provide a basis for growth.

BACKGROUND

Concepts of mental illness

Until the late eighteenth century, people who had experiences that we now define as 'mental illness' were treated no differently from any other dependent person referred to as the 'needy and worthy poor', a group that included people with physical disabilities, chronic illnesses and dementia. The parish provided some financial assistance to enable people to continue to live in the community and very few 'dangerous and troublesome lunatics' were segregated from society in specialised houses of correction. The rise of industrialisation brought about very significant changes in nineteenth-century society with an increasing need for labour and an expectation that 'able bodied' people would work, leaving those who were not 'able bodied' to be supported by the poor houses to the point at which the poor houses began to overflow. People whose differences of behaviour set them apart from others in the poor houses began to be problematic in the overcrowded conditions and this led to the development and rise in provision of private care provided by doctors specialising in the care of people thought to be 'mad'. It was in the middle of the nineteenth century that the development of asylums was mandated and they, like the poor houses, filled quickly with a wide range of people whose differences and behaviour could not be tolerated (Jenkins 1994). The Alleged Lunatics' Friends Society was established by John Perceval in 1845 (Frese and Davis 1997).

So original concepts of 'mental illness', if defined by those who were admitted to the asylums, were very broad indeed including people with a range of physical difficulties, tertiary syphilis, diabetes and even malnutrition. There were almost as many classification systems as there were experts! It was with the publication of the sixth edition of Emil Kraepelin's *Lehrbuch* (1904) that classification of mental disorders began to stabilise. However, with the establishment of the World Health Organisation (WHO) in 1948 and the publication of an international classification of diseases, ICD-6 (WHO 1948), a more internationally recognised classification was achieved, although only adopted by six nations. The publication of ICD-8 (WHO 1967) provided a classification based on new principles proposed in a report commissioned by WHO from the English psychiatrist Erwin Stengel (1959) and finally achieved broad international agreement. However, there has always been an issue between the importance of empirical as opposed to non-empirical evidence in classification, with empirical views dominating to the exclusion of non-empirical views (Fulford 1989).

Recovery narratives strengthen the importance of non-empirical views that are meaningful to the people whose experiences mental health services and psychiatry aim to address. Perhaps with the significant contribution now being made by 'expert patients', by learning what helps people on their recovery journeys and by giving greater weight to this qualitative experience, ICD-11 and DSM-V will see in a new era of understanding that gives at least equal weight to evaluative information.

The concept of recovery

The experiences of the service users of mental health services, those people who seek support for their mental distress, have generally been excluded since the rise of industrialisation, due to poverty or social exclusion on the basis that people with 'mental illness' were perceived not to have the capacity for sound reasoning. However, there have been many people with experiences of recovery from mental illness/distress throughout history whose stories were often not told and, if they were, were not heard or were discounted. It was not until the rise of the civil rights movement in the United States and the publication of books like Judi Chamberlin's *On Our Own* (1978) that a new sense of hope among people diagnosed as having a 'mental illness' seemed at all possible.

The 1990s was seen as the 'decade of the brain' from the perspective of biological psychiatry and, in apparent direct contradiction to this medical philosophy, mental health recovery was seen as 'a guiding vision for the 1990s' (Anthony 1993) from a service user and family perspective, a more values-based thinking. The concept of mental health recovery was not taken up in the UK until the mid- to late 1990s when a few people began to embrace the concept in their work, although in those early days there was little in-depth understanding of the concept or its practice. However, with the publication of research into coping and adaptation (Hatfield and Lefley 1993) and *Accepting Voices* (Romme and Escher 1993), together with the development of user groups and organisations such as the Hearing Voices Network, the development of concepts of coping with symptoms began to become more prominent and 'experts by experience' began to develop their own writing (Coleman and Smith 1999).

What underpins the development of recovery is a value base that respects the differences between people. The announcement by the government in July 2001 of the establishment of the National Institute for Mental Health in England (NIMHE) was accompanied by an announcement that one of the first tasks of NIMHE would be the development of a national framework of values for mental health. A draft national framework of values (see Box 1.1) was delivered to the e-conference hosted by the Mental Health Foundation at the end of March 2003 (NIMHE 2003) and the link between the concept and practice of mental health recovery and values-based practice connected by two of the participants now appointed as Fellow for Recovery and Fellow for Values-Based Practice at NIMHE. A literature review of recovery that includes a commentary on the role of values can be found in Allott, Loganathan and Fulford (2002).

Box 1.1 National Framework of Values for Mental Health (draft, March 2003)

The National Institute for Mental Health in England (NIMHE)'s work on values in mental health is guided by three principles of values-based practice:

1. *Recognition* – NIMHE recognises the role of values alongside evidence in all areas of mental health policy and practice

2. *Raising awareness* – NIMHE is committed to raising awareness of the values involved in different contexts, the role/s they play and their impact on practice in mental health

3. *Respect* – NIMHE respects diversity of values and will support ways of working with such diversity that makes the principle of service user-centrality a unifying focus for practice. This means that the values of each individual service user/client and their communities must be the starting point and key determinant for all actions by professionals.

Respect for diversity of values encompasses a number of specific policies and principles concerned with equality of citizenship. In particular, it is anti-discriminatory because discrimination in all its forms is intolerant of diversity. Thus respect for diversity of values has the consequence that it is unacceptable (and unlawful in some instances) to discriminate on grounds such as gender, sexual orientation, class, age, abilities, religion, race, culture or language.

Respect for diversity within mental health is also:

- *user-centred* – it puts respect for the values of individual users at the centre of policy and practice
- *recovery oriented* – it recognises that in building on the personal strengths and resiliences of individual users, and on their cultural and racial characteristics, there are many diverse routes to recovery
- *multi-disciplinary* – it requires that respect be reciprocal, at a personal level (between service users, their family members, friends, communities and providers), between different provider disciplines (such as nursing, psychology, psychiatry, medicine, social work), and between different organisations (including health, social care, local authority housing, voluntary organisations, community groups, faith communities and other social support services)
- *dynamic* – it is open and responsive to change
- *reflective* – it combines self-monitoring and self-management with positive self-regard
- *balanced* – it emphasises positive as well as negative values
- *relational* – it puts positive working relationships supported by good communication skills at the heart of practice.

NIMHE will encourage educational and research initiatives aimed at developing the capabilities (the awareness, attitudes, knowledge and skills) needed to deliver mental health services that will give effect to the principles of values-based practice.

MENTAL HEALTH, POVERTY, CULTURE AND SOCIAL JUSTICE

Prilleltensky (2001a, p.253) defines mental health as 'a state of psychological wellness characterised by the satisfactory fulfilment of basic human needs'. Prilleltensky highlights that some of the basic human needs for mental health include a sense of mastery, control, and a sense of efficacy; emotional support and secure attachment; cognitive stimulation; sense of community and belonging; respect for personal identity and dignity; and others identified by the Basic Behavioral Science Task Force of the National Advisory Mental Health Council (1996a, 1996b).

Given the above it is not surprising that the experiences we identify as 'mental illness' are closely connected with poverty and social injustice and what might more accurately be referred to as 'disempowerment' or 'losing control over one or more aspects of one's life'. Prilleltensky (2001a, p.254) highlights the importance of cultural assumptions on mental health, particularly cultural assumptions about poverty and social justice, the way this is framed and society's response to it. He summarises his view that:

> cultural assumptions exert a direct influence on mental health through definitions of the good life and the good society and through psychological definitions and solutions to problems. Notions of the good life derived from competition and individualism lead to social isolation and psychological stress. When these problems are defined in individualistic terms, the person is viewed as responsible for her or his suffering. But cultural assumptions also exert an indirect influence on mental health via society's definitions of social justice. The way we frame justice determines how we allocate resources, and the way we allocate resources has a direct impact on the mental health of the poor and the vulnerable.

Psychiatry is part of Western medical science and as such has developed within the context of Western cultures. When one considers, in addition to the cultural assumptions identified above, the cultural differences between nations including differences of ethnicity and race and the way these issues are dealt with in a multicultural society, concepts of mental illness become very much more complex. Until relatively recently the significance and importance of differences in cultural meanings of mental health have gone unrecognised, or been ignored, and this has led to considerable social injustice; in particular the fact that many more people from African Caribbean backgrounds in the UK experience considerably greater levels of coercion both on entry to and within the mental health system.

The importance of culture has been recognised since the beginnings of psychiatric classification (Kraepelin 1904), but the Western societies in which we now live and our ability to travel and communicate around the world easily have created a very different context to that experienced by Kraepelin. Culture within these societies has become very much more complex. Marsella and Yamada define culture as:

> Shared learned meanings and behaviors that are transmitted from within a social activity context for purposes of promoting individual/societal adjustment, growth, and development. Culture has both *external* (i.e., arti-

facts, roles, activity contexts, institutions) and *internal* (i.e., values, beliefs, attitudes, activity contexts, patterns of consciousness, personality styles, epistemology) representations. The shared meanings and behaviors are subject to continuous change and modification in response to changing internal and external circumstances. (Marsella and Yamada 2000, p.12)

They highlight the work of Murdock (1980), an American anthropologist, who separated Western views from non-Western views of disease causality. He reported that Western models were based on *naturalistic* views of disease causation, including infection, stress, organic deterioration, accidents and acts of overt human aggression. In contrast, among many non-Western societies, disease models were based on *supernatural* views (i.e. any disease which accounts for impairment of health as being a consequence of some intangible force) including:

1. theories of mystical causation because of impersonal forces such as fate, ominous sensations, contagion, mystical retribution

2. theories of animistic causation because of personalised forces such as soul loss and spirit aggression

3. theories of magical causation or actions of evil forces including sorcery and witchcraft.

It is considered significant that many people in the United Kingdom who are 'experts by experience' (people who experience mental illness/distress, their families and friends) and have been diagnosed as 'mentally ill' have adopted a mixture of Western naturalistic models of disease – including stress, accidents and acts of human aggression, including abuse – and non-Western models that are more supernaturally or spiritually based, while rejecting naturalistic biological concepts of infection and organic deterioration.

Anam Cara is the service-user-run crisis alternative to psychiatric hospital inpatient treatment reported on in *Being There in a Crisis* (Mental Health Foundation 2002). This work and the Foundation's *Strategies for Living with Mental Illness* (Mental Health Foundation 2000) highlight the importance to experts by experience of Eastern concepts of 'illness' and 'healing' that have an emphasis on spiritual beliefs and 'energy healing': the use of Bach or Australian bush flower essences, Reike, Shiatsu and meditation practices, to name but a few. The work at Anam Cara proved very effective in supporting the recovery of many people and the service

was valued by both its 'guests', who reported 100 per cent excellent satisfaction with the service, and the staff that worked alongside the Anam
Cara 'recovery guides' from the local home treatment team. The national
MIND survey (Baker and Strong 2001) confirms that 'spirituality' was
important to roughly half of the respondents. This reflects the fact that in
1997 42 per cent of the UK population used alternative therapies, an
increase from 34 per cent in 1990 (Eisenberg *et al.* 1998), with 70–90 per
cent of all episodes of illness managed outside the established health care
system – through self-care and alternative therapies (Melmed 2001).

Each one of us has a different background; our personal upbringing
has unique characteristics. The cultural context provided by our family,
our local community and the wider society in which we grow up has a significant impact on the way in which each of us views the world. In
Western societies the development of biological medicine has led to the
belief that the functioning of mind and body are separate, whereas in
Eastern societies beliefs are much more holistic in nature and there is a
recognition that mind and body are interrelated. In fact, Western
medicine is reported to be only the fourth most commonly practised
system of medicine in the world today, preceded by Chinese medicine,
homoeopathy and herbal medicine (van Kooten-Prasad 2000); and if
studies of recovery from serious mental illness, including schizophrenia,
report that recovery rates are significantly higher in developing countries
than they are in Western countries (Warner 1994) then, in terms of our
definitions of mental health, illness and wellness, we must, at least,
consider what we can learn from different cultures as well as begin to
understand how people from different cultures in Western societies may
experience difficulties with Western ways of conceptualising 'mental
illness'.

SEEKING DEFINITIONS

What we call 'mental illness' in Western society describes differences of
perceptions, feelings and behaviour that are perceived to vary significantly from those of the majority population. At the simplest level, mental
illnesses can be defined as severe disturbances of behaviour, mood,
thought processes and/or social and interpersonal relationships. In psychiatric diagnosis these experiences are grouped under a range of
common headings that enable the use of similar responses and treat-

ments to be offered to people with the same diagnoses. The most common groupings are anxiety, affective disorders, psychotic disorders, including schizophrenia, and personality disorders.

However, it is argued that what is more important to the individual is a description of the issues as perceived by the person rather than a diagnosis. This is because people can only begin to look for solutions to issues that are identified by them, whether with or without professional or non-professional assistance, and can then begin to contextualise, understand and perhaps find meaning in the experiences (Bracken and Thomas 2001). If diagnoses are given within a Western medical context and the response, as is often the case, is only to prescribe medication, then there is an assumption that both the problem and the solution can be simply dealt with by the 'third party' rather than the person seeking solutions that are considered effective and have meaning to him or her. This is a common course of action within Western medicine that is comfortable for both the person and the general practitioner or psychiatrist, although it is one through which personal growth of the individual may well be impeded. This is not to argue that diagnosis is unimportant but rather that it has less relevance for the person than for the professional, and that at least part of the solution rests with respecting the values of individuals who approach services for support.

Mental health and mental wellness are more than an absence of mental illness. All of us have experiences of mental distress at some points in our lives and the experience of mental illness or even clinically diagnosable psychosis is much more common in our societies than has previously been identified. Van Os et al.'s (2000) study of a population of 7076 people in the Netherlands found an occurrence of psychosis in the general population of 17.5 per cent, some fifty times more than expected. This suggests that a significant proportion of the population may have experiences of 'the psychosis phenotype' that indicates the continuum of 'mental illness' in our communities and that even those forms of mental disorder considered the most serious are significantly more prevalent than previously identified. Therefore, if some 17 per cent of people with clinically diagnosable 'psychosis' are not in contact with mental health services, we must assume that a person who can be clinically diagnosed as having a 'mental illness' can also be 'mentally healthy'. This will be particularly so if in addition to their symptoms of 'mental illness' they experience 'a state of psychological wellness characterised by the satisfactory fulfilment of basic human needs' (Prilleltensky 2001a, p.253). They may have high self-esteem and feel good about who they are, they may have loving relationships and family lives and be successful in their chosen occupation, in spite of diagnosable symptoms. So the presence of symptoms, in themselves, is not sufficient to determine 'mental illness' or to exclude 'mental health'. This view is supported by Repper and Perkins (2003, p.viii), who contend that approaches that focus on deficits limit our view of people who experience mental health problems. They point out: 'People whose symptoms continue or recur can, and do, live satisfying lives and contribute to their communities in many different ways and the alleviation of such symptoms does not necessarily result in the reinstatement of former, valued, roles and relationships.' Mental wellness or well-being might be defined by each of us within our own culture, experience and expectations of life, so that what is mental wellness for one person may well not be for another.

Prilleltensky (2001b, p.7) defines mental wellness as 'the simultaneous, balanced, and contextually-sensitive satisfaction of personal, relational, and collective needs' and particularly identifies the importance of 'relationality'. Two sets of needs are considered to be essential in pursuing healthy relationships among individuals and groups: respect for diversity, and collaboration and democratic participation. Respect for diversity ensures that people's unique identities are affirmed by others, while democratic participation enables community members to have a say in decisions affecting their lives.

This has been clearly demonstrated in the Department of Health's (DH) *Black and Ethnic Minority Drug Misuse Needs Assessment* completed in May 2003 (Winters and Patel 2003) that highlights the benefits of true democratic participation and community engagement, referred to by the author as 'community recovery'. The project defined 'community engagement' as 'The simultaneous and multifaceted engagement of supported and adequately resourced communities and relevant agencies around an issue, or set of issues, in order to raise awareness, assess and articulate need and achieve sustained and equitable provision of appropriate services' (Patel, Winters and McDonald 2002, p.12) – so much so that a community engagement approach is now being considered to address the mental health issues of black and minority ethnic communities. It is thought that the outcome of such a process will significantly support and extend the views expressed in this chapter and confirm approaches underpinned by the concept of recovery and values-based practice.

There is much to learn from this experience and the developing methodology of engaging people from different cultures, black and minority ethnic communities. People from these communities have experiences of exclusion through prejudice, discrimination and racism. New approaches to addressing these issues and their consequences, as well as other community issues, must have meaning to these people in ways that enable them to take control of their lives and to take the actions they believe necessary for their communities. The process of development and consultation adopted in producing *Inside Outside* (DH 2003), like the above, clearly demonstrates this in the true and meaningful engagement of some 4000 people from local communities.

Respect for diversity and democratic participation are essential principles for enabling concepts of mental health, illness and wellness to be understood and are encapsulated in the developing NIMHE National Framework of Values for Mental Health (see Figure 1.1).

RECOVERY AND VALUES-BASED PRACTICE

It has been argued that the concept of recovery is not new (Roberts and Wolfson 2004), although what might be referred to as the emerging 'recovery movement', that is enabling significant potential change in the way services are delivered, *is* new. This follows a decade of writing, research and identification of emerging best practices in mental health recovery in a number of states in the US (United States Public Service Office of the Surgeon General 1999), New Zealand (Mental Health Commission 1998) and Canada (Everett *et al.* 2003).

What is recovery?

'Recovery' is a concept that has been introduced primarily by people who have recovered from mental health problems often in spite of and outside of the 'mental health system'. At its simplest 'recovery' can be defined as a subjective experience of having regained control over one's life. 'Recovery' is not simply a reframing of current professional approaches, such as rehabilitation or psychosocial intervention. Recovery is in the control of each person. The achievements of those who have recovered embrace hope, empowerment and social connectedness.

In the UK, the West Midlands Regional Health Authority commissioned a piece of work in 1997 that led to the development and publication of a series of five directional papers with the intention of 'helping to articulate the direction of the mental health system of the future'. The first paper set out a vision of a modern community mental health system that 'is rooted, first and foremost, in the desired goal or outcome for the individuals it seeks to support: service users and their families' (Carling and Allott 1999, p.1). The core concept within the series of directional papers is therefore the concept of recovery that:

> refers to an active, ongoing and highly individual process through which a person assumes responsibility for his/her life, and develops a specific set of strategies not only to cope with symptoms, but also to address secondary assaults of the disability, including stigma discrimination and social exclusion. (Carling *et al.* 1999, p.1)

However, it appears to have taken some five years for the concepts contained in the directional paper series to begin to become more widely known. The changes in services demanded by these new concepts, even though now underpinned by national policy, *Modernising Mental Health Services: Safe, Sound and Supportive* (DH 1998), *The National Service Framework for Mental Health: Modern Standards and Service Models* (DH 1999), and the *NHS Plan: A Plan for Investment. A Plan for Reform* (DH 2001), will still take time to be accepted requiring, as they do, the need for new ways of thinking and approaching issues of respect for difference, personal autonomy and power.

In New Zealand there is a clear policy for the adoption of recovery in the blueprint that states:

> Recovery is a journey as much as a destination. It is different for everyone. For some people with mental illness, recovery is a road they travel on only once or twice, to a destination that is relatively easy to find. For others, recovery is a maze with an elusive destination, a maze that takes a lifetime to navigate. Recovery is happening when people can live well in the presence or absence of their mental illness and the many losses that may come in its wake, such as isolation, poverty, unemployment, and discrimination. Recovery does not always mean that people will return to full health or retrieve all their losses, but it does mean that people can live well in spite of them. (Mental Health Commission 1998, p.1)

The concept of recovery within professional circles in the United States became more widely recognised following the publication of 'Recovery from mental illness: The guiding vision for the 1990s', in which William Anthony synthesised the writings of people with experience of recovery into his definition:

> ...a person with mental illness can recover even though the illness is not 'cured'... [Recovery] is a way of living a satisfying, hopeful, and contributing life even with the limitations caused by illness. Recovery involves the development of new meaning and purpose in one's life as one grows beyond the catastrophic effects of mental illness. (Anthony 1993, p.15)

People who have experienced mental illness/distress and been treated by the mental health system have been writing about recovery for many years, even if the word 'recovery' has not been used. This has occurred particularly since the 1980s, including works written in the UK such as *I'm Not a Bloody Label, I am Graham Myerscough* (Myerscough 1981). The author wrote:

> My perception of myself and the world around me has almost completely reversed. I have abilities now that as far as I was concerned those years ago did not exist. I have uncovered creative thinking and abilities, a creative perception to go with those abilities that I did not have, was buried. In the process I have exploded many myths about human behaviour through my own thinking and experiencing, for myself that is... I can say and do, that Manic-Depression is not an illness, on the contrary it was for me a fundamental part of my growth process; from my experiences. (Myerscough 1981, p.14)

Many stories of recovery have a very positive sense of discovering self, finding meaning and personal growth as described in the quote from Myerscough above. The benefits of a recovery approach appear to be very significant and we must ask why, if we have known about these experiences, have we not explored, researched and implemented ways in which these recovery experiences can be supported for the majority of people who experience mental illness/distress?

The growing recovery movement is not anti-psychiatric since it recognises and respects differences between people, and many people choose to take medication and even have ECT. There is tension between traditional views and approaches to mental illness and alternative views and approaches that exists in all groups, both professionals and people with lived experiences of distress themselves. It is the freedom to make informed choices that is considered of central importance. This requires a different relationship with services, one in which true collaboration and partnership are acknowledged and individual differences respected.

Values-based practice (VBP)

In order to manage the tensions mentioned above, it is essential that we adopt a values process that can enable this. 'Values-Based Practice (VBP) is the theory and practice of effective healthcare decision-making for situations in which legitimately different (and hence potentially conflicting) value perspectives are in play' (Fulford, forthcoming).

VBP, like recovery, starts from respect for the values of each individual (in this VBP differs fundamentally from 'ethics', in so far as ethics aim to tell people what is right); VBP, like recovery, emphasises the importance of strengths and positive values rather than focusing on deficits and negative values; VBP, like recovery, is concerned as much with process as with outcomes, building on skills of communication, awareness and engagement; VBP, like recovery, provides options in care, genuine choices that are built on the diverse skills and resources of different disciplines, and that reflect the strengths and resources of each individual rather than the demands of 'authority' (professional, ideological or political); and finally, VBP, like recovery, puts decision-making firmly in the hands of those most directly concerned, individual users and providers working together in the real-life contingencies of day-to-day care (Allott *et al.* 2002).

PRACTISING IN RECOVERY-ORIENTED WAYS

On the one hand, changing practices requires what appear to be small and cost-limited investments, but on the other, they are changes that Western societies seem to have had great difficulty implementing and sustaining over the last thirty years or so. In the early 1970s Paul Polak and his colleagues (Polak and Kirby 1976, p.13) in south-west Denver delivered a service that 'reduced the need for total adult psychiatric inpatient beds to less than 1/100,000 population'. This, described as a 'total community care system', has a bearing on current discussions about 'whole systems of care'. In south-west Denver the structure of mental health services began with 'citizen participation and community control', in what today we might refer to as 'citizenship' but in fact is much more than this. The service system included a network of small, specific community environments, such as Anam Cara, as well as private homes, called family sponsor homes in Birmingham (Mental Health Foundation 2002). This was supported by an 'intensive observation apartment', 'home day care' and 'back-up hospital beds'. The primary treatment approach was 'social systems intervention and crisis intervention' with a philosophy based on the ability of the person's 'social system' to take control and for individuals within the system to be empowered and to learn to deal with and resolve their crises.

The messages then are clear; it is possible to do things differently but:

> Recovery requires the right atmosphere or organizational climate in your mental health organization – one that is sensitive to consumers, and values [the] independence of the individual. It allows consumers to risk, to fail. It holds that every consumer has a right to the same pleasures, passions, and pursuits of happiness that we have. It looks at potential, not deficits. (Weaver 1998, p.1)

For practitioners, Weaver advises what mental health provider staff might need to think in order to assist a service user with recovery:

1. I will stop trying to control the consumer's life.

2. My professional success is based on the consumer's recovery progress.

3. I listen to, believe, and value what the consumer says.

4. I will not treat a consumer any different than anyone else.

5. I have in-depth knowledge about and sympathy for the consumer's disability.

6. I will not allow a consumer to become overly dependent upon me.

7. I can give a consumer hope or helplessness – it is my choice.

8. I see potential in the consumer.

9. I serve as a 'coach', not as an authoritative mental health professional.

10. I will not become discouraged when a consumer fails or rejected when a consumer succeeds.

11. I will take care of my whole being – dealing truthfully and realistically with the spiritual, mental, emotional, and physical aspects of my life.

(Weaver 1998, p.4)

IMPLICATIONS FOR EDUCATORS AND SERVICE COMMISSIONERS

If we are to implement recovery concepts and practices in all of our services, then we need to find ways of commissioning services that will enable the process to begin and developing education programmes that recognise that this is a new way of thinking about what is diagnosed as mental illness.

There is no simple or single answer to commissioning services or educating and training the workforce. As with the individual recovery of people who experience distress, the pathway to recovery for each professional and service will be different and services too must be allowed 'to risk, to fail' and to learn from these experiences.

Each service should have clearly stated and *active* vision and mission statements underpinned by an agreed values process that will provide the foundation on which to build. These must include recovery as the core vision driving the system. Recovery measures should be used to identify the effectiveness of the system. In particular, these measures must include quality of life and empowerment. In order to deliver effective outcomes for people with lived experiences in these domains a comprehensive framework is provided in the *Emerging Best Practices in Mental Health Recovery* (Townsend *et al.* 1999), developed by people with lived experience. The core set of service domains are:

- clinical care
- family support
- peer support and relationships
- work/meaningful activity
- power and control
- stigma
- community involvement
- access to resources
- education.

It is important that the role of each stakeholder is identified: this will include the person with lived experience, the clinician and the community in each of these service domains and at each of the four stages of recovery:

1. dependent/unaware
2. dependent/aware
3. independent/aware
4. interdependent/aware.

In order to achieve such a service, significant interagency and interdisciplinary collaboration is required, demanding investment in training and education of the current workforce as well as redesign of basic professional training courses to include recovery as a core concept.

We need to ensure that all educational programmes address the issue of values and adopt a process that recognises and values differences between people, particularly differences of culture and race. Emphasis should be placed on training that can support people to self-manage, develop their resilience and contribute their skills and abilities.

Essential to delivering this major change, which will bring significant benefits for people with lived experiences of mental distress, will be truly putting the service user at the centre of everything we do. To achieve this we need to ensure significant investment in peer operated services, initially in the region of 15 per cent of overall mental health spend, as well as developing a workforce that values lived experience of recovery from mental distress as well as experience by training.

To conclude, the following quote from Octavio Paz (1967, accessed via web) challenges us all:

> What sets worlds in motion is the interplay of differences, their attractions and repulsions. Life is plurality, death is uniformity. By suppressing differences and peculiarities, by eliminating different civilizations and cultures, progress weakens life and favors death. The ideal of a single civilization for everyone, implicit in the cult of progress and technique, impoverishes and mutilates us. Every view of the world that becomes extinct, every culture that disappears, diminishes a possibility of life.

REFERENCES

Allott, P., Loganathan, L. and Fulford, K.W.M. (2002) 'Discovering hope for recovery from a British perspective: A review of a selection of recovery literature, implications for practice and systems change.' In S. Lurie, M. McCubbin and B. Dallaire (eds) *International Innovations in Community Mental Health: Special Issue of Canadian Journal of Community Mental Health 21*, 3.

Anthony, W.A. (1993) 'Recovery from mental illness: The guiding vision of the mental health service system in the 1990s.' *Psychosocial Rehabilitation Journal 16*, 4, 11–23.

Baker, S. and Strong, S. (2001) *Roads to Recovery – How People with Mental Health Problems Recover and Find Ways of Coping.* London: MIND.

Basic Behavioral Science Task Force of the National Advisory Mental Health Council (1996a) 'Basic behavioral science research for mental health: Family processes and social networks.' *American Psychologist 51*, 622–30.

Basic Behavioral Science Task Force of the National Advisory Mental Health Council (1996b) 'Basic behavioral science research for mental health: Vulnerability and resilience.' *American Psychologist 51*, 22–8.

Bracken, P. and Thomas, P. (2001) 'Postpsychiatry: A new direction for mental health.' *British Medical Journal 322*, 724–7.

Carling, P. and Allott, P. (1999) *Core Vision and Values. Helping to Articulate the Direction of the Mental Health System of the Future – A Series of Directional Papers on Developing Modern Community Mental Health Systems*. Birmingham: West Midlands Regional Health Authority.

Carling, P., Allott, P., Smith, M. and Coleman, R. (1999) *Principles of Recovery for a Modern Community Mental Health System. Helping to Articulate the Direction of the Mental Health System of the Future – A Series of Directional Papers on Developing Modern Community Mental Health Systems*. Birmingham: West Midlands Regional Health Authority.

Chamberlin, J. (1978) *On Our Own: Patient-controlled Alternatives to the Mental Health System*. New York: McGraw-Hill.

Coleman, R. and Smith, M. (1999) *Working with Voices*. Gloucester: Handsell.

DH (Department of Health) (1998) *Modernising Mental Health Services: Safe, Sound and Supportive*. London: DH.

DH (Department of Health) (1999) *The National Service Framework for Mental Health: Modern Standards and Service Models*. London: DH.

DH (Department of Health) (2001) *NHS Plan: A Plan for Investment. A Plan for Reform*. London: DH.

DH (Department of Health) (2003) *Inside Outside, Improving Mental Health Services for Black and Minority Ethnic Communities in England*. London: DH.

Eisenberg, D.M., Davis, R.B., Ettner, S.L., Appel, S., Wilkey, S., Van Rompay, M. and Kessler, R.C. (1998) 'Trends in alternative medicine use in the United States, 1990–1997 – Results of a follow-up national survey.' *The Journal of the American Medical Association 280*, 1569–75.

Everett, B., Adams, B., Johnson, J., Kurzawa, G., Quigley, M. and Wright, M. (2003) *Recovery Rediscovered: Implications for the Ontario Mental Health System*. Ontario: The Canadian Mental Health Association, Ontario Division (*www. ontario.cmha.ca*).

Frese, F.J. and Davis, W.W. (1997) 'The consumer-survivor movement, recovery, and consumer professionals.' *Professional Psychiatry, Research and Practice 28*, 243–5.

Fulford, K.W.M. (1989) *Moral Theory and Medical Practice*. Cambridge: Cambridge University Press.

Fulford, K.W.M. (forthcoming) 'Ten principles of values-based medicine.' In J. Radden (ed.) *Companion to the Philosophy of Psychiatry*. New York: Oxford University Press.

Hatfield, A. and Lefley, H. (1993) *Surviving Mental Illness: Stress, Coping and Adaptation*. London: Guilford Press.

Jenkins, J.B. (1994) 'International perspective of community mental health services.' In C. Dean (ed.) *A Slow Train Coming – Bringing the Mental Health Revolution to Scotland. Glasgow*. Glasgow: The Greater Glasgow Community and Mental Health Services NHS Trust.

Kraepelin, E. (1904) *Ein Lehrbuch für Studiereinde und Ärzte. Siebeite, vielfach umgearbeitete Auflage. II. Band: Klinische Psychiatrie*. Leipzig: Barth Verlag.

Marsella, A.J. and Yamada, A.M. (2000) 'Culture and mental health: An introduction and overview of foundations, concepts, and issues.' In I. Cuellar and F. Paniagua (eds) *The Handbook of Multicultural Mental Health: Assessment and Treatment of Diverse Populations 3–24*. New York: Academic Press.

Melmed, R. (2001) *Mind, Body, and Medicine*. Oxford: Oxford University Press.

Mental Health Commission (1998) *Blueprint for Mental Health Services in New Zealand – How Things Need to Be*. Wellington, New Zealand. Accessed from *www.mhc.govt.nz/publications/1998/Blueprint1998.pdf* on 11.09.2003.

Mental Health Foundation (2000) *Strategies for Living with Mental Illness*. London: MHF.

Mental Health Foundation (2002) *Being There in a Crisis*. London: MHF.

Murdock, G. (1980) *Theories of Illness: A World Survey.* Pittsburgh, PA: University of Pittsburgh Press.

Myerscough, G. (1981) *I'm Not a Bloody Label, I am Graham Myerscough.* Southsea: ISSNESS.

NIMHE (National Institute for Mental Health in England) (2003) *National Framework of Values for Mental Health.* Draft. *www.connects.org.uk/conferences*

Patel, K., Winters, M. and McDonald, B. (2002) *Community Engagement: A Paper Prepared to Support the Development of a Brief to be Submitted to the Department of Health.* Preston: University of Central Lancashire.

Paz, O. (1967) *The Labyrinth of Solitude: Life and Thought in Mexico.* London: Penguin Press. Accessed from *www.owenbarfield.com/imaginativethinker/authors/ pauthors/paz.htm* on 11.09.2003.

Polak, P. and Kirby, M. (1976) 'A model to replace psychiatric hospitals.' *Journal of Nervous and Mental Disease 162,* 1, 13–22.

Prilleltensky, I. (2001a) 'Cultural assumptions, social justice, and mental health.' In J. Shumaker and T. Ward (eds) *Cultural Cognition and Psychopathology.* Westport, CO: Praeger.

Prilleltensky, I. (2001b) *The Role of Power in Wellness, Oppression, and Liberation: The Promise of Psychopolitical Validity.* Accessed from *http://members.optushome.com. au/psydeas/power.htm* on 05.09.03.

Repper, J. and Perkins, R. (2003) *Social Inclusion and Recovery: A Model for Mental Health Practice.* London: Baillière Tindall.

Roberts, G. and Wolfson, P. (2004) 'The rediscovery of recovery: Open to all.' *Advances in Psychiatric Treatment 10,* 37–49.

Romme, M. and Escher, S. (1993) *Accepting Voices.* London: MIND Publications.

Stengel, E. (1959) 'Classification of mental disorders.' *Bulletin of the World Health Organisation 21,* 601–63.

Szasz, T.S. (1960) 'The myth of mental illness.' *American Psychologist 15,* 113–18.

Townsend, W., Boyd, S., Griffin, G. and Hicks, P.L. (1999) *Emerging Best Practices in Mental Health Recovery.* Columbus, OH: Ohio Department of Mental Health.

United States Public Service Office of the Surgeon General (1999) *Mental Health: A Report of the Surgeon General.* Rockville, MD: Department of Health and Human Services, U.S. Public Health Service.

van Kooten-Prasad, M. (2000) 'Mental health in the global village.' *Balance: The Magazine of the Mental Health Association.* Brisbane, Australia: QLD Inc.

Van Os, J., Hanssen, M., Bijl, R.V. and Ravelli, A. (2000) 'Strauss (1969) revisited: A psychosis continuum in the general population?' *Schizophrenia Research 45,* 11–20.

Warner, R. (1994) *Recovery from Schizophrenia: Psychiatry and Political Economy.* Second edition. New York: Routledge.

Weaver, P. (1998) 'Recovery: Plain and simple.' Keynote Address, State Case Management Conference, Tulsa, Oklahoma, Oklahoma Department of Mental Health.

Winters, M. and Patel, K. (2003) *The Department of Health's Black and Ethnic Minority Drug Misuse Needs Assessment – Community Engagement, Report 1: The Process.* Preston: University of Central Lancashire.

WHO (World Health Organisation) (1948) *Manual of the International Statistical Classification of Diseases, Injuries and Causes of Death (ICD-6).* Geneva: WHO.

WHO (World Health Organisation) (1967) *Manual of the International Statistical Classification of Diseases, Injuries and Causes of Death (ICD-8).* Geneva: WHO.

CHAPTER 2

HUMAN RIGHTS AND MENTAL HEALTH LAW

DAVID HEWITT

INTRODUCTION

This chapter will consider how the Human Rights Act 1998 (HRA 1998) has affected mental health law in England and Wales.

The Mental Health Act 1983

At the moment, practitioners must use the Mental Health Act 1983 (MHA 1983). The main provisions of the MHA 1983 are set out in Box 2.1.

Box 2.1 Mental Health Act 1983

- Admission for assessment (max 28 days, non-renewable)   s 2
- Admission for treatment (6 months, renewable)   s 3
- Holding power (doctor, 72 hours)   s 5 (2)
- Holding power (nurse, 6 hours)   s 5 (4)
- Emergency admission (max 72 hours)   s 4
- Guardianship   s 7
- Leave of absence   s 17
- Transfer   s19
- Renewal of detention   s 20
- Discharge   s 23
- Supervised discharge   s 25A–J
- Nearest relative: appointment   s 26

- Nearest relative: displacement   s 29
- Criminal detention   ss 35–55
- Consent to treatment: general   ss 56–64
- Consent to treatment: medicine for mental disorder   s 58
- Consent to treatment: urgent   s 62
- Consent to treatment: other forms   s 63
- MHRT*: general   ss 65–79
- MHRT*: applications   ss 66 and 67
- MHRT*: discharge criteria   ss 72 and 73
- Aftercare   s 117
- Removal to a place of safety – from a private place   s 135
- Removal to a place of safety – from a public place   s 136

*Mental Health Review Tribunal

The government plans to introduce new mental health legislation (Department of Health 2002a, b, c).

The Human Rights Act 1998

HRA 1998 came into force on 2 October 2000. It introduced into domestic law the European Convention on Human Rights and Fundamental Freedoms (ECHR).

As far as mental health law is concerned, the main implications of the HRA 1998 are as follows:

- all 'public authorities' – including NHS bodies and local authorities – must interpret legislation in a way that is compatible with the ECHR
- the ECHR can be enforced in every court and tribunal
- the victim of an act that is incompatible with the ECHR can sue for damages and/or seek judicial review
- if an Act of Parliament is incompatible with the ECHR, the courts can make a formal Declaration to that effect.

So, HRA 1998 introduces the ECHR into domestic law. But what does the ECHR say?

The European Convention on Human Rights

For present purposes, the most significant parts of the ECHR are set out in Box 2.2.

Box 2.2 European Convention on Human Rights

- The right to life   Article 2
- The prohibition on torture and inhuman and
  degrading treatment   Article 3
- The right to liberty   Article 5
- The right to a fair trial   Article 6
- The right to respect for one's private and
  family life   Article 8

PSYCHIATRIC PRACTICE UNDER THE ECHR

Although the ECHR has been available in the English courts only since HRA 1998 came into force in October 2000, UK citizens have been able to appeal to the European Court of Human Rights (ECtHR) in Strasbourg since 1966. So, the ECHR has been influencing domestic law for several decades.

The purpose of this chapter is to consider what the ECHR requires – and what it permits. It will do this by looking at various significant features of psychiatric care.

REGULATIONS

Mental health law isn't all contained in the MHA 1983. Various regulations have been made under the Act, such as the Mental Health (Hospital, Guardianship and Consent to Treatment) Regulations 1983, and some government departments issue directions that affect psychiatric patients. Now HRA 1998 is law, such regulations and guidance must be interpreted so as to comply with the ECHR (HRA 1998, s 3).

What this means was considered in *Ex parte L*, which came before the High Court in December 2000 and was the first significant mental health law decision since the coming of HRA 1998 (*R. (L) v Secretary of State for Health* 2001). The case involved ECHR, Article 8 (1), which is set out in Box 2.3.

Box 2.3 Article 8 (1), European Convention on Human rights

Everyone has the right to respect for his private and family life, his home and his correspondence

---

Significantly, Article 8 (2) says this right can be interfered with in certain circumstances. Those circumstances are set out in Box 2.4.

Box 2.4 Article 8 (2), European Convention on Human Rights

- National security, public safety or the economic well-being of the country
- The prevention of disorder or crime
- The protection of health or morals, or
- The protection of the rights and freedoms of others

In *L*, a patient challenged new restrictions on visits by children to high secure hospitals (*Directions and Guidance for Visits by Children to Patients in High Security Hospitals*, HSC 1999/160). However, the Court found against him. It said that although the restrictions breached Article 8 (1), the breach was justified on some of the grounds in Article 8 (2).

Shortly afterwards, in *R. (N) v Ashworth Special Hospital Authority and Secretary of State for Health* (2001), a patient tried to challenge security arrangements in the high secure hospitals that allow staff to monitor patients' telephone calls (*Safety and Security in Ashworth, Broadmoor and Rampton Hospitals Directions 2000*, Dir 29 (1) and (3)). Again, the High Court held that any breach of Article 8 (1) could be justified under Article 8 (2) (*R. (N) v Ashworth Special Hospital Authority and Secretary of State for Health* 2001).

These cases show why some people have argued that the ECHR is of little help to psychiatric patients: its key provisions, including Article 8, are subject to a large number of very wide exceptions.

DETENTION

Although Article 5 of the ECHR gives everyone the 'right to liberty', it does not apply when someone is detained because of mental disorder. The relevant parts of Article 5 (1) are set out in Box 2.5.

Box 2.5 Article 5 (1), European Convention on Human Rights

Everyone has the right to liberty and security of person. No one shall be deprived of his liberty save in the following cases and in accordance with a procedure prescribed by law:

[...]

(e) the lawful detention of persons for the prevention of the spread of infectious diseases, of persons of unsound mind, alcoholics or drug addicts, or vagrants

---

The most significant case on this point is *Winterwerp*, in which the ECtHR imposed further conditions (*Winterwerp* v *Netherlands* 1979). It said that, except in an emergency, someone of unsound mind might be detained only in the circumstances set out in Box 2.6.

Box 2.6 The Winterwerp conditions

(i)   The patient has a true mental disorder that can be proved by objective medical expertise; and

(ii) the mental disorder is of a kind or degree that warrants detention; and

(iii) detention can only continue while the disorder persists

---

The domestic courts have accepted these conditions (e.g. *Anderson, Reid and Doherty* 2002). What do they mean?

A true mental disorder

Generally, MHA 1983 complies with this *Winterwerp* condition:

- the detention provisions – e.g. ss 2 and 3 – can be used only on someone suffering from mental disorder (MHA 1983, s 1 (1))
- *Winterwerp* said that a person isn't 'of unsound mind' simply because his/her behaviour is different to other people's; MHA 1983 says the same thing (MHA 1983, s 1 (3)).

Article 5 also requires that a detained person's 'unsoundness of mind' is shown by 'objective medical expertise' – in other words, by medical evidence. That evidence:

- needn't come from a psychiatrist, and may be provided by a GP (*Schuurs* v *The Netherlands*)
- will usually involve an examination, although a review of the medical records may suffice (*X* v *United Kingdom* 1981)
- will have to be up to date (*Varbanov* v *Bulgaria* 2000).

A patient detained in hospital by order of a criminal court may subsequently be given a 'conditional discharge'. However, the Home Secretary may recall a conditionally discharged patient to hospital, and English law doesn't require him/her to have medical evidence before doing so. This probably *does* breach Article 5.

A kind or degree warranting detention

This part of the *Winterwerp* test is replicated in MHA 1983, which asks 'whether it can "reliably be shown" that [a person] suffers from a mental disorder sufficiently serious to warrant detention' (*R. (H)* v *Mental Health Review Tribunal* 2001). If not, s/he cannot be detained.

English legislation says detention will only be justified if it represents the 'least restrictive alternative' (MHA 1983, ss 2 (2) (a), 3 (2) (c), and 37 (2) (b); MHA Code of Practice, para 3.6). The ECtHR has said the same thing (*Litwa* v *Poland* 2001).

The persistence of the disorder

Under *Winterwerp*, a patient can only be detained for as long as s/he is 'of unsound mind'. However, the ECtHR and the English Court of Appeal have each held that a person doesn't stop being 'of unsound mind' merely because his/her symptoms have disappeared (*R. (H)* v *Mental Health Review Tribunal* 2001).

The ECtHR court has also accepted that a patient needn't be discharged immediately his/her unsoundness of mind comes to an end, and that s/he may continue to be detained while appropriate aftercare facilities are put in place (*Johnson* v *United Kingdom* 1999).

Other conditions

The detention of persons of unsound mind is subject to more restrictions than those established in *Winterwerp*. Some of them are as follows:

- someone of unsound mind must be told why s/he has been detained in simple language (*Van der Leer* v *Netherlands* 1990; *Fox et al.* v *United Kingdom* 1991), otherwise there will be a breach of Article 5 (4) (*Conka* v *Belgium* 2002; *X* v *United Kingdom* 1981)

- a person lawfully detained under Article 5 retains the Article 8 right to respect for his/her family life (*Messina* v *Italy* 2000)

- a patient retains all the Article 5 rights where s/he *agrees* to enter hospital for psychiatric treatment and isn't detained there (*De Wilde et al.* v *Belgium* 1971)

- a patient may be 'detained' even though the authorities don't regard him/her as being so (*Ashingdane* v *United Kingdom* 1985)

- a child may be admitted to a psychiatric hospital with the permission of his/her parents, and will not be 'detained' even if s/he objects to that admission (*Neilsen* v *Denmark* 1989)

- a child who is detained has the added protection of the United Nations Convention on the Rights of the Child (*R. (SR)* v *Nottingham Magistrates' Court* 2001).

THE TREATABILITY TEST

In order for someone to be detained under MHA 1983, s/he must be suffering from 'mental disorder'. In section 1, the Act refers to four classes of mental disorder:

- mental illness
- severe mental impairment
- mental impairment
- psychopathic disorder.

Anyone suffering from either of the first two may be detained under MHA 1983 without a 'treatability test' being met; those from either of the last two may be detained – and the detention of anyone with 'mental disorder' may be renewed – only if treatment 'is likely to alleviate or prevent a deterioration of his condition' (MHA, s 3 (2) (b) and s 20 (3) (b) and (4) (b)). This 'treatability test' is very controversial.

After *R. v Canons Park Mental Health Review Tribunal, ex parte A* (1994), the treatability test could have been summarised as follows:

- a patient is 'treatable' if hospital treatment will stop his/her condition worsening, even if it won't alleviate it
- the condition will be alleviated if the patient gains insight or becomes less uncooperative
- the alleviation of a patient's condition will be sufficient even if it is only likely in the future.

The case of *R. v Secretary of State for Scotland* (1998) added the following further principles:

- a patient is 'treatable' if treatment will affect his/her symptoms, even if it won't affect the illness itself
- many things amount to 'treatment', and it 'may extend from cure to containment'.

Some commentators have suggested that as a result of these cases, and the very broad definition of 'treatment' they create, virtually every psychiatric patient is 'treatable'.

Nevertheless, the new Scottish Parliament found it necessary to abolish the 'treatability test' in certain circumstances. In 1999 it introduced legislation to ensure that patients with severe anti-social personality disorders about whom there are public safety concerns may continue to be detained in hospital even though they are not 'treatable' (Mental Health (Public Safety and Appeals) (Scotland) Act 1999, s 1).

That legislation was soon challenged, on the grounds that it must breach the 'right to liberty' in Article 5 of the ECHR. The challenge failed at every stage:

- the senior Scottish Court said that detention would comply with Article 5 (1) (e) even if the patient wasn't 'treatable', provided it is necessary to serve a legitimate social purpose, which may be the protection of the public (*A v The Scottish Ministers* 2000)

- on appeal, the Privy Council in London held it was lawful to detain a patient for medical treatment *or* public protection (*A* v *The Scottish Ministers* 2002)
- and the ECtHR agreed (*Alexander Lewis Hutchison Reid* v *United Kingdom* 2003).

The current position with the 'treatability test' is as set out in Box 2.7.

Box 2.7 Treatability – The current position

- The 'treatability test' is still relevant because the MHA still contains it, but
- almost any health care will be 'treatment', and
- the fact that an untreatable patient can be detained won't breach the ECHR

THE NEAREST RELATIVE

Under MHA 1983, a patient's 'nearest relative' has a significant role to play (MHA 1983, ss 11 (1) and (4), 23 (2), and 66 (1) (g) and (h)). However, s/he is chosen according to rigid criteria in section 26, which take no account of the patient's wishes. This can make a patient vulnerable to abuse (Mental Health Act Commission 1998, para.10.10.3, and 2000, para.4.46).

Abusive nearest relatives

In *JT* v *United Kingdom* (2000), a woman claimed that MHA 1983 breached Article 8 of the ECHR because it imposed upon her a nearest relative who had abused her, and allowed her no say in his selection. Before the case could come before the ECtHR, the UK government admitted the breach and promised to amend MHA 1983.

The government first set out its proposed amendments in its Draft Mental Health Bill (Department of Health 2002a, Part 1, Chapter 7). However, it has still not made a change, and in the spring of 2003 the High Court formally declared that the nearest relative provisions in MHA 1983 breach Article 8. It noted that, although the incompatibility had been identified 'a considerable time ago', it hadn't yet been removed (*R. (M)* v *Secretary of State for Health* 2003).

However, practitioners should resist the temptation to anticipate the government's amendments, because:

- if they stick to the MHA 1983 (even though it breaches Article 8), they will have a defence to any claim
- if they take a different route (for example, by allowing a patient to choose his/her nearest relative), they won't.

Same-sex cohabitants

Until recently, although one heterosexual cohabitant would be the 'husband or wife' of the other – and therefore qualify as his/her 'nearest relative' after six months – the same was not true of homosexual cohabitants (MHA, s 26 (1) and (6)). This has changed.

In *Ex parte SSG* (2002), the High Court made a declaration to the effect set out in Box 2.8 (*R. (SSG)* v *Liverpool City Council and the Secretary of State for Health* 2002; see also Cho 2002).

Box 2.8 The declaration in Ex Parte SSG

- The homosexual partner of a MHA 1983 patient may be regarded as 'living with the patient as the patient's husband or wife' under section MHA 1983 26 (6); and
- provided the two have lived together for six months, each may therefore be the 'nearest relative' of the other within MHA 1983, section 26 (1)

The Department of Health has confirmed that all public authorities should respect this declaration (see *www.doh.gov.uk/mhact1983/consentorders.htm*).

THE CONDITIONS OF DETENTION

It is very hard for a patient to succeed in a claim that the conditions in which s/he is being detained breach the ECHR. The relevant articles are Article 5 (which is set out in Box 2.5) and Article 3 (set out in Box 2.9).

Box 2.9 Article 3, European Convention on Human Rights

No one shall be subjected to torture or to inhuman or degrading treatment or punishment

---

Strasbourg has repeatedly said that for Article 3 to be breached, the conditions have to reach a minimum level of severity. That level is so high that it wasn't reached where:

- a patient was detained in a high secure hospital in what he claimed were tense, overcrowded, uncomfortable and insanitary conditions (*B* v *United Kingdom* 1984)
- a patient who required hospital psychiatric treatment was kept for seven months on the hospital wing of a Belgian prison (*Aerts* v *Belgium* 2000).

However, where someone is mentally ill, the following factors will apply:

- the conditions may breach Article 3 even though s/he can't point to specific ill-effects (*Keenan* v *United Kingdom* 2001)
- s/he must not be subjected to distress or hardship over and above the suffering unavoidably caused by detention
- s/he must be given all necessary medical assistance (*Kudla* v *Poland* 2002)
- *anti*-therapeutic conditions may breach Article 5 even if they don't breach Article 3
- detention will only comply with Article 5 if it takes place in a clinical setting (*Aerts* v *Belgium* 2000).

No UK psychiatric patient has yet succeeded in a claim under Article 3, and anyone wishing to complain about the conditions in which s/he is detained will have a better chance if they use Article 5.

MEDICAL TREATMENT
General

The decisions summarised in Box 2.10 show that the ECHR provides only limited protection for psychiatric patients. Although the required standard may be getting higher (*Selmouni* v *France* 2000), most current psychiatric practice is probably consistent with ECHR, Article 3.

Recently, there has been a suggestion that patients who are mentally capable cannot be forced to accept psychiatric medication, even if they are detained under MHA 1983.

Box 2.10 The European Convention on Human Rights and Medical Treatment

- It won't breach Article 3 to force-feed someone who is mentally competent (*X* v *Germany* 1984) (this would be unlawful in the UK, where a capable adult who is not detained under MHA 1983 may not be forcibly treated against his/her will)
- Provided treatment is clinically necessary, it won't breach Article 3 (*Herczegfalvy* v *Austria* 1993). So, it was permissible to force-feed a psychiatric patient, sedate him against his will, handcuff him and tie him to a bed
- Psychiatric treatment won't breach Article 3 merely because it has side effects; and any interference with Article 8 may be justified by the need to protect the patient's health or preserve public order (*Grare* v *France* 1992)

This suggestion was made in the *Wilkinson* case, by Lord Justice Simon Brown (*R. (Wilkinson)* v *RMO, SOAD and Health Secretary* 2002: see also Hewitt 2002b, pp.194, 195). It wasn't binding, and neither of the other two Court of Appeal judges who heard the case adopted it. In any case, Simon Brown LJ has subsequently adjusted his view (see *R. (B)* v *Ashworth Hospital Authority* 2003). However, the Courts have accepted that now the HRA 1998 is in force, compulsory treatment will be permissible only if it doesn't breach a patient's ECHR rights. At the very least, this has given patients the right to have the reasons for their treatment explained to them (see *R. (John Wooder)* v *Dr Graham Feggetter and the Mental Health Act Commission* 2002; *R. (N)* v *Dr M and others* 2003).

SECLUSION

Before the HRA 1998 came into force, the practice of secluding patients was thought to be vulnerable to challenge under the ECHR. However, as a result of two recent cases, it is now more strongly established, and the safeguards for its use are far weaker, than for some time.

It was already known that:

- Article 3 might be breached where a detained person is removed from association (*Koskinen* v *Finland* 1994)

- there will be no such breach where seclusion is for security, disciplinary or protective reasons (*Dhoest* v *Belgium* 1987)

- but the arrangements made for each secluded patient must be reviewed continuously (*McFeely* v *United Kingdom 1981*).

That seclusion is now incontestably lawful is the result of two cases that were made possible by HRA 1998.

Following *R. (Munjaz)* v *Ashworth Hospital Authority (No 2)* (2002) and *S* v *Airedale NHS Trust* (2003; see also Hewitt 2002b) the position with regard to seclusion is as follows:

- Even though it contains no express provision, the power to seclude a detained patient may be implied from MHA 1983 (*R.* v *Bracknell JJ, ex parte Griffiths* 1976).

- Seclusion doesn't breach ECHR, Article 3, even where it is something other than a short-term, emergency measure (*A* v *United Kingdom* 1980).

- Article 5 is not relevant, because patients who are detained have been deprived of their liberty, even before they are secluded and even if that step is never taken.

- Seclusion may be 'medical treatment' under section 145 of MHA 1983, and if it isn't, the decision to begin or end it, and the management and review of its conditions, *is* (*B* v *Croydon Health Authority* 1995).

- An NHS trust must consider the MHA Code of Practice when drafting its seclusion policy, but it may lawfully depart from it if it has sensible reasons for so doing.

The *Munjaz* and *Airedale* cases show that as far as the management of psychiatric patients is concerned, the standard set by the ECHR is not particularly high.

MENTAL HEALTH REVIEW TRIBUNALS

Introduction

The Mental Health Review Tribunal (MHRT) is the body through which the state fulfils its obligations under ECHR, Article 5 (4), whose provisions are set out in Box 2.11.

Box 2.11 Article 5 (4), European Convention on Human Rights

Everyone who is deprived of his liberty by arrest or detention shall be entitled to take proceedings by which the lawfulness of his detention shall be decided speedily by a court and his release ordered if the detention is not lawful

---

Because this burden does not fall upon the 'hospital managers', their proceedings need not comply with Article 5 (4).

But what does Article 5 (4) require?

The right to review

All patients detained under MHA 1983 – whether they are unrestricted (MHA 1983, ss 66 and 69) or restricted (MHA 1983, s 71) – have the right to challenge their detention in a MHRT. Therefore, it is likely that, at least in theory, the MHRT system complies with Article 5 (4). However, in *practice*, the situation is a little less clear.

Delay

Anyone of 'unsound mind' is entitled to a 'speedy' review of his/her detention. What 'speedy' means has been examined in a number of cases, which may be summarised as follows:

- a gap of eighteen weeks between application and hearing is not speedy enough (*Barclay-Maguire* v *United Kingdom* 1981)
- a delay of five months is 'excessive' (*Van der Leer* v *Netherlands* 1990)
- a wait of four months is 'unreasonable' (although a hearing may not need to be arranged as quickly upon a subsequent review as upon initial detention) (*Koendjbihaire* v *Netherlands* 1990)

- the current benchmark is eight weeks (*E* v *Norway* 1994).

These decisions have led the state to seek to speed up MHRT procedures. However, where it tried to do so by listing all unrestricted cases for hearing after a fixed eight-week period, that was held to breach Article 5 (4). The High Court said that each application should be heard as soon as reasonably practicable, and *in any event* within eight weeks (*R. (C)* v *Mental Health Review Tribunal* 2002).

More recently, eight English psychiatric patients won a claim that the MHRT hadn't heard their cases 'speedily' enough (*R. (KB and 6 others)* v *Mental Health Review Tribunal and Health Secretary* 2002; *B* v *Mental Health Review Tribunal and Home Secretary* 2002; see also Hewitt 2002c). The High Court held that the delays, which were as great as twenty weeks, were due to a shortage of MHRT staff for which the government was responsible. Subsequently, six of these patients were awarded damages of between £750 and £4000 in respect of the delays (*R. (KB and others)* v *Mental Health Review Tribunal and Health Secretary* 2003).

As far as conditionally discharged patients are concerned, Strasbourg has found a breach of Article 5 (4) where it has taken, respectively, six months (*X* v *United Kingdom* 1981) and five months (*Kay* v *United Kingdom* 1994) to arrange a MHRT following their recall to hospital. A further challenge (*Pauline Lines* v *United Kingdom 1997*) resulted in the UK government amending the MHRT Rules 1983 to impose a limit of eight weeks between recall and hearing (SI 1998 No 1189; see r 2 (4)).

The regularity of review

The ECHR also guarantees anyone detained because of 'unsound mind' the right to challenge detention 'at reasonable intervals' (*Megyeri* v *Germany* 1993).

Every patient detained under ss 2, 3, 7 and 37 of MHA 1983, together, in some circumstances, with the 'nearest relative' of an unrestricted patient, may apply to the MHRT for release at least once in every period of detention (MHA 1983, ss 66 (1) and (2) and 70). This probably complies with the ECHR.

Some patients have their detention under MHA 1983, section 2, extended indefinitely because an application has been made to displace their 'nearest relative' (MHA 1983, s 29 (4)). The Secretary of State has indicated that he will use his power to refer those cases back to an MHRT

(MHA 1983, s 67 (1)), so that patients are able to go before the tribunal once in every 28-day period for which they are detained under section 2.

The medical member

Each three-member MHRT will have at least one 'medical member' (MHA 1983, Sched 2, para 4).

Because s/he both interviews the applicant and determines his/her application, it is sometimes argued that the medical member is witness and judge in the same case.

Although the High Court has dismissed this argument, it has said that if the medical member is going to take into account a view that s/he formed after meeting the patient, or if s/he is going to discuss it with other MHRT members, s/he should disclose that view to the patient (*R. (H)* v *Mental Health Review Tribunal* 2001).

These safeguards may not be sufficient. The ECtHR has held that a tribunal's impartiality may be called into question, and Article 5 (4) may be breached, where it has to assess evidence given by one of its own members (*DN* v *Switzerland* 2002).

In *R. (S)* v *Mental Health Review Tribunal and Health Secretary* (2002), a patient argued that, because he had to be examined by the MHRT medical member (MHRT Rules 1983, r 11), there was a breach of Article 5 (4). The High Court held:

- the medical member shouldn't use the examination of the patient to form a settled view of his/her mental state
- provided the medical member keeps an open mind until the conclusion of the hearing, s/he may express a provisional view.

The burden of proof

The coming of the HRA 1998 forced the government to adjust the grounds upon which a patient may be discharged from detention by a MHRT.

A patient may be detained if s/he can be shown to fulfil the relevant admission criteria (see, for example, MHA 1983, ss 2 (1) and 3 (2)). However, a patient who sought discharge had to show that s/he now satisfied different *discharge* criteria (MHA 1983, ss 72 (1) and 73 (1)).

The purpose of a patient's right of access to a court under Article 5 (4) is to 'take proceedings by which *the lawfulness of his detention* shall be decided', and it was not the reasonableness of discharge that should have been in issue.

In *R. (H)* v *Mental Health Review Tribunal* (2001), the Court of Appeal held that the relevant provision of MHA 1983, sections 72 (1) and 73 (1), breached ECHR, Article 5 (1) and (4). The Court made a formal declaration to that effect, and in response the UK government introduced the Mental Health Act 1983 (Remedial) Order, which requires those who detain a patient to show why s/he should not be discharged (SI 2001 No 3712).

Conditional discharge

In the case of 'restricted' patients, who will have been detained in hospital by order of a criminal court, an MHRT may grant discharge subject to conditions (and the patient may be recalled to hospital if those conditions are broken).

A conditional discharge may be deferred so that the necessary arrangements can be made (MHA 1983, s 73 (7)). Those arrangements would form part of the aftercare services to which a patient would be entitled under MHA 1983, section 117. In some cases the inability to make them has been the subject of legal challenge.

- In *Johnson* v *United Kingdom* (1999) a patient had received a conditional discharge on four occasions, and each had been frustrated because no suitable hostel accommodation could be found for him. The Commission ruled that the 'lack of adequate safeguards [...] to ensure that [his] release from detention was not unreasonably delayed' violated ECHR, Article 5 (1).

- In *R.* v *Mental Health Review Tribunal and others, ex parte Hall* (2000), a patient continued to languish in prison because a requirement of his conditional discharge could not be satisfied. The High Court had ruled that his discharge had been unlawful, saying that the MHRT should have taken steps to police the conditions it had imposed. However, the Court of Appeal ruled that the MHRT had no such power.

The Courts have followed this line in most subsequent cases. The decisions of the High Court and the Court of Appeal in *R.* v *Camden and*

Islington Health Authority, ex parte K (2001) may be summarised as follows:

- NHS bodies have no *absolute* obligation to ensure that the conditions of a conditional discharge are satisfied (*R. v Mental Health Review Tribunal and others, ex parte Hall* 2000).

- If adequate community facilities are not available, a patient may have to remain in hospital.

- The NHS may decide what 'section 117' facilities to provide, and may make this decision on financial grounds.

- ECHR, Article 5, does not stipulate *what* community facilities must be provided.

- A patient's detention won't breach Article 5 if s/he is still of 'unsound mind' and it is impossible to provide the community care the MHRT considers necessary.

- Doctors cannot be forced to implement aftercare arrangements with which they don't agree.

This position is widely regarded as being favourable to NHS trusts and local authorities and *un*favourable to the patients whose discharge from hospital may depend upon them.

Precisely how an MHRT might resolve an impasse has been the subject of keen debate over the last few years:

- In *R. v Camden and Islington Health Authority, ex parte K* (2001), the Court had suggested that the health authority might refer the matter to the Home Secretary, who might then refer it back to the MHRT under MHA 1983, section 71.

- However, in *R. (C) v Secretary of State for the Home Department* (2001), the High Court held that a deferred conditional discharge is a final order, which the MHRT may not reconsider (see also *Secretary of State for the Home Department v Oxford Regional Mental Health Review Tribunal and another* 1987).

This issue has been resolved by the case of *R. (IH) v Secretary of State for the Home Department and Secretary of State for Health* (2002).

Here, a patient's conditional discharge was frustrated because no one could find a forensic psychiatrist who was prepared to supervise him in the community. He sought judicial review, claiming that the relevant discharge criteria were incompatible with the 'right to liberty' contained in ECHR, Article 5. He argued that the MHRT should have the power to enforce any conditions it imposed upon discharge.

The Court of Appeal dismissed the patient's case. Its decision is summarised in Box 2.12.

Box 2.12 The case of IH

- After HRA 1998, the case law must be re-considered
- If an MHRT couldn't revisit a conditional discharge that had been frustrated, that might breach the ECHR
- However, MHA 1983, section 73 (7) – which allows an MHRT to defer conditional discharge until suitable arrangements can be made – also allows it to monitor the making of those conditions
- Therefore, there is no breach of the ECHR

Here, the Court of Appeal was keen to comply with its duty under HRA 1998, section 3 (1), to read primary legislation 'in a way which is compatible with the Convention rights'.

Re-detention

Another way in which the will of an MHRT may be frustrated is by the re-detaining of a patient shortly after s/he has been granted a discharge.

In *R. v East London and the City Mental Health NHS Trust, ex parte Von Brandenburg* (2001), a patient to whom an MHRT had granted a deferred discharge was re-detained one day before it came into effect. The High Court said the new detention was perfectly lawful, and the Court of Appeal agreed. It said:

- Under MHA 1983, there needn't be a change in circumstances before a patient who has been discharged by a MHRT can be re-detained.
- However, where re-admission is proposed 'within days' of an MHRT discharge, the MHRT's view should prevail.
- In such circumstances, it is unlikely, in the words of MHA 1983, section 13, that an Approved Social Work could be satisfied that an application 'ought to be made', and any

subsequent admission may be unlawful (see also Hewitt 2002d).

This decision was vague, and it no longer holds good.

The current legal position was set out in the case of *H* v *Ashworth* (2002; see Hewitt 2002e; Stern and Hewitt 2002). Here, a patient in a high secure hospital who was discharged at short notice was soon re-detained under MHA 1983, section 3. He sought to challenge his re-detention, and for its part, the hospital sought to challenge his discharge.

Box 2.13 summarises the guidelines set down by the Court of Appeal for when consideration is being given to a patient who has only recently been discharged by an MHRT.

Box 2.13 H v Ashworth

- Those who wish to re-detain must ask themselves whether the ground on which they rely is one that has been rejected by the MHRT
- If so, they should not 're-section'
- In deciding whether the grounds were rejected by the MHRT, the professionals should not be too zealous in seeking to find new circumstances

---

COMMUNITY TREATMENT

As we have seen, the ECHR imposes no particular standard for aftercare services (*R.* v *Camden and Islington Health Authority, ex parte K* 2001). However, the ECHR has held that a refusal to provide assistance with housing to someone suffering from 'serious disease' may breach Article 8 (*Marzari* v *Italy* 1999).

In terms of the current aftercare regime, it is unlikely that 'supervised discharge' under MHA 1983, section 25A–J, breaches the ECHR.

Nationals of other states have used Article 5 to attack other forms of community treatment, but few have succeeded:

- The fact that a woman was required to accept outpatient psychiatric treatment as a condition of her discharge from hospital was held not to amount to a deprivation of her liberty under Article 5 (*W* v *Sweden* 1988).

- It could be justified under Article 8 to grant a woman provisional discharge from hospital where it was feared that she would stop taking her medication if she were absolutely discharged (*L* v *Sweden* 1986).
- Although medical treatment with adverse side-effects may breach the right to private life, its compulsory use in the community may be justified by, amongst other things, the need to preserve public order (*Grare* v *France* 1992).

CONCLUSION

It would be wrong to suggest that the HRA 1998 has had no impact upon mental health law in England and Wales. In some areas – especially MHRT practice – it has been responsible for some real changes, and it may affect the care and treatment that is given to many detained patients. However, those areas are relatively few and far between. Many litigants have discovered that the ECHR is a mixed blessing, and the cases they have brought – and lost – have begun to reveal as much about the Convention and its limitations as about the state of domestic law. Nevertheless, the fact that change is incremental need not prevent it, in time, being deeply significant.

REFERENCES

Cho, N. (2002) 'Nearest relatives of gay and lesbian patients.' *Journal of Mental Health Law*, December, 323–7.

Department of Health (2002a) *Draft Mental Health Bill*, Cm 5538–I. London: The Stationery Office.

Department of Health (2002b) *Draft Mental Health Bill: Explanatory Notes*, Cm 5538–II. London: The Stationery Office.

Department of Health (2002c) *Mental Health Bill: Consultation Document*, Cm 5538–III. London: The Stationery Office.

Hewitt, D. (2002a) 'An end to compulsory psychiatric treatment?' *New Law Journal*, 8 February, 194, 195.

Hewitt, D. (2002b) 'A room of one's own – seclusion is at last lawful.' *The Times*, 26 November.

Hewitt, D. (2002c) 'Delays have dangerous ends.' *New Law Journal*, 10 May, 694.

Hewitt, D. (2002d) 'Detention of a recently-discharged psychiatric patient.' *Journal of Mental Health Law*, February, 50–9.

Hewitt, D. (2002e) 'Challenging unwelcome MHRT decisions.' *Solicitors Journal*, 12 April, 338, 339.

Mental Health Act Commission (1998) *Seventh Biennial Report, 1995–1997*. London: The Stationery Office.

Mental Health Act Commission (2000) *Eighth Biennial Report, 1997–1999*. London: The Stationery Office.

Stern, K. and Hewitt, D. (2002) 'Re-admission under the Mental Health Act following discharge by a Mental Health Review Tribunal.' *Journal of Mental Health Law*, July, 169–78.

STATUTES
Human Rights Act 1998
Mental Health Act 1983

CASES
A v The Scottish Ministers [2000] SLT 873.
A v The Scottish Ministers [2002] 3 WLR 1460.
A v United Kingdom, Application No 6840/74, Decisions and Reports, Vol 10, 5 and Vol 20, 5.
A v United Kingdom [1980] 3 EHRR 131.
Aerts v Belgium [2000] 29 EHRR 50.
Anderson, Reid and Doherty v The Scottish Ministers and the Advocate General for Scotland [2002] 3 WLR 1460.
Ashingdane v United Kingdom [1985] 7 EHRR 528.
B v Croydon Health Authority [1995] Fam 133.
B v Mental Health Review Tribunal and Secretary of State for the Home Department [2002] EWHC 1553 (Admin).
B v United Kingdom [1984] 6 EHRR 204.
Barclay-Maguire v United Kingdom, Application No 9117/80, Decision as to admissibility, 9 December 1981.
Conka v Belgium [2002] 34 EHRR 54.
De Wilde, Ooms and Versyp v Belgium [1971] 1 EHRR 373.
Dhoest v Belgium [1987] 12 EHRR 135.
DN v Switzerland [2002] BMLR 221.
E v Norway [1994] EHRR 30.
Fox, Campbell and Hartley v United Kingdom [1991] 13 EHRR 157.
Grare v France [1992] 15 EHRR CD 100.
Herczegfalvy v Austria [1993] 15 EHRR 437.
Johnson v United Kingdom [1999] 27 EHRR 296.
JT v United Kingdom [2000] 1 FLR 909.
Kay v United Kingdom, Application No 17821/91, Report of the Commission, adopted 1 March 1994.
Keenan v United Kingdom [2001] 33 EHRR 38.
Koendjbihaire v Netherlands [1990] 13 EHRR 820.
Koskinen v Finland [1994] 18 EHRR CD 146.
Kudla v Poland [2002] 35 EHRR 11.
L v Sweden [1986] 8 EHRR 269.
Pauline Lines v United Kingdom [1997], Application No 2451/94.
Litwa v Poland [2001] 33 EHRR 53.
Marzari v Italy, Application No 00036448/97, European Court of Human Rights, 4 May 1999.
McFeely v United Kingdom [1981] 3 EHRR 161.
Megyeri v Germany [1993] 15 EHRR 584.
Messina v Italy (No 2), Application No 00025498/94, European Court of Human Rights, 28 September 2000.
Neilsen v Denmark [1989] 11 EHRR 175.
R. v Bracknell Justices, ex parte Griffiths [1976] AC 314.
R. v Camden and Islington Health Authority, ex parte K [2001] COD 483 and [2001] 3 WLR 553.
R. v Canons Park Mental Health Review Tribunal, ex parte A [1994] 1 All ER 481 and [1994] 2 All ER 659.
R. v East London and the City Mental Health NHS Trust, ex parte Von Brandenburg [2000] 3 CCL Rep 189 and [2001] 3 WLR 588.
R. v Mental Health Review Tribunal and others, ex parte Hall [2000] 1 WLR 1323.
R. v Secretary of State for Scotland [1998] SC 49, 2 Div and [1999] 1 All ER 481.
R. (on the application of Ashworth Hospital Authority) v Mental Health Review Tribunal, West Midlands and North West Region and R. (on the application of H, a patient) v Ashworth Hospital

Authority, Lorraine Berry, Edward Silva and Melanie Frances Croy [2001] EWHC 901 (Admin) and *R.* v *Ashworth Hospital Authority and others, ex parte H: R.* v *(1) Mental Health Review Tribunal for West Midlands and North West Region (2) London Borough of Hammersmith and Fulham (3) Ealing, Hounslow and Hammersmith Health Authority, ex parte Ashworth Hospital Authority* [2002] EWCA Civ 923.

R. (on the application of B) v *Ashworth Hospital Authority* [2003] EWCA Civ 547.

R. (on the application of C) v *Secretary of State for the Home Department* [2001] EWHC 501 (Admin).

R. (on the application of C) v *Mental Health Review Tribunal, London South and South West Region* [2002] 1 WLR 176.

R. (on the application of H) v *Mental Health Review Tribunal, North and East London Region* [2001] 3 WLR 512 and [2001] EWCA Civ 415.

R. (on the application of IH) v *Secretary of State for the Home Department and the Secretary of State for Health* [2002] 3 WLR 967.

R. (on the application of KB and 6 others) v *Mental Health Review Tribunal and Secretary of State for Health* [2002] ACD 85.

R. (on the application of KB and others) v *Mental Health Review Tribunal and Secretary of State for Health* [2003] 2 All ER 209.

R. (on the application of L) v *Secretary of State for Health* [2001] 1 FLR 406.

R. (on the application of M) v *Secretary of State for Health* [2003] EWHC 1094 (Admin).

R. (on the application of Munjaz) v *Ashworth Hospital Authority (No 2)* [2002] EWHC 1521.

R. (on the application of N) v *Ashworth Special Hospital Authority and the Secretary of State for Health* [2001] HRLR 46.

R. (on the application of N) v *Dr M and others* [2003] 1 WLR 562.

R. (on the application of S) v *Mental Health Review Tribunal and Department of Health* [2002] EWHC 2522 (Admin).

R. (on the application of SR) v *Nottingham Magistrates' Court* [2001] EWHC 803 (Admin).

R. (on the application of SSG) v *Liverpool City Council and the Secretary of State for Health, LS (Interested party)* CO/1220/2002.

R. (on the application of Wilkinson) v *The Responsible Medical Officer Broadmoor Hospital, the Mental Health Act Commission Second Opinion Appointed Doctor and the Secretary of State for Health* [2002] 1 WLR 419.

R. (on the application of John Wooder) v *Dr Graham Feggetter and the Mental Health Act Commission* [2002] 3 WLR 591.

Alexander Lewis Hutchison Reid v *United Kingdom*, Application No 00050272/99, European Court of Human Rights, 20 February 2003.

S v *Airedale NHS Trust* [2003] Lloyd's Rep Med 21.

Schuurs v *Netherlands*, 41 D and R 186.

Secretary of State for the Home Department v *Oxford Regional Mental Health Review Tribunal and another* [1987] 3 WLR 522.

Selmouni v *France* [2000] 29 EHRR 403.

Van der Leer v *Netherlands* [1990] 12 EHRR 567.

Varbanov v *Bulgaria*, Application No 31365/96, 5 October 2000.

W v *Sweden* [1988] D and R 59, 158–61.

Winterwerp v *Netherlands* [1979] 2 EHRR 387.

X v *Germany* [1984] 7 EHRR 152.

X v *United Kingdom* [1981] Application No 6998/75.

X v *United Kingdom* [1981] 4 EHRR 181

CHAPTER 3

THE CARE PROGRAMME APPROACH

LYNN AGNEW

INTRODUCTION

The Care Programme Approach (CPA) is the framework set out by the government for the delivery of effective mental health care. This chapter discusses the reasons why it was introduced, and how it now fits into the government's agenda for mental health. The core elements of the approach are the subject of extensive Department of Health (DH) guidance, summarised here along with some notes on good practice. The CPA applies to all those in contact with secondary mental health services regardless of setting; however, who is included and how the levels of the approach are applied may vary in local mental health services. The CPA is inextricably linked to the creation and maintenance of community mental health teams (CMHTs). Some of the problems that teams commonly find in its implementation are discussed later in this chapter.

THE CPA, CARE MANAGEMENT AND THE MODERNISATION AGENDA

The Care Programme Approach (DH 1990) was introduced to provide a framework for the care of mentally ill people outside hospital, requiring health and social care authorities to work together. It would help to solve the problems flowing from the closure programme for large psychiatric institutions of the previous two decades. Closure had led to problems of inaccessibility, confusion and duplication of effort caused by the attempt to meet needs through a number of physically separate and differently managed services. Concerns with public safety and the failures of community care were high on the agenda. It was feared that people with mental health problems 'fell through the net' too easily and with potentially tragic consequences.

At the same time social services departments were developing care management systems (DH/SSI 1991) following the National Health Service and Community Care Act 1990. Both systems were intended to provide a better focus on need and reduce the fragmentation of provision. Both involved the same processes of systematic assessment, planning and review, focused on the individual and coordinated by a single worker. Care Management differed by including the responsibility for commissioning and purchasing care.

In the real world of supporting people with long-term mental health problems, demarcation lines between health and social care support were never clear, and the two systems obviously overlapped. *Building Bridges* (DH 1995), in providing detailed guidance on the CPA, stated that both systems were 'in essence' doing the same thing and should be integrated. *Effective Care Co-ordination* (DH 1999a) stated that 'CPA *is* care management' in mental health services, and that integration should proceed apace in order to spare users and carers needless distress and confusion.

As the political landscape changed in the late 1990s, mental health policy began to reflect New Labour's social inclusion agenda alongside continuing worries about public safety. The stated aims of the government's wider health agenda (DH 2000) go beyond the provision of health care, narrowly conceived as a range of treatment responses, to the eradication of health inequalities and improvement of the quality of life for all citizens. In order to deliver this in the field of mental health, health and social services must integrate and work with the rest of the mental health community: users, carers, and voluntary and private sectors.

The CPA, integrated with Care Management and updated to support the *National Service Framework for Mental Health* (NSFMH) (DH 1999b), reflects this wider agenda through the coordination of health and social care for individuals, with an increasing emphasis on promoting social inclusion. Its key elements, and notes for practitioners, are set out below.

WHAT IS THE CPA?

The CPA is a delivery system for mental health care with four essential elements:

- a systematic *assessment* of health and social care needs (see Box 3.1)
- an agreed *care plan* (see Box 3.2)
- the assignment of a named *care coordinator* (see Box 3.4)
- regular *reviews* to reconsider need and change plans necessary (see Box 3.3).

The guidance, standards and targets for each element summarised here are taken from *Effective Care Co-ordination* (DH 1999a) and the NSFMH (DH 1999b).

Box 3.1 Assessment

Covers the following:
- Psychiatric, psychological and social functioning
- Risks to the individual and others, including previous violence and criminal record
- Any needs arising from comorbidity (e.g. drugs, alcohol misuse)
- Personal circumstances including family or other carers
- Housing, financial and occupational status
- Physical health needs
- Communication, cultural, gender, religious and access needs

Approached as follows:
- Multidisciplinary, undertaken in partnership between health and social care staff
- Undertaken collaboratively with the individual, and carer where the individual agrees
- Involving advocates, and/or interpreters as necessary

In addition, where assessment of the individual reveals that another is providing regular and substantial care, the Carers (Recognition and Services) Act 1995 must be complied with. The carer should have:
- An assessment of the individual's caring, physical and mental health needs, repeated on at least an annual basis
- His or her own written care plan

Good Practice Point

Assessment of need must be distinct from the consideration of resources available to meet need. The statement 'X needs residential
care' does not describe need, it proposes one solution to the difficulties an individual is experiencing. A relevant expression of need
could be 'X needs care around the clock' supported by a risk assessment which considers the likely consequences if such care is
not provided. Consideration could then be given to how resources
could be assigned to X in order to meet this need. This could include consideration of residential care amongst other options.
Needs should be recorded when services are lacking, as this information can inform service planning.

Box 3.2 Care planning

All service users on the CPA must have written copies of their care
plans, containing:
- Plans for action in relation to all aspects of the individual's life
  that need support, which *must* cover accommodation,
  occupation and benefit entitlement for enhanced CPA
- Agreed goals of intervention and, in the event of
  disagreement, reasons for this
- Estimated time scale for achievement or review of goals
- Contributions of all the agencies involved
- Name of care coordinator
- Crisis and contingency plans (mandatory for enhanced-level
  CPA)
- Advice to GPs on how they should respond if the service user
  needs additional help
- Date of next planned review

The plan should:
- Clearly relate to the assessment of need
- Involve service users and, where appropriate, their carers
- Focus on strengths and promote recovery

- Recognise diversity, reflect culture and ethnicity, gender and sexuality
- Use accessible language, and if necessary be translated or provided in other formats

There is a further standard that each service user 'requiring a period of care away from their home' will have a copy of a written aftercare plan agreed on discharge.

Good Practice Point

Care plans are not simply timetables. So when, for example, Y attends day care, s/he may receive a timetable that details the days on which s/he attends, the times of activities, groups and so on. This will be helpful to the service user (s/he needs to know when to turn up), and should form an adjunct to the care plan but should not be the whole of it. The care coordinator must develop with the user a care plan that indicates what the purpose of day care is in his/her life and how it relates to other goals, such as making friends or learning something new. It will link day care to other interventions, such as taking medication, help with finances, and so on, which will also contribute to his/her recovery and quality of life.

Box 3.3 Reviews

There is no timetable laid down for reviews. Rather, the care coordinator should ensure that the review and evaluation of care plans is ongoing.

Reviews should consider:
- How far the care plan is meeting the assessed needs
- Any change in those needs
- Any necessary changes to the care plan, in light of the above
- The date of next review, which must be recorded

Reviews of care plans must be:
- Held on a service user's discharge from hospital
- Considered at the request of any member of the care team, user or carer at any time. If a review is not held to be necessary, reasons for this must be recorded
- Checked by the annual audit of the CPA

Good Practice Point

It is necessary to check that care is being delivered, or to make minor adjustments sometimes, but this is monitoring – not review. To review the day care element of Z's care, the care coordinator must consider not just whether s/he is turning up and joining in, but how his/her needs may have changed and how far day care is meeting those needs as part of a comprehensive package. Adding to or decreasing services can flow from such a re-assessment. Care plans should change as needs change, and CPA level can be adjusted. Service gaps found at review should be recorded and used to inform service planning and commissioning.

Box 3.4 The care coordinator

This role is not specifically linked to any one of the mental health professions.

Assignment of care coordinator to a case should:
- Consider who is best placed to oversee care planning and resource allocation
- Take account of user needs and preferences in respect of gender, ethnicity, culture, language and religion
- Reflect where major issues in the care plan lie: medical or social?
- Consider the training, experience and current workload of proposed care coordinator

Key duties of a designated care coordinator will be to:

- Keep in contact with the service user
- Oversee both health and social care aspects of the care package
- Advise other team members of any changes that call for review of the care plan
- Ensure ongoing review and evaluation of the care plan

Good Practice Point

Building Bridges (DH 1995) states that the care coordinator role should not be assigned to someone in their absence or without their agreement. It does not make clear what needs to happen when such agreement cannot be obtained. Issues relating the role are considered in more detail below.

TO WHOM DOES THE CPA APPLY?

Focus on severe and enduring mental Illness

The CPA is 'applicable to all adults of working age in contact with the secondary mental health system (health and social care)' (DH 1999a, p.4). Since the early 1990s policy has stressed that all secondary mental health care should be focused on those with severe and enduring mental illness. This is locally defined, drawing on the framework recommended in *Building Bridges* (DH 1995), with its five dimensions of safety, informal and formal care, diagnosis, disability and duration, and should not be based on diagnosis alone. Recent guidance (DH 2002a, 2003a) emphasises that personality disorder and dual diagnosis, often marginalised by mainstream services, must also be considered within this framework.

Within the group thus defined as having severe and enduring mental illness there are clearly differing levels of vulnerability and risk, not all requiring the same intensive multi-agency approach. The potential for the full CPA to be applied indiscriminately to a large and poorly defined group has caused some to question whether it can meet its core purposes effectively (Burns and Liebowitz 1997).

It has been suggested that increased access to secondary services may lead to resources drifting towards those with less severe mental disorders. However, recent research has found that within one CMHT over a ten-year period, comparing case mix and service provided before and after the introduction of the CPA, the focus on patients with the most severe disorders increased (Cornwall *et al.* 2001). Nevertheless, achieving and maintaining such a focus may challenge community teams. Two approaches to this may be found in current policy guidance. The first relates to primary care, the second to the two tiers of the updated CPA.

CPA and primary/secondary care interface

The first approach focuses on the interface between primary and secondary care. GPs are faced with many patients with a wide range of mental health problems, and may refer them even if they do not fall within the agreed definition for secondary care. Recent policy implementation guidance on CMHTs (DH 2002b) suggests how, over time, GPs may be encouraged to refer fewer mild and self-limiting mental health problems, through measures such as screening by GP link workers, assessment of all those referred beyond the initial screening, advice on management and ready access to re-referral following discharge from secondary care. GP access to counselling and psychology services is also likely to reduce such referrals to secondary care, although this varies around the country.

CASE STUDY 3.1

Susan is a 45-year-old woman. She is divorced and her grown-up family have left home. She has not worked outside the home since having children. She has been recently treated for depression and agoraphobia by the community mental health team using an approach combining medication with psychological and social support. The support worker was important in encouraging Susan to put into practice the coping strategies she was learning.

Initially Susan refused to go out with the worker, although she welcomed the visits as an antidote to the loneliness and boredom of her day. The worker persisted and gradually Susan began to regain her independence. She attended a day centre and started some voluntary work. The

---

team returned her care to her GP with Susan's agreement, although she expressed her sadness at losing the support worker, 'a real friend'.

Susan's GP has now referred her back to the team. She is 'back at square one'. There has been an unspecified family upset. Susan is depressed, although not as low as last time, but is not going out at all. The GP says that she 'needs the support worker to visit her at home again'. Susan would like this at least twice a week and says it must be the original support worker.

Questions for discussion

1. Should the first response to this request be to reinstate the support worker, or are there other options?

2. What issues are raised here about the relationship between primary and secondary care?

3. What information do we have here about Susan's needs, as communicated through her GP?

4. What are the possible benefits and costs to Susan of reinstating the service according to her wishes?

The tiered CPA

In the second approach, providing levels of service clearly linked to levels of need allows teams to focus their efforts more effectively. Recent guidance (DH 2002b) suggests that people accepted into secondary care fall into two groups: the larger with 'time-limited disorders' and a substantial minority needing care for periods of several years. The latter group will include those with psychotic disorders, but also others needing care beyond the resources of primary care; examples include those with any disorder associated with significant risk of self-harm and those with severe disorders of personality. The CPA will apply to all accepted, but differentially depending on the intensity and complexity of care needed and related level of risk.

The updated CPA (DH 1999a) has two levels, *standard* and *enhanced*, based on complexity of individual need. The level may change as needs and risks vary. At standard level, needs will be assessed as for enhanced CPA, but usually by a single practitioner whose clinical notes will then constitute the care plan and record of review. This allows those who, for example, attend a psychiatrist's outpatient clinic or a depot clinic only to be dealt with in a manner that is not unnecessarily bureaucratic and time consuming. The time- intensive multidisciplinary effort is reserved for those with more complex needs at enhanced level, thus allowing teams to focus most resources on those in most need.

Providing a framework for care regardless of setting

The CPA applies to all those with serious mental illness wherever they happen to be, including hospitals, residential care and prisons in the statutory, voluntary and private sectors. Admission is simply a shift in the location of care.

Box 3.5 summarises guidance on discharge arrangements (DH 1999a) to ensure continuity between hospital and community and could be usefully applied to discharge from other institutions.

Box 3.5 Effective care coordination
guidance on discharge

- Preparation for discharge involving community-based staff, including children's services staff where relevant, should start early in admission
- Plans should cover all areas necessary to ensure safe discharge
- Hospital and community staff should be trained in discharge and care planning
- CPA meetings timetabled separately from ward rounds should be considered
- Implementation of the care plan should be assessed in the first month post-discharge

---

The CPA applies to those in settings beyond local hospital and community. Local mental health communities are now required to strengthen the application of the CPA to prisoners known to have serious mental health problems before imprisonment, and those found to have them whilst in custody. This links the CPA to strategies for improving mental health care for offenders (DH/HMPS/NAW 2001).

Not only prisoners may be considered here. Trusts and local authorities sometimes find that a lack of appropriate local resources to meet specific needs leads to individuals being placed outside their boundaries, perhaps in residential or inpatient care purchased within the private sector. The CPA framework of named care coordinator, care plan and review applies equally to those placed at a distance, and should promote active consideration of the potential of the individual for rehabilitation and return to his/her home area.

IMPLEMENTING THE CPA: PRACTITIONER ISSUES

DH guidance on the CPA sets out its key elements and objectives. How services organise themselves in order to deliver the CPA, however, is locally determined. Implementation is clearly linked to the development of effective multidisciplinary teams. The CMHTs continue to be the 'mainstay of the system' (DH 2002b, p.3) with the assertive outreach, crisis intervention teams and so on envisaged in the NHS Plan (DH 2000) arranged around them.

Just as this development process differs around the country, so too does the implementation of the CPA. This section, which is not exhaustive, looks at some of the issues that teams may encounter in putting the CPA into practice.

CASE STUDY 3.2

Wayne is a 38-year-old man recently released from prison. Much of his adult life has been spent in prison, serving sentences for offences such as aggravated burglary. He has been diagnosed as having a psychopathic personality disorder by a forensic psychiatrist who saw him during his last period of imprisonment. A possible underlying psychotic illness was queried, and he has been prescribed anti-psychotic drugs. He had no contact with local mental health services before going to prison. He has been placed on parole in a probation hostel away from his home area. The hostel workers have contacted the local CMHT, alarmed by Wayne's behaviour. They do not know much about his medication and wonder if aspects of his behaviour are to do with that, or with his personality. Also, Wayne would very much like to return to his former home area, but no one knows how that might be achieved.

Questions for discussion

1.   How does the CPA apply to Wayne?

2.   Whose responsibility could it be to place Wayne on the CPA?

3.   When should the process have started?

4.   What must an assessment of Wayne's needs cover?

5.   What consequences could ensue from failing to place Wayne on the CPA?

The role of care coordinator

As care management and the CPA are integrated, mental health professionals will find that as care coordinators they take on unfamiliar tasks and responsibilities; for example, purchasing care. They may feel ill-prepared for this, or even feel that professional boundaries are being transgressed. Where this is linked to a degree of alienation from the whole multidisciplinary project, as found by some researchers (Peck and Norman 1999), it may need to be addressed as a team development issue. Helpful approaches could include sharing information about professional roles and the positive recognition of differences in perspective between team members, as well as training on unfamiliar issues. At the organisational level, clear agreements allowing practitioners access to the resources of both health and social care, with use of pooled budgets, should reduce confusion.

Norman and Peck (1999) found psychiatrists, psychologists and occupational therapists in their study doubtful about how their professional expertise was used within the multidisciplinary team. Recent guidance (DH 2002b) makes it clear that psychiatrists should not usually be care coordinators for those on enhanced CPA. This acknowledges that the role of care coordinator for enhanced CPA does not make best use of their time and expertise. For those on standard CPA, however, the psychiatrist may be well placed to act as care coordinator.

CPA meetings

Care coordinators have a key role in organising CPA meetings and will usually but not always chair them. Finding time for meetings is an issue and it is important to avoid duplication. For example, where aftercare is arranged under Section 117 (Mental Health Act 1983) there is no need to hold one meeting to consider this and another to review the care plan prior to discharge from hospital, as the latter meeting can cover the requirements of Section 117. Equally, it is unnecessary to hold reviews related to each separate element of a care package, such as day care, home care, support workers and so on. CPA reviews should consider all needs and all aspects of care provided. Care may be increased or decreased at review, and the CPA level varied accordingly.

The care coordinator has responsibility for ensuring that meetings are accessible and comprehensible to the service user, and that full account is taken of diversity. The care coordinator should prepare the person by explaining what the meeting is about beforehand, and ensure that the person is enabled to take as full a part as possible. Interpreters or advocates should be brought in as needed. Supporters such as family and friends should also be encouraged to attend if that is what the service user wants.

Recording and sharing information
All those on CPA must receive a care plan in writing (or other format such as tape or Braille as appropriate). The written care plan should contain no surprises, as it will have been built as far as possible in partnership with the service user, and will reflect goals of real relevance. This does not mean that the care plan is a service user's wish list, nor should it be a way simply of setting out the care coordinator's preferred therapeutic method. Rather it should show that the care coordinator has sought to understand with the service user where his/her priorities lie, and to work out how they could be met.

Unlike service users, families and other carers have no absolute right to copies of the care plan without the knowledge and consent of the service user (although the Crime and Disorder Act 1998 allows for consent to be overridden where an individual's safety may be directly at issue; practitioners should seek advice here). However, where family and others form part of the care plan and have been involved in its development, it makes sense for them to receive a copy, and if consent is an issue it will help to make agreements about sharing care plan contents during stable times, not at crisis points.

CASE STUDY 3.3

Tom is nineteen years old. He has been admitted to hospital under a section of the 1983 Mental Health Act. Before admission Tom had not spoken to his parents, with whom he lives, for twelve months and had not been outside in daylight for the last six months. He kept to his room apart from midnight forays into the kitchen for food, and became seriously underweight. He was admitted to hospital after police found him wandering by the railway line in the early hours, muttering to himself.

Two years before he had stopped going to college after suffering a major loss of confidence. Before that his college work had been good and he had been planning to go on with his education.

Tom has improved on anti-psychotic medication, although there remains doubt over his diagnosis. On the ward it has become clear that he has many issues in common with others of his age, wanting financial independence, opportunities to meet and impress girls and less interference from mum and dad.

Tom's care coordinator has created a discharge plan for him. Ignoring the layout of the CPA form, which required a list of needs and proposals for meeting them, he opted instead for an elaborate formulation of the family's communication difficulties, complete with diagrams. Underneath was a space for the service user to record his view of his needs. Tom had written 'A flat and a car'. His parents are not sure that they can cope with Tom, but feel sure he could not survive living independently.

Questions for discussion

1.   Has the care coordinator described Tom's needs?

2.   Has Tom described his needs?

3.   What do you consider Tom's needs to be at this time, and in the longer term?

4.   What are the likely consequences of the evident disparity between Tom's views and his care coordinator's?

5.   Who else needs to contribute to the care plan?

6.   How should Tom's parents' views come into the planning process?

7.   What might a plan to meet Tom's needs contain, and who could be involved in delivering it?

CASE STUDY 3.4

John is a 30-year-old man of mixed racial heritage. He has learning disabilities and lives in a local authority residential scheme. He had a period of inpatient care in a unit for people with learning disabilities and psychiatric disorder some years ago. He is thought to have been diagnosed with schizophrenia and to have been compulsorily detained, but no one is certain. No notes can be found. The unit has since closed and there is no consultant psychiatrist for learning disabilities locally. John, like others in the residential scheme, has no GP and no contact with the local community mental health team, which has a robustly defended view that their services are for people with serious mental illness, not learning disabilities.

The duty approved social worker (ASW) receives a telephone call from a care worker in the scheme who says that John is 'kicking off'. He can be heard shouting in the background. On asking for more details, the ASW is told that John is very large and 'violent', that he has a 'mental history', and that he needs to be sectioned. The care worker asks if he should order an ambulance.

Questions for discussion

1.   Should the CPA apply to John?

2.   What should an assessment of his needs cover? Who should be involved?

3.   How can the application of the CPA help prevent such situations developing?

4.   Who should be involved in John's care?

5.   Is there evidence of stereotyping here, and what are the likely consequences of this for John?

The sharing of information between agencies may easily give rise to uncertainty for practitioners. It is good practice to explain to service users, as early as possible, that some information may need to be shared between professionals and agencies in order to gain access to the full range of support needed, and to gain consent on this basis. Multi-agency involvement in enhanced CPA (such as probation, police and housing) will necessitate the sharing of information. This should be governed by protocols to ensure that all concerned, including the service user, are aware of how information will be used, who will have access to it and how it will be safeguarded. There is now extensive confidentiality and data protection guidance on health records, of which a summary may be found in *The Protection and Use of Patient Information* (DH 1996). Generally, patient consent to sharing information is essential but, as stated above when the prevention, detection or reduction of crime is at issue, there may be grounds to override this (Crime and Disorder Act 1998).

CONCLUSIONS

Recent consultation and NSFMH implementation guidance on dual diagnosis, women's mental health, personality disorder, and black and minority ethnic issues (DH 2002a, 2003a, 2003b, 2003c) all describe how the CPA will apply as services bring marginalised groups into the mainstream of provision. As mental health services modernise, care will continue to be a multidisciplinary endeavour. The efficacy of medication and psychological treatments in supporting people with severe and enduring illness cannot be discussed other than in the context of building comprehensive care packages, as the CPA allows. The views of service users themselves that adequate housing, income and social and occupational aspects of daily living are important in reducing disability cannot be ignored. The aim of the CPA is to draw together all aspects of health and social care not only to prevent people with serious mental health problems falling through the net, but also to meet their aspirations for better lives.

REFERENCES

Burns, T. and Liebowitz, J. (1997) 'The Care Programme Approach: Time for frank talking.' *Psychiatric Bulletin of the Royal College of Psychiatrists 21*, 426–9.

Cornwall, P., Gorman, B., Carlisle, J. and Pope, M. (2001) 'Ten years in the life of a community mental health team: The impact of the care programme approach in the UK.' *Journal of Mental Health 10*, 4, 441–7.

DH (Department of Health) (1990) *Joint Health and Social Services Circular: The Care Programme Approach for People with a Mental Illness Referred to the Specialist Psychiatric Services* (HC (90) 23/LASSL(90/11). London: DH.

DH (Department of Health) (1995) *Building Bridges: A Guide to Arrangements for Inter-agency Working for the Care and Protection of Severely Mentally Ill People.* London: DH.

DH (Department of Health) (1996) *The Protection and Use of Patient Information.* (HSG(96)18: LASSL(96)5). London: DH.

DH (Department of Health) (1999a) *Effective Care Co-ordination: Modernising the Care Programme Approach.* London: DH.

DH (Department of Health) (1999b) *National Service Framework for Mental Health: Modern Standards and Service Models.* London: DH.

DH (Department of Health) (2000) *The NHS Plan: A Plan for Investment, a Plan for Reform.* London: DH.

DH (Department of Health) (2002a) *Dual Diagnosis Good Practice Guide.* London: DH.

DH (Department of Health) (2002b) *Mental Health Policy Implementation Guide: Community Mental Health Teams.* London: DH.

DH (Department of Health) (2003a) *Personality Disorder: No Longer a Diagnosis of Exclusion.* London: DH.

DH (Department of Health) (2003b) *Women's Mental Health: Into the Mainstream.* London: DH.

DH (Department of Health) (2003c) *Inside Outside: Improving Mental Health Services for Black and Minority Ethnic Communities in England.* London: DH.

DH/HMPS/NAW (Department of Health, HM Prison Service and The National Assembly for Wales) (2001) *Changing the Outlook: A Strategy for Developing and Modernising Mental Health Services in Prisons.* London: DH.

DH/SSI (Department of Health/Social Services Inspectorate) (1991) *Care Management and Assessment: Practitioners' Guide.* London: DH.

Norman, I.J. and Peck, E. (1999) 'Working together in adult community mental health services: An inter-professional dialogue.' *Journal of Mental Health 8*, 3, 217–30.

Peck, E. and Norman, I.J. (1999) 'Working together in adult community mental health services: Exploring inter-professional role relations.' *Journal of Mental Health 8*, 3, 231–42.

STATUTES

Mental Health Act 1983. London: HMSO.
National Health Service and Community Care Act 1990. London: HMSO.
Carers (Recognition and Services) Act 1995. London: HMSO.
Crime and Disorder Act 1998. London: HMSO.

USEFUL CONTACT

The Care Programme Approach Association is a network organisation providing support to CPA coordinators and managers and all those involved in the operation of the CPA.

Tel: 01246 552889

Email: cpa.association@chcsnd-tr.trent.nhs.uk

ACKNOWLEDGEMENT

I would like to thank Tony Ryan for his patient encouragement and support throughout the writing of this work.

CHAPTER 4

INTERVENTIONS IN MENTAL HEALTH
PROMOTING COLLABORATIVE WORKING AND MEANINGFUL SUPPORT

SIMON RIPPON

INTRODUCTION

This chapter will guide the reader on some key interventions and strategies that are relevant to mental health practice. The approaches used
have an emphasis on promoting collaboration between the practitioner,
the service user and the service user's social networks. The interventions
illustrated are intended in principle to be transferable across a range of
problem areas experienced by service users seeking support from practitioners in a range of mental health settings, the caveat here being that the
practitioner will need to ensure that the approaches are relevant at all
times to the needs of the service user. In essence the chapter is intended as
a practice guide and serves to translate evidence-informed practice into
the mainstream of mental health work. The interventions used assume
that the practitioner will have grounding in mental health work and an
understanding of some of the established models and approaches
currently profiled in education and training and mental health services.

Context and contemporary issues for mental health practitioners

The current context of mental health and social care provision is steering
practitioners toward models of intervention and support that are increasingly focused on specific service user groups and mental health and
related issues. In turn practitioners are expected to be able to deliver
support and interventions that are based on sound evidence and information and which are congruent or show fidelity to preferred models of

working and organising services. In line with this focus there are emerging national guidelines on the management of particular mental health problems, which articulate a clear position as to what the range and emphasis needs to be in delivering intervention and treatment (NICE 2003).

The development of specific and structured interventions for specific service users in particular environments has been further emphasised by the focus on national competency and capability statements for mental practitioners in health and social care settings. The focus on training and education linked to these key competencies for practice is also a major driver in mental health services currently.

Establishing focused interventions in practice

We noted earlier that modern mental health interventions are shaped around established evidence and practice guidelines, and are underpinned by practitioners who have a demonstrable level of capability and competence. Given this context it is important for practitioners to plan and implement interventions in a methodical and responsive way.

For those practitioners working in community and primary mental health settings there will be a range of needs presented by individuals and families, which will require focused and specific intervention. One of the growing issues facing such practitioners is the frequency with which people present within such services when experiencing a change in mood, often described as low mood, or mild or moderate depression. The national statistic for the prevalence of depression is shown to be 21/1000; where there are less specific and broader changes in mood, often seen as mixed depression and anxiety, the figure rises to 98/1000 (Meltzer *et al.* 1995). These rates are seen to differ significantly across age groups, between gender and for those who are economically and socially deprived. The experience of low mood and depression in women is more marked during early to mid-adulthood, and prevalence is highest among those who have separated; more so among males. Female prevalence is higher among those who are cohabiting or single rather than those who are married. In terms of education and other social indicators, males who complete education have progressively lower rates of depression and unemployment is also seen as being a factor in depression. In terms of social class, those in class 3 and below have higher rates than those in classes 1 and 2 – this is for both sexes. Lone parents have the highest overall rates and couples with children show a higher rate of prevalence than those without.

The experience of depression is seen to be the fourth commonest cause of loss of disability-adjusted life years in the world and is predicted to become the second most common by 2020 (World Bank 1993).

The vast majority of people experiencing such life events as unemployment, marital and relationship breakdown and changes in social circumstances will be treated and supported in primary care and community settings and have a range of interventions open to them. For many, the experience will be short-lived with minimal disruption to their lifestyle; for some, the experience will lead to marked changes in their social and life circumstances, bringing them into contact with specialist mental health services. The need, therefore, to provide meaningful and effective interventions and support is indicated.

DEPRESSION, LOW MOOD AND CORE INTERVENTIONS

There is an established literature in mental health practice related to the management of depression and low mood and the emergence of short-term and specific psychological interventions. This literature articulates models and conceptual frameworks for understanding the advent of depression and the underlying intra-personal phenomena that play a part in the development of the experience. One of the most prominent models for understanding depression is that described by Beck *et al.* (1979), which suggests that life experience leads people to form assumptions about themselves and others, the event itself and a subsequent view of the world as a whole. This is often referred to as the *cognitive triad of depression*. These assumptions and views are then developed and used to organise, govern and evaluate later personal experiences and inform resulting behaviours. It is this ability to evaluate and predict events from a particular perspective, in a way that is automatic, that gives rise to biased interpretations and leads to behaviours which can be seen as dysfunctional and which impact in a variety of ways on the lifestyle of the individual and his or her social networks.

CASE STUDY 4.1 HOW THINKING STYLES INFLUENCE MOOD CHANGE

Martin was asked to make a presentation to colleagues at work. At once he began to think that he would make a mess of the presentation and that his colleagues would think he was no good at his job. He began to recall similar events where things had not worked out as he had planned. As a result, over the next few weeks he became increasingly preoccupied with the planned presentation and his potential performance. Martin frequently questioned his ability to communicate in this way, he thought that his colleagues would be embarrassed at his performance and he regularly stated to himself that he was useless. Martin noticed that he was unable to concentrate on his usual work; he found it difficult to relax and was becoming frequently irritable in respect of minor events. He was reluctant to socialise with work colleagues and he was generally unhappy and had lost interest in his usual lifestyle. His relationship with his partner became difficult as he became more frequently tearful, lacking in motivation and enjoyment.

Martin went to see his GP for a physical health problem; he disclosed in conversation that he was feeling unhappy and was not sleeping. The GP became concerned after further conversation. He suggested a referral to the mental health practitioner attached to the practice.

Questions for disucssion

1.   What might be some of the useful conceptual models for developing your understanding of Martin's situation?

2.   What might be the benefit of sharing these with Martin?

Achieving collaborative understanding: Introducing the core elements of a cognitive behavioural approach to aid learning and understanding

As noted earlier there are specific conceptual frameworks for understanding the onset and recurrence of low mood and depression. The way the practitioner incorporates these into everyday practice is key as it enables relevant interventions to be identified and implemented.

It is important in the initial stages of work with Martin to spend time discussing the detail of his experiences. This phase of assessment and information gathering should aim to promote learning and to build consensus between the practitioner and service user. The emphasis in cognitive behavioural therapy (CBT) is on establishing an educative and collaborative focus where the individual learns to recognise negative and unhelpful thoughts and evaluate thinking patterns and behaviours that occur during and following such thought episodes. The interventions also focus on helping the individual to *practise* new approaches to managing behaviours and thinking patterns.

Following this stage the practitioner will be more informed as to the duration of the problem(s), the impact on broader biological, psychological and social well-being and have an understanding as to the interplay between these features in maintaining the service user's current situation. It will become important for the practitioner to offer a resumé of his/her understanding in respect of these experiences. Such a resumé should aim to clarify information and seek to confirm the relationship between events, thoughts, behaviours and emotional states. This will demonstrate that both the practitioner and the service user are working together in a collaborative manner to reach a point where interventions can be identified for specific issues and problems.

The opportunity to review the information disclosed during the sessions will enable the practitioner to provide a key part of CBT's conceptual framework. This stage is the formulation phase; it is a central tenet of the model and serves to help the service user to understand his/her situation, the interaction between the key features and the resultant emotional experiences and behaviour. The formulation resulting from this series of interviews and conversations is an integral part of the therapeutic relationship. Often formulation is best illustrated in diagrammatic form where key thoughts, behaviours and emotional and physiological states can be expressed in a sequential way. The timing in presenting the formulation may depend on the detail gathered during the assessment phase; it may be that an initial formulation is offered as a means of illustrating broad problems and issues related to thoughts with a more specific formulation being made at a later stage that represents a key or singular issue. In the case of low mood or depression any formulation should focus on the relationship between key thinking patterns and symptom experiences such as low mood, poor concentration or loss of motivation (Blackburn and Twaddle 1996).

Reflective Practice Questions: Establishing a Mutual Understanding of the Issues

1. What are the benefits of offering Martin a formulation based on his descriptions of his experiences?

2. What potential learning can be generated from such an intervention as this?

3. What methods will aid you in conveying the formulation?

4. How important will language and terminology be in this session?

INTERVENTIONS FOR MANAGING LOW MOOD AND EXPERIENCES OF DEPRESSION

Cognitive behavioural therapy

The emphasis in this section is toward developing interventions that will lead to self-management and which will foster personal learning and coping. These principles are congruent to those within a CBT approach.

CASE STUDY 4.2: EARLY PRIORITIES FOR INTERVENTION

Martin had discussed with the practitioner about his motivation to engage in and undertake regular lifestyle activities, being often variable. He had noticed a decrease in his level of enjoyment and was often unable to make necessary decisions to organise aspects of his daily routine. As a result Martin was experiencing frequent discord with his partner.

Secondary to this, Martin was also aware that he was having thoughts that were self-deprecating and critical, which impacted on his behaviour in terms of irritability and tearfulness.

There are a number of practical and helpful interventions that can be offered to service users in order to help during this time. Initially the practitioner will have agreed with the service user which issues and areas of his/her life require urgent attention. This will have been achieved following careful assessment. A significant part of this phase of information gathering will result in the practitioner presenting a formulation to the service user; this formulation will illustrate key features of the service user's experiences and the interplay between environmental situations, thinking patterns and resultant behaviours.

From this point the duration and frequency of contact with the practitioner can be determined, and the agenda for support and intervention outlined and then agreed. There are a range of interventions that could be utilised to support Martin and aid change and self-management of his experience.

Recent literature relating to the management of low mood and depression offers a range of interventions that are relevant to Martin's current situation (NICE 2004). The practitioner could begin by helping Martin monitor the extent and frequency of his unhelpful and self-deprecating thinking. Linked to this it would be useful for him to identify the situation he is in, who is present and the behaviours which he demonstrates during and following the experience. In order to do so Martin will need to keep a log or diary, which can then be used in follow-up sessions to review the impact and also to illustrate his change and self-management over a period of time.

Problem solving

An initial approach to supporting Martin may be introducing a problem-solving approach to help manage his current situation. Problem solving is a systematic method that has a focus on defining the issues and problems currently being faced, identifying the possible solutions and testing out these solutions (Andrews and Jenkins 1999). This approach also includes identifying difficulties that are related to practical lifestyle issues as well as issues connected to cognitive (thought) patterns. It is important that the practitioner helps in identifying support networks during the period when Martin is testing out this approach. This should include support from family members or friends (Hawton and Kirk 1998), and identify a range of situations where a problem-solving approach may be appropriate, covering crisis situations, personal conflicts and marital and relationship difficulties. The process by which a problem-solving approach should be introduced needs to illustrate collaboration and learning. The emphasis is on assisting Martin to incorporate the principles of problem solving into everyday aspects of his life and not on the practitioner solving problems on behalf of Martin (Andrews and Jenkins 1999). The process will follow a sequential pattern (see Box 4.1).

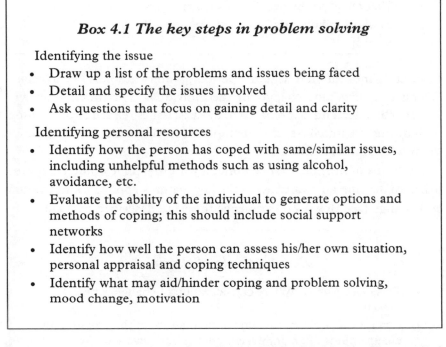

Box 4.1 The key steps in problem solving

Identifying the issue
- Draw up a list of the problems and issues being faced
- Detail and specify the issues involved
- Ask questions that focus on gaining detail and clarity

Identifying personal resources
- Identify how the person has coped with same/similar issues, including unhelpful methods such as using alcohol, avoidance, etc.
- Evaluate the ability of the individual to generate options and methods of coping; this should include social support networks
- Identify how well the person can assess his/her own situation, personal appraisal and coping techniques
- Identify what may aid/hinder coping and problem solving, mood change, motivation

Furthermore, the practitioner should establish with Martin the practical arrangements for utilising the problem solving approach. This may include keeping a personal record or 'homework diary', of when it was applied, and what were the benefits and outcomes. Emphasis may also be given to the support needs of friends and partners who may be helping Martin utilise this approach.

Reflective Practice Questions: Developing a Question Style to Aid Problem Solving

1. What might be the types of questions you may need to ask in the early stages of using a problem-solving techique?

2. How might you enable the individual to detail and explain events and responses to situations in a way that focuses on enhancing motivation and self-awareness?

3. How might you demonstrate the use of methods involved in the approach?

4. What could be the benefits of such an approach in terms of relationship building?

Promoting motivation during the period of intervention is key to establishing and sustaining change for the individual. The practitioner will need to consider, and be prepared to discuss, issues related to motivation both during the initial stages of therapeutic engagement and throughout the phases of intervention.

In terms of the practitioner working with Martin it would be appropriate to develop an awareness of the key features applied to motivation and change (see Box 4.2). In essence these are described in stages.

Box 4.2 Cycle of change

- *Pre-contemplation*: Where consideration of change is not present
- *Contemplation*: Here the individual is aware of the potential to change but is often ambivalent, being both aware of the reasons for change and the reasons staying the same
- *Preparation*: Here the individual is prepared to take needed action to access help and support and make initial changes
- *Action*: At this stage the individual is engaged in elements of change
- *Maintenance*: Successful change has been achieved in elements of behaviour

---

It is once again important that the motivational strategies reflect the overall objectives and needs of the individual. In terms of constructing a dialogue with the individual there are a number of routes that need to be considered; exploring the good and less good aspects of the behaviour and discussing issues related to satisfaction with life – this could include a focus on how life has been, could be and in fact is. It is important also to focus on decision-making dialogue that will help the individual prepare for, and undertake, key incremental changes.

In addressing the issues related to motivation it would also be important to consider the involvement of significant others, both professional peers and, importantly, those from within the individual's social networks. These people can act as a supportive resource to augment and endorse the individual's moves toward change.

Martin may require help with self-management of unhelpful thinking and what are often described as *automatic thoughts*. It would be relevant for the practitioner to recap on any explanation previously given related to illustrating the frameworks and concepts for the model of intervention being used. In this example the practitioner would revisit the explanations as to the core concepts of the framework for CBT. Such an explanation would focus on issues in relation to low mood and depression; using language and illustrations to emphasise key points within the model may help understanding. The relationship of thinking styles to Martin's overall situation should be a main point of emphasis in generating understanding as to why behaviours and emotional states occur.

In terms of interventions for managing such thoughts the practitioner may introduce guided learning (guided discovery) within the sessions to enable Martin to understand further the relationship between events, thoughts, behaviours and emotional feelings. The practitioner may use the information shown in Martin's 'homework diary' as a means of making the exercise appropriate and meaningful.

INTERVENTIONS TO MANAGE RELAPSE AND RECURRENCE OF MENTAL DISTRESS

Relapse in psychosis

The last decade has seen a significant shift in terms of how mental health practitioners are working with and supporting those individuals experiencing episodes of psychosis; with an emphasis on 'rebuilding a meaningful and valuable life...that involves taking control of cognitive and emotional difficulties as well as making decisions...' (Repper and Perkins 2003, p.109). There have been developments in terms of training and research that have encouraged organisations and teams within services to refocus aspects of practice toward interventions that promote and contribute to self-management and personal coping (Brooker, Falloon and Butterworth 1994).

Early intervention in psychosis has three key themes: interventions that are based in primary health care settings which focus on screening and early detection (Falloon *et al.* 1996), interventions that target individuals with a recent onset of psychosis and provide a range of support (McGorry *et al.* 1996) and interventions that are aimed at recognition and early detection of relapse in those who experience recurrent episodes of psychosis (Birchwood *et al.* 1989).

Early detection of relapse in psychosis and management interventions

Recognition of the early signs of relapse in psychosis has received much attention within both the research field and related practice literature (McCandless-Glincher, McKnight and Hamera 1986). The emphasis in the UK stems from the work of Birchwood and colleagues (see Birchwood *et al.* 1989, 1991) through the last decade. The focus on recognition of early signs enables the practitioner to work with the individual and his/her social networks in such a way as to help identify the key personal experiences that indicate progress toward psychotic relapse and which mark the way for deterioration in both personal lifestyle and functioning.

Therapeutic engagement

The essence of the relationship between the practitioner and individual will have a focus on positive engagement strategies that enhance relationship formation, open communication, mutual understanding and collaborative enquiry toward self-discovery and personal learning. These features enable the individual and practitioner to reach both a shared conceptual understanding as to the nature and meaning of psychotic phenomena and the potential for self-management and coping.

The importance of engagement in therapeutic relationships as a means of establishing effective therapeutic working cannot be understated. The core elements and prerequisites for such relationships have been discussed recently within the mental health literature (Repper and Perkins 2003; Rogers and Pilgrim 1994). Key skills include building a rapport that facilitates disclosure of personal information and experi-

CASE STUDY 4.3

Jasmin is a 27-year-old Afro-Caribbean woman who has recently moved back to live with her parents. She has been in receipt of services from a community mental health team following an initial episode of psychosis three years ago. The initial episode occurred shortly after Jasmin had left university and at a time where she was using illicit substances (smoking cannabis and using ecstasy and similar dance drugs with increasing frequency). At the time of her first episode she was admitted to a local mental health unit after she became involved with police following an argument in a lecture.

Jasmin spent six weeks in hospital and was discharged to her home with contact from a community mental health nurse and a psychiatrist in the outpatient department. She had also begun to work as a volunteer in a housing shelter in the city.

After a number of months Jasmin became reluctant to interact with her peers and was increasingly withdrawing from her social networks. Her manager at the housing shelter suggested she take time out from being a volunteer. It became apparent to the community nurse that she was keen to talk more about her psychosis and the impact this experience had had on her since leaving hospital.

ences as well as helping to identify the issues for change and exploration (Birchwood *et al.* 1989); other skills may be focused on exploring issues with regards to motivation to change, and the barriers and boosters to making such change (Miller and Rollick 1991). The importance at this stage, however, is to establish a realistic focus for the work in hand and to work towards therapeutic optimism, and relationships that inspire and sustain hope (see Repper and Perkins 2003).

The elements of relationship formation and engagement have been recently described as 'not necessarily "therapy", it is simply what some staff would recognise as caring, the development of empathy or just being with' (Bowles *et al.* 2002, p.257), and the aim of 'engagement is to understand the present situation of the person, which includes the relationship with illness and health...this is in pursuit of knowledge of what is happening within the person's world, self and colleagues and what this might mean in terms of essential care of the person' (Barker 2001, p.234).

The importance of this element of therapeutic work cannot be understated and is perhaps the platform for all future work and conversation with the user.

Good Practice Point

As a practitioner it may be useful to spend the initial sessions with Jasmin talking through her views on recent experiences; this way you can demonstrate that you are prepared to listen and hear her story. You can also get a real-time account of how she is understanding the issues involved in readiness for more structured or deliberate work together in later stages.

Reflective Practice Questions: Establishing a Focus on Understanding and Relationship Formation

1. Why might Jasmin be withdrawing from her social netorks?

2. What could a series of discussions about Jasmin's expeiences of psychosis lead to in terms of intervention and support?

3. How might the practitioner introduce and set the scene for such dialogue?

4. What key skills and knowledge would the practitioner need to achieve such a dialogue?

Identifying the stages of relapse

Following the steps that have enabled therapeutic engagement, the practitioner and service user will be now be able to focus down on further meaningful aspects of relapse management. The next stages may include the mapping of chronological and sequential events and key experiences that illustrate either a recent relapse or acute crisis or which are the milestones which are indicative of increasing distress and which may challenge existing coping strategies. The identification of such patterns and sequences is important for two main reasons. First, such patterns often herald learning for both the practitioner and the service user;

indeed, these patterns are key to determining the future stages of support from mental health services and the service user's social networks. Second, identifying relapse patterns enables the practitioner to become more aware of the strengths and deficits of the individual in terms of personal coping and self-management. The practitioner can then become attuned to when such personal elements may become compromised and, in turn, when a relapse may herald a possible acute crisis. There is need for a caveat here: the onset of relapse indicators may not always herald an acute phase of psychosis. Indeed, the individual may experience a low level of psychotic phenomena over a period of weeks which may ameliorate with support of positive coping and management strategies.

Reflective Practice Questions: Focus on Gathering Detail of Personal Experience

1. How might I help the individual to build up a chronology of his/her relapse features?

2. What are the implications for doing this in terms of relationship building?

3. What could be the helpful/unhelpful implications of this for the individual?

4. How might I set the tone for this work with the service user?

When the practitioner has helped the service user identify the chronological and recurrent trends of personal and life experience that constitutes a move towards relapse or crisis it is important to frame this in the context of personal 'relapse signature' (Birchwood 1996), which has within it the core and common features of psychosis but which is unique to the individual in terms of occurrence, meaning and experience.

Good Practice Points

Key considerations for creating the context for identifying relapse indicators:

- Identify time, via a series of appointments with the service user, in which to begin to map the chronology of personal events.
- There should be a series of discussions with the service user wherein you can put forward your observations and perspectives on his/her experiences in respect of phenomena, relapse and coping – this serves to foster collaboration and understanding.
- Consideration should be given to the preferences of the service user in terms of language, phrases and terminology used to describe the relapse experiences. These should be incorporated into the dialogue of the sessions with appropriateness and regard.
- Consider a range of media to enable the service user to articulate his/her relapse indicators. Often visual mapping is useful – drawing a personal time line and filling key dates and events that correspond to personal change and emotional distress.
- Suggest that significant others (partners, spouses, friends and family members) involved in supporting the individual have an opportunity to participate in the sessions when appropriate – this may strengthen options for social support and involvement.
- Continually review progress with the service user – sounding out ideas and his/her perspectives on experiences, their impact on his/her self, social role and participation in meaningful lifestyle events, etc.
- Create a climate that fosters learning and shares coping.
- Be clear about next stages following the identification of the chronology of personal events – knowing isn't enough!
- Foster hope and optimism.

Planning support and intervention

The objective of identifying the relapse signature with the service user is then to plan the needed and appropriate levels of support and intervention in order to reduce the potential for an actual relapse and escalation in psychotic phenomena. Such a plan must be tailored to the needs of the service user and reflect his/her existing and developing coping mechanisms, as well as being structured around the distinct phases of the relapse, and any increase in core psychotic phenomena.

Each of the staged components will be indicated by a time limit which, when expired, indicates the next stage of intervention either as an adjunct to, or replacement for, the previous intervention. It is at this time in the relationship and stage of delivering interventions that the practitioner will need to coordinate a number of approaches to support the service user effectively should a relapse be evident. This planned support and intervention should include contingencies to manage emerging needs and events. Frequent appointments and arrangements for access to services will need to be defined; levels of input from other workers and services will also be identified so as to enable a responsive and needs-led package of intervention to be offered. All of this work needs to be undertaken with the involvement of the service user.

It is also imperative that family members, carers and the service user's social networks are part of any plan to support the service user in times of crisis and relapse. Information, support and service access will all need to be communicated to these people in advance and as part of the wider ethos of managing relapse and supporting the service user.

The practitioner should give careful thought to how carers, service users and their social support networks are involved in the development of the relapse plan.

SUMMARY

The focus in mental health services is now firmly upon developing treatments and interventions that impact positively on the individul's life situation, thereby increasing both self-management and determination and contributing to recovery. More recently, professional mental health practice has seen an increase in practice guidelines which describe key interventions and models of service provision that reflect the evidence from research in terms of effectiveness and efficacy.

There are many challenges facing the mental health practitioner. The need to develop skills and knowledge is imperative if practitioners are to demonstrate contemporary practice that contributes to and reflects the focus toward delivering services that promote collaboration with users.

This chapter has offered an overview of a number of practical approaches to delivering interventions in mental health. It is important that practitioners recognise that this is indeed an overview of some of the principles involved in delivering what are often quite sophisticated models of intervention. However, that said, the fundamental principles of collaboration, therapeutic and meaningful engagement are interventions that all practitioners need to be skilled in, for it is these principles that will form the platform for more intensive and structured programmes of intervention.

REFERENCES

Andrews, G. and Jenkins, R. (1999) *Management of Mental Disorders*, UK edition. Sydney: World Health Organisation Collaborating Centre for Mental Health and Substance Misuse.

Barker, P. (2001) 'The tidal model: Developing an empowering, person centred approach to recovery within psychiatric and mental health nursing.' *Journal of Psychiatric and Mental Health Nursing 8*, 233–40.

Beck, A.T., Rush, A.J., Shaw, B.F. and Emery, G. (1979) *Cognitive Therapy of Depression*. New York: John Wiley and Sons.

Birchwood, M. (1996) 'Early intervention in psychotic relapse: Cognitive approaches to detection and management.' In G. Haddock and P.D. Slade (eds) *Cognitive-Behavioural Interventions with Psychotic Disorders*. London: Routledge.

Birchwood, M., Smith, J., MacMillan, F., Hogg, B., Prasad, R., Harvey, C. and Bering, S. (1989) 'Predicting relapse in Schizophrenia: The development and implementation of an early signs monitoring system using patients and families as observers, a preliminary investigation.' *Psychological Medicine 19*, 649–56.

Birchwood, M., Smith, J., MacMillan, F. and McGovern, D. (1991) *Early Intervention in Psychotic Relapse: A Controlled Trial*. London: Department of Health.

Blackburn, I.M. and Twaddle, V. (1996) *Cognitive Therapy in Action: A Practitioner's Casebook*. London: Souvenir Press.

Bowles, N., Dodds, P., Hackney, D. Sunderland, C. and Thomas, P. (2002) 'Formal observations and engagement: A discussion paper.' *Journal of Psychiatric and Mental Health Nursing 9*, 255–60.

Brooker, C. Falloon, I. and Butterworth, A. (1994) 'The coutcome of training community psychiatric nurses in psychosocial intervention.' *British Journal of Psychiatry 165*, 222–30.

Falloon, I., Kydd, R., Coverdale, J. and Laidlaw, T. (1996) 'Early detection and intervention for initial episodes of schizophrenia.' *Schizophrenia Bulletin 22*, 271–82.

Hawton, K. and Kirk, J. (1989) 'Problem solving.' In K. Hawton, P. Salkovskis, J. Kirk and D.M. Clark (eds) *Cognitive Behavioural Therapy for Psychiatric Problems: A Practical Guide*. Oxford: Oxford University Press.

McCandless-Glincher, L., McKnight, S. and Hamera, E. (1986) 'Use of symptoms by schizophrenics to monitor and regulate their illness.' *Hospital and Community Psychiatry 37*, 929–33.

McGorry, P., Edwards, J., Mihalopoulos, C., Harrigan, S. and Jackson, H. (1996) 'EPPIC: An evolving system of early detection and optimal management.' *Schizophrenia Bulletin 22*, 305–26.

Meltzer, H., Gill, B., Petticrew, M. and Hinds, K. (1995) 'The prevalence of psychiatric morbidity among adults living in private households.' *OPCS Survey of Psychiatric Morbidity. Report 3*. London: HMSO.

Miller, W. and Rollick, S. (1991) *Motivational Interviewing: Preparing People to Change Addictive Behaviour*. New York: Guildford Press.

NICE (National Institute of Clinical Excellence) (2003) *Schizophrenia: Core Interventions in the Treatment and Management of Schizophrenia in Primary and Secondary Care*. London: NICE.

NICE (National Institute of Clinical Excellence) (2004) *The Management of Depression in Primary and Social Care*. Second consultation draft. London: NICE.

Repper, J.M. and Perkins, R. (2003) *Social Inclusion and Recovery: A Model of Mental Health Practice*. London: Baillère Tindall.

Rogers, A. and Pilgrim, D. (1994) 'Service users' views of psychiatric nurses.' *British Journal of Nursing 3*, 16–18.

World Bank (1993) *World Development Report: Investing in Health Research Development*. Geneva: World Bank.

CHAPTER 5

MEDICATION MANAGEMENT

JACQUIE WHITE

INTRODUCTION

The most common therapeutic intervention throughout the NHS is prescribed medication. Medicines management can include all aspects of
supply and therapeutic use of medicines, from individual service-user
level to the organisational delivery of an entire service (National Prescribing Centre and National Primary Care Research and Development
Centre 2002). This chapter will consider good practice in meeting the
individual needs of service users who are prescribed psychotropic medication within secondary mental health services, and this primarily
clinical activity will be referred to as 'medication management'. The term
'non-compliance' is used to describe a failure to take medicines as prescribed. This is to enable the difference between compliance and concordance to be emphasised, i.e. that one describes a behaviour or action in
accordance with prescription from a health professional and the other is a
process of collaboration where the service user can exercise choice (i.e.
not to take their medication if s/he so chooses).

Secondary mental health services focus on the needs of people with
serious and enduring mental health problems. Although a whole range of
psychotropic medication is prescribed to this population, anti-psychotic
and/or mood-stabilising medication is most likely to be the main prescription over the short term to treat acute episodes and over the long
term to prevent relapse. All psychotropic medications have the potential
to cause side-effects, which range from the mildly irritating to the chroni-
cally disabling and potentially fatal. Evidence from surveys of
anti-psychotic prescribing suggests more than half (and maybe even the

majority) of service users experience distressing and probably unnecessary side-effects (Taylor *et al.* 2000).

Non-compliance amongst people who are prescribed medications for chronic conditions is estimated at 50 per cent and is no different in mental health service users (Haynes, Montague and Oliver 1999). A number of factors can be identified which influence compliance, including agreement between the service user and clinician about the presence and severity of illness, beliefs about medication and the presence of side-effects (Gray, Wykes and Gournay 2002). The impact of non-compliance on individuals and the service is high, correlating with high rates of relapse and poorer long-term outcomes such as chronic disability and early death (Helgason 1990). Rates of cardiovascular disease, diabetes, HIV/AIDS and substance use are much more prevalent in the population of users of mental health services than in the general population (Harris and Barraclough 1998). Although the coexistence of other conditions makes prescribing decisions complex due to the many interactions that can occur, these risks can only be considered when they are identified.

DRIVERS FOR A CHANGE IN PRACTICE

There are several drivers towards change in current practice:

- the negative experience of service users and carers
- sub-optimal (least favourable) prescribing
- development of evidence-based interventions
- clinical governance.

Since the community care reforms of the late 1980s, service users and carers groups have been increasingly vociferous in their condemnation of medicines management services that have predominantly been experienced as negative. In 1989 one group of service users made some criticisms of their medicines management service which would have resonated with many other users. These criticisms included the failure to communicate information about medication benefits and risks, the disregard of the right to informed consent, the lack of recognition of the validity of the subjective experience of medication, the tendency to view side effects as pathological symptoms of mental disorder, the lack of consultation with the user about his or her experiences and the use of threats of evoking the Mental Health Act 1983 to coerce compliance (Islington Mental Health Forum 1989).

More recent reports highlight a 'postcode lottery' of prescribing practice, lack of choice and high numbers of service users experiencing distressing side-effects (Consumer's Association 2003; National Schizophrenia Fellowship, MIND and Manic Depression Fellowship 2000, 2001). It is recommended that all service users should have access to newer medicines with better side-effect profiles, have their clinical progress and side-effects effectively and systematically monitored and reviewed, be offered choice and be actively included in decision making (DH 1999, 2001; NICE 2002a, 2002b).

A national shortage of psychiatrists leaves limited time for prescribing decisions, reviews and monitoring. Evidence from a number of studies has demonstrated a lack of awareness of guidelines, unacceptable rates of polypharmacy, inappropriate uses of high doses, and a failure to utilise new treatments, use effective monitoring strategies and carry out interventions (e.g. Taylor et al. 2000). A shortage of pharmacists with expertise in mental health threatens to compound these difficulties by limiting access to expert information, support and monitoring.

Sharing information about the rationale for the prescription, alongside the potential effects and side-effects, with the service user and carer can facilitate both a process of informed consent and conordance (Harris, Lovell and Day 2002). However, information- giving or education interventions alone do not promote compliance or improve health outcomes (Gray et al. 2002). A structured and pragmatic medication management intervention based on motivational interviewing and cognitive behavioural therapy techniques has been demonstrated to increase compliance, promote the potential for recovery and improve mental health in people with a diagnosis of schizophrenia (Gray 2001).

Since the White Paper *The New NHS: Modern and Dependable* (DH 1997), there has been an increasing emphasis on using the framework of clinical governance to improve the quality of patient care. Awareness of the latest clinical evidence, standards and guidelines, access to continuing education and clinical supervision, transparent and well-documented decision making, risk management strategies, evaluation and audit processes have all become increasingly important.

POLICY, GUIDELINES AND PRACTICE ROLES

Since the early 1990s there has been a focus on expanding the traditional medication role of mental health nurses from a task-orientated, administrative activity to a variety of roles aimed at addressing unmet medication management need. As well as checking the prescription and administering safely, this includes ensuring information has been given about the benefits and the risks of treatment, checking the service user has given informed consent, monitoring effects and side-effects and communicating with the prescriber.

The role of *systematic* side-effect assessment was added in 1994 (DH 1994; Department of Health and the Royal College of Nursing 1994). This role has been repeated in a variety of policy documents ever since and the specific focus of antipsychotic medicines has been replaced with a general statement about the need to systematically monitor all side-effects. This has occurred despite a paucity of validated measures for other medications. The information-giving role has also expanded to one of educating service users and carers about diagnosis, treatment and the prevention of relapse. The role of checking informed consent now includes a need to demonstrate the concordance process. There is an expectation that, alongside side-effects, efficacy and compliance with treatment will also be systematically monitored so that the data can be used to inform regular reviews and clinical audit.

There is increasing recognition that people need to maintain and/or learn self-medication skills whilst in hospital in preparation for discharge, and nurses are increasingly expected to support, teach and assess these skills. Motivational interviewing and cognitive behavioural therapy skills are also needed, to both promote compliance with long-term maintenance regimes and address substance misuse issues. There is the further expectation that practitioners will maintain their own professional competence to perform these roles through continuous professional development.

The initial focus of policy upon nursing has been replaced with an acknowledgement that nursing roles can be provided from within the multidisciplinary care team from any practitioner with appropriate skills (Sainsbury Centre for Mental Health 2000). However, the burden of change remains within nursing practice due to the greater numbers of nurses than other professionals, the opportunity for intervention within the nurse–patient relationship and an expectation that medication management is a natural extension of the traditional administration role. Little attention appears to have been paid to the medication management role of social workers or other professionals, despite increasing integration and blurring of roles within multidisciplinary teams. Despite national shortages of mental health nurses and pharmacists, both these professions are also included in recent policy developments and legislation to bring about the new role of supplementary prescriber from April 2003. However, for this new role to benefit mental health service users psychiatrists will need to find time within their workloads to accommodate the changes. This includes a commitment to supervise trainees directly and meet regularly with the supplementary prescriber and service user to agree and review clinical treatment plans (DH 2003).

Curricula for all mental health professionals have yet to address the array of skills required by the new medication management roles described in policy over the last decade. There is an absence of NHS commissioned and funded courses to address this deficit amongst qualified staff, with an almost total reliance on education provided by or funded through the pharmaceutical industry. Criticism of the ethics of this position and calls for a greater distance from the marketing power of this global industry, for both doctors and mental health nurses, are becoming more prevalent (Abbasi and Smith 2003; Ashmore and Carver 2001). The alternative argument is that many innovative projects would never have occurred without such funding.

GOOD MEDICATION MANAGEMENT PRACTICE

There are a variety of roles and activities which need to take place to meet the needs of people who are prescribed psychotropic medication. It is no longer acceptable merely to write the standard statement 'monitor for effects and side-effects' in care plans. It is the view of the author that the complexity of medication management need is best addressed within a team approach. Ten rules can be identified as a checklist to stimulate debate and guide this process (Box 5.1).

Box 5.1 Ten rules for effective medication management

1. Engage service users in a comprehensive assessment of their physical and mental health

2. Inform and educate service users and carers of the purose, benefits and risks of proposed medication (verally and in writing)

3. Facilitate concordance by agreeing a care/treatment plan with the service user

4. Prescribe safely and appropriately within the scope of current evidence and guidelines

5. Make sure informed consent has been given and is onoing

6. Administer safely

7. Monitor outcomes systematically

8. Initiate regular reviews

9. Maintain clear communication with service users and their carers, across service interfaces and between practitioners

10. Maintain own professional competence

Assessment

At the initial assessment it is important to take a comprehensive history and establish baselines to minimise risks, inform clinical decision making and allow an effective review of treatment in the future. Many of these actions will be recognised as a typical part of any assessment, with a great deal of overlap with the information needed to inform other clinical interventions. These may include:

- medical history (including all allergies)
- medication history (to include everything the person takes)
- physical parameters
- symptoms and coping strategies
- health and medication beliefs
- side-effects
- substance use

- cognitive function
- practical issues
- support network and the views of carers and significant others.

Before medication is prescribed, a medical history should be taken alongside a thorough physical examination. It is particularly important to check for previous adverse events and allergies including food allergies (nut oils are a common constituent of depot preparations – long-acting anti-psychotic medications given by injection).

An accurate and detailed medication history is rarely available and often very time consuming, if not impossible, to collate from old volumes of case notes. It is, however, a very useful tool which aids clinical decision making as well as enabling an illustration of change (e.g. it is possible to use the history to visually illustrate the link between stopping medication and relapse). It is good practice for the team (and the organisation) to agree a process and format for recording medication histories. A practical record would include the date, names and doses of medications as well as the rationale for the choice, change or stopping of medication, including details of adverse events. Although it is rare to see documented rationales for prescribing, it is interesting to note that clinical treatment plans in supplementary prescribing have to include a documented reason for the prescription as well as a diagnosis (DoH 2003).

It is also important for those administering and/or prescribing medication to have access to information about all the medicine that the person is prescribed and/or currently taking. There is often some difficulty with this where this information is held by two or more care providers (e.g. between primary and secondary care). It is therefore good practice to ask service users to bring all the medicines they are currently taking to a consultation or on admission. This has the advantage of enabling a conversation to be facilitated about the service user's knowledge of the medicines, e.g. 'What do you take that one for?', 'When do you take it?', as well as enabling a comparison with the current record. Alongside prescribed medication, it is necessary to assess everything the person takes which has the potential to interact or interfere with the prescribed medicine. This should include questions about the use of over-the-counter medicines, herbal remedies, vitamins, caffeine, nicotine, alcohol and street drugs.

After prescribing it is necessary to monitor physical parameters, so baselines need to be established before administration. This includes basic observations of vital signs (blood pressure, pulse, temperature, respirations), body mass index, a range of blood/urine tests and a baselines electrocardiogram. Routine drug and alcohol screening on admission is now commonplace and is particularly important where the person is not known to the service or where rapid tranquillisation (RT) may be required. Where there is use of high doses, RT and/or medication initiation or change, more frequent monitoring is appropriate and this should be planned for and documented. Electronic vital signs monitoring should be considered following RT due to the need to maintain almost constant observation. For comprehensive monitoring guidance see Taylor, Paton and Kerwin (2003).

Efficacy cannot be evaluated without measuring the symptoms the medication is aiming to treat. Many outcome measures developed for research are inappropriate clinically due to their length, narrow focus or cost. Useful scales include the Brief Psychiatric Rating Scale (Overall and Gorham 1962) and, in psychosis, the KGV-M Version 5 (Lancashire 2001). The KGV-M promotes assessment of coping strategies as well as symptom severity, allowing an individualised formulation that can help the service user to build on his/her strengths. This information can be supplemented by an assessment of function and/or quality of life. All scales require short training courses in their application. This is best done via a team approach so that videos or live subjects can be rated and compared to enable the achievement of inter-rater reliability.

Some of the most important aspects of medication management which determines whether people will take their prescribed medication or not is their belief about the severity of their 'illness', the treatment, their own susceptibility to relapse and attitudes towards medicines in general. It is also possible to gather this information and, indeed, predict compliance by using a tool which measures beliefs, such as the Hogan Drug Attitude Inventory (Hogan, Aswad and Eastwood 1983). Completing the scale can stimulate discussion about beliefs which may otherwise have remained hidden.

Side-effects can only be systematically assessed using a validated measure. Perhaps the most well-known tool used in clinical practice is the Liverpool University Neuroleptic Side Effect Rating Scale (LUNSERS)

(Day *et al.* 1995). This is a subjective, self-rating scale which covers a full range of anti-psychotic side-effects. It can stimulate discussion about side-effects which are often overlooked, sometimes because staff are too embarrassed to ask about some, such as sexual dysfunction, and prompt further investigation.

Knowledge and observation skills are important to identify when action is needed for painful, distressing side-effects (e.g. acute dystonia – muscle spasm), potentially fatal side-effects (e.g. neuroleptic malignant syndrome) and chronic side-effects such as tardive dyskinesia (TD), an involuntary movement disorder that affects the limbs and face. TD can develop within as little as three months' exposure to anti-psychotic medication. Symptoms of TD such as abnormal mouth movements and unusual gait are often more obvious to an observer than the person and therefore require both objective and subjective assessment. Signs of TD may be masked in people on long-term depot medication and anti-cholinergics (medications designed to counteract involuntary movements), only becoming apparent when changes are made. It should be assessed using the Abnormal Involuntary Movement Scale (National Institute for Mental Health 1975).

A common scenario in clinical practice is the need to differentiate between agitation and akathisia (a side effect characterised by subjective and objective restlessness). PRN (as required) anti-psychotic medication is often given for agitation but can increase akathisia, as can anti-cholinergic medication. Akathisia can have a (hidden) subjective component, so patients should be questioned about their feelings of restlessness or 'inner turmoil' and a tool which has a subjective as well as an objective component should be used, e.g. the Barnes Akathisia Scale (Barnes 1989).

Cognitive function may be impaired by the disorder itself, relapse and/or the side-effects of medication (e.g. anti-cholinergics may impair memory). Cognitive impairment is an important consideration when assessing self-medication skills, providing information and structuring education and other interventions. The Mini Mental State Examination (Folstein, Folstein and McHugh 1975) is a useful, validated tool with which many mental health practitioners are familiar. Individual literacy and English language skills should also be considered to enable appropriate information resources to be selected.

Apart from the increase in use of substances in society in general, service users may use substances to self-medicate both their symptoms and/or their side-effects. It is, therefore, important to assess this, to evaluate the risk of interactions and to inform interventions about methods of coping, risk taking and relapse prevention. Information from the clinical interview can be supplemented with a drug screen and/or a scale which measures the level of use and dependence, e.g. Drug Use Scale, Alcohol Use Scale (Drake, Mueser and McHugo 1996).

Practical considerations can be very important and may include those which may impair access, such as problems (physical, psychological or financial) in getting to the chemist to collect prescriptions. It is also useful to ask people which pharmacy they usually use so that links with the community pharmacist can be made. This can enable an individualised service with many benefits, such as being able to organise more frequent dispensing, explaining any changes in packaging and advising on suspected side-effects. It can also promote normalisation as people commonly consult their local pharmacist for information and advice on medicines.

People are more likely to take their prescribed medication if they have the support of families and/or friends. Carers often hold important information about medication management skills, and experiences of effects and side-effects. A common complaint from carers is that they have been excluded from contributing their perspective or have not been given basic information. The benefits of including carers in the assessment and treatment process can be explained to the service user so that consent to include them can be actively sought rather than being automatically dismissed due to confidentiality concerns.

Medication management care planning

There is an opportunity afforded by the care planning process to facilitate shared decision making and collaborative care. The specific and individual rationale for the medication can be documented and need, based on the assessment process, can be formulated and documented. This can all be done in the language of the service user, avoiding jargon. Goals and targets can be jointly decided, the interventions selected and frequency of monitoring and review established (Box 5.2).

Box 5.2 Example from a medication management care plan

Summary of client's perception of her problem area:

- When I am out in busy places I hear people whispering about me and how I am going to die soon. On a good day I can distract myself and get on with things
- My medication used to make me feel stiff but this has got better since I stopped taking anti-depressants. I don't want to go back into hospital again
- I want to remember to take my medication, continue with my voluntary job and be able to visit my friends

Please summarise your perception of the client's problem area:

- Jenny hears voices telling her she is terminally ill. She is prescribed Amisulpiride 400 mg twice a day to help control these voices and protect her from relapse. She is also prescribed Procyclidine 5 mg daily to control the stiffness she sometimes experiences
- Jenny sometimes forgets to take her medication in the mornings and does not always remember to order and collect her repeat prescriptions

What goals are you and your client hoping to achieve?

- To maintain medication at a level to help Jenny cope with her voices
- For Jenny to remember to take her medication and collect her repeat prescriptions before running out of tablets
- To discontinue the Procyclidine within the next six months

What is your agreed plan of action to work towards these goals?

- Jenny is to experiment with reducing her Procyclidine over the next three months with the aim of stopping altogether within six months. Paula is to help Jenny to self-monitor this using LUNSERS ratings every month and repeating KGV-M ratings before the next review
- Scores and test results are to be fed back to the consultant psychiatrist to allow a comparison with baseline and medication review in six months
- Jenny is to make a chart to remind her to take her medication. Jenny is to ask her community pharmacist for suggestions about how she might remember to order her repeat prescriptions on time and be alerted if she forgets

> • A medication review can be requested by Jenny or Paula at any time if there are any indications of relapse or medication concerns

Medication management interventions

Possible interventions may include the following:

- information giving
- medication review
- medication change
- education and health promotion
- promoting self-medication skills
- using concordance skills.

Information giving should include planning about who should be included (e.g. carers) as well as the frequency of giving and the format of information. Care must be taken to select appropriate materials that meet individual needs and do not inadvertently promote a particular product. All medication dispensed in the community must include a standard patient information leaflet (PIL) by European law. These are taken from the data sheet for a particular product and have been criticised for their complexity and use of jargon and the failure to consult service users in their design and evaluation (Consumer's Association 2003). PILs are rarely available in hospitals. Information, designed particularly for the individual needs of mental health service users, is available from the United Kingdom Psychiatric Pharmacy Group (UKPPG) (see the useful contact section at the end of this chapter).

The aim of a medication review is to ensure that the service user is receiving a treatment regime that is evidence based and the most effective possible. Medication is reviewed and compared to evidencebased prescribing guidelines. The rationale for any discrepancies (e.g. polypharmacy, use of very high doses or long-term use of anticholinergics) is reviewed and discussed with the service user and the prescriber. Medication changes may be needed to maximise effects, limit side-effects, prevent interactions and maximise the ability to self-medicate. Practical solutions to tackling side-effects can also be initiated (e.g. changing the dose, timing or route of administration).

Regular health checks can be promoted by liaison with the GP and service user. This should include advice about the need, content and frequency of physical monitoring. Interventions can be initiated for a whole range of health promotion needs including education in meal planning, shopping and cooking skills and/or facilitation of an appropriate and achievable exercise regime. In some areas it may be possible to facilitate access to exercise ('exercise on prescription') and/or subsidised fresh fruit and vegetables.

Interventions to promote self-medication skills often include a graded, structured programme, giving increasing responsibility and reduced prompts while assessing progress. In preparing for discharge service users may also need support to adopt processes to remind them to take their medication (and order repeat prescriptions). This can include behavioural tailoring techniques (e.g. twinning medication times with meal times) and/or choosing appropriate reminders (e.g. calendars). Compliance aids such as daily dose reminder devices ('Dosett' boxes) should not be seen as a universal solution. They may contribute to a further loss of self-care skills and have safety and cost implications associated with dispensing. They should only be used following a comprehensive multidisciplinary assessment. Transfer of medicines from their original container to the device incurs a risk of error and potential loss of stability of the product for which the person who transfers the medicines becomes accountable. Pharmacists should, therefore, load and label the device.

Ambivalence about taking medication should be seen as an opportunity for therapeutic intervention that aims to improve health. Practitioners trained in 'concordance skills' work with the service user to build awareness of the importance of medication and develop confidence in taking it. Specific therapeutic interventions include helping the service user to explore their previous experience of medication and their current ambivalence, examine the evidence for their beliefs and concerns about medication and use problem-solving strategies. The service user is encouraged to take an active role in the negotiation of decisions about his/her own treatment with health care workers through developing skills in self-monitoring and communication.

CASE STUDY 5.1

John had been taking Risperidone 6 mg daily since stopping his depot four years ago. He had a good relationship with his community psychiatric nurse, Dawn, and he told her he had a swollen chest which he had interpreted as a sign that he was changing sex. This idea was compounded by his inability to gain an erection and as he found this so embarrassing he did not tell anyone.

Dawn and John completed the LUNSERS together and a high hormonal side-effect score was highlighted. This was fed back to John's consultant psychiatrist who wrote to the GP to request a blood test. John's prolactin levels were very high and this was explained to John who agreed to change from Risperidone to Quetiapine.[1] Six-monthly monitoring of side-effects and symptoms has provided John, with valid evidence that his mental and physical health has improved. He has now joined an exercise group with other service users.

SYSTEMS AND PROCESSES TO SUPPORT PRACTICE

Several systems and processes which aim to aid the effective delivery of medication management can be identified and include:

- multidisciplinary working
- communication, IT and recording systems
- guidelines
- policies, procedures and care pathways
- medication review clinics

---

1   Prolactin is a hormone that is involved with several aspects of reproduction, most notably lactation (milk production). The neurotransmitter dopamine serves as the major brake on prolactin secretion. Some anti-psychotics can lead to a release of prolactin from the pituitary gland due to their blockade of dopamine in the hypothalamus. High levels of prolactin, detected by a blood test, are known as hyperprolactinaemia. Hyperprolactinaemia may cause a variety of unwanted and unpleasant effects in both men and women. These may include menstrual disturbances, breast enlargement, milk production, osteopoerosis, ejaculation/erectile difficulties and a loss of libido.

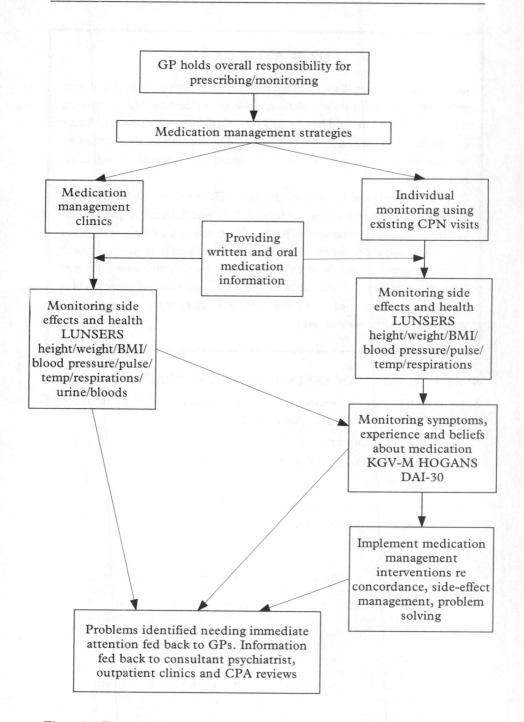

Figure 5.1 Example of a medication review clinic within a rural CMHT

- staff development and updating
- medication management supervision
- audit and clinical governance.

SUMMARY

Good medication management practice is best achieved through working alongside the service user and any carers, along with a team approach and a sharing of skills and expertise. A comprehensive assessment that pays attention to physical health status and uses validated tools to establish baselines should be followed by a collaborative care-planning process. The care plan should include rationales, interventions and outcomes agreed with the service user in clear language that avoids medical jargon. Attention must be paid to systems within the service and across service interfaces that support this good practice.

There is an urgent need to improve communication pathways and address the practice–theory–policy gap for all health care professionals. This is particularly important in the current climate where there appears to be a rush to supplementary prescribing without attention being paid to underpinning skills. Nurse-led clinics may be a useful way for practitioners to start to address the needs of service users who already receive medication but are not yet receiving an appropriate medication management service (see Figure 5.1).

REFERENCES

Abbasi, K. and Smith, R. (2003) 'No more free lunches: Patients will benefit from doctors and drug companies disentangling.' *British Medical Journal 326*, 1155–6.

Ashmore, R. and Carver, N. (2001) 'The pharmaceutical industry and mental health nursing.' *British Journal of Nursing 10*, 21, 1396–1402.

Barnes, T.R.E. (1989) 'A rating scale for drug induced akathisia.' *British Journal of Psychiatry 154*, 672–6.

Consumer's Association (2003) *Patient Information: What's the prognosis?* London: Consumer's Association.

Day, J.C., Wood, G., Dewey, M. and Bentall, R.P. (1995) 'A self-rating scale for measuring neuroleptic side-effects: Validation in a group of schizophrenic patients.' *British Journal of Psychiatry 166*, 650–3.

DH (Department of Health) (1994) *Working in Partnership: A Report by the Review Team of Mental Health Nursing*. London: Department of Health.

DH (Department of Health) (1997) *The New NHS: Modern and Dependable*. London: Department of Health.

DH (Department of Health) (1999) *National Service Framework for Mental Health: Modern Standards and Service Models*. London: Department of Health.

DH (Department of Health) (2001) *National Service Framework for Older People: Modern Standards and Service Models*. London: Department of Health.

DH (Department of Health) (2003) *Supplementary Prescribing by Nurses and Pharmacists within the NHS in England: A Guide for Implementation*. London: Department of Health.

Department of Health and the Royal College of Nursing (1994) *Good Practice in the Administration of Depot Neuroleptics: A Guidance Document for Mental Health and Practice Nurses*. London: Department of Health.

Drake, R.E., Mueser, K.T. and McHugo, G.J. (1996) 'Clinician rating scales: Alcohol Use Scale (AUS), Drug Use Scale (DUS), and Substance Abuse Treatment Scale (SATS).' In L.I. Siderer and B. Dickey (eds) *Outcomes Assessment in Clinical Practice*. Baltimore, MD: Williams and Wilkins.

Folstein, M., Folstein, S. and McHugh, P. (1975) 'Mini mental state: A practical method for grading the cognitive state of patients for the clinician.' *Journal of Psychiatric Research 12*, 189–98.

Gray, R. (2001) *Medication Management. Working to Improve the Health of People with Schizophrenia. A Randomised Control Trial of Medication Management Training for Community Psychiatric Nurses*. London: Institute of Psychiatry, King's College.

Gray, R., Wykes, T. and Gournay, K. (2002) 'From compliance to concordance: A review of the literature on interventions to enhance compliance with antipsychotic medication.' *Journal of Psychiatric and Mental Health Nursing 9*, 277–84.

Harris, E.C. and Barraclough, B. (1998) 'Excess mortality of mental disorder.' *British Journal of Psychiatry 173*, 11–53.

Harris, N.R., Lovell, K. and Day, J.C. (2002) 'Consent and long-term neuroleptic treatment.' *Journal of Psychiatric and Mental Health Nursing 9*, 475–82.

Haynes, R.B., Montague, P. and Oliver, T. (1999) *Interventions for Helping Patients Follow Prescriptions for Medications (Cochrane Review)*. In The Cochrane Library, Issue 4. Oxford: Update Software.

Helgason, L. (1990) 'Twenty-year follow-up of first psychiatric presentation for schizophrenia: What could have been prevented?' *Acta Psychiatrica Scandinavica 81*, 231–5.

Hogan, T.P., Aswad, A.G. and Eastwood, R. (1983) 'A self report scale predictive of drug compliance in schizophrenics: Reliability and discriminative validity.' *Psychological Medicine 13*, 177–83.

Islington Mental Health Forum (1989) *Fit for Consumption? Mental Health Users' Views of Treatment in Islington*. London: Islington Mental Health Forum.

Lancashire, S. (2001) *KGV (M) Symptom Scale. Manchester University Version 5*. Manchester: University of Manchester.

NICE (National Institute for Clinical Excellence) (2002a) *Guidance on the Use of Newer (Atypical) Antipsychotics in the Treatment of Schizophrenia: Technology Appraisal Guidance – No 43*. London: NICE.

NICE (National Institute for Clinical Excellence) (2002b) *Clinical Guideline 1: Schizophrenia. Core Interventions in the Treatment and Management of Schizophrenia in Primary and Secondary Care*. London: NICE.

National Institute for Mental Health (1975) 'Abnormal Involuntary Movements Scale.' *Early Clinical Drug Evaluation Unit Intercom 4*, 3–6.

National Prescribing Centre and National Primary Care Research and Development Centre (2002) *Modernising Medicines Management: A Guide to Achieving Benefits for Patients, Professionals and the NHS: Books 1 and 2*. Liverpool: National Prescribing Centre.

National Schizophrenia Fellowship, MIND and Manic Depression Fellowship (2000) *A Question of Choice?* London: NSF.

National Schizophrenia Fellowship, MIND and Manic Depression Fellowship (2001) *That's Just Typical*. London: NSF.

Overall, J.E. and Gorham, D.E. (1962) 'The Brief Psychiatric Rating Scale.' *Psychological Reports 10*, 799–812.

Sainsbury Centre for Mental Health (2000) *The Capable Practitioner*. London: The Sainsbury Centre.

Taylor, D., Mace, S., Mir, S. and Kerwin, R. (2000) 'A prescription survey of the use of atypical antipsychotics for hospital inpatients in the United Kingdom.' *International Journal of Psychiatry in Clinical Practice 4*, 41–6.

Taylor, D., Paton, C. and Kerwin, R. (2003) *The Maudsley 2003 Prescribing Guidelines*. Seventh edition. London: Martin Dunitz.

FURTHER READING

Harris, N. (1998) *Long-term Neuroleptic Treatment and the Role of the Community Mental Health Worker*. Salisbury: Quay Books.
Healy, D. (2002) *Psychiatric Drugs Explained*. Third edition. London: Churchill Livingstone.

USEFUL CONTACT

United Kingdom Psychiatric Pharmacy Group
62 Park Hill,
Moseley,
Birmingham B13 18DT
Web: www.ukppg.co.uk

ACKNOWLEDGEMENT

I would like to acknowledge the work of members of the Hull and East Yorkshire Medication Management Network, particularly Keith Lambeth, who was responsible for initiating the nurse-led clinic described in this chapter.

CHAPTER 6

THE ROLE OF PRIMARY CARE

DEBBIE NIXON AND TIM SAUNDERS

INTRODUCTION

This chapter describes the context of primary care and the associated development of high quality mental health services. It outlines national policy and describes the structure and delivery of primary care services. The prevalence and range of mental health problems that present in primary care are considered. These are summarised as a number of clinical case studies that outline the scale and complexity of presenting issues to which front-line staff respond. These are set within the context of the current capacity and capability to respond of clinicians working in primary care. Models of best practice are discussed and a summary of the key issues underpinning effective approaches to service development and modernisation presented. In summary the challenges and opportunities facing primary care to deliver the required agenda are considered within the context of current organisational structures, needs, cultures and resources.

PRIMARY CARE: THE CONTEXT

Primary care has been placed at the cornerstone of the NHS. *Shifting the Balance of Power* (DH 2001) identifies primary care trusts (PCTs) as having the lead NHS role in developing strategic partnerships that improve health and reduce health inequalities within local communities.

Primary care is an open, free-at-the-point-of-use and demand-led service. It is also generally the first point of contact for people entering the health care system. It provides care to people who are ill, or believe themselves to be ill, and also a range of chronic disease management services.

Problems are undifferentiated and people are often seen for short appointments over long periods of time.

Typically the service is provided in independent general medical practices usually run as partnerships between general medical practitioners (GPs). GPs are considered specialists in 'generalism' who take an interest in whatever is of interest to their patients. Practices vary in size from 'single-handed GP' practices to large multi-doctor partnerships. These practices operate as 'small businesses' and employ support staff such as reception staff, administration clerks and practice managers. They also employ other clinical staff, typically practice nurses, but other clinical staff can be directly employed. They also frequently provide premises and other infrastructure which is 'leased back' to the NHS for use by NHS patients and staff.

Under the new general medical services (GMS) contract (DH 2003) practices will contract with local PCTs to provide a range of services to their registered patients. These are classified into 'essential' and 'additional' services, which most practices will provide, and a further range of services known as 'enhanced services'. These will be commissioned by the PCT and may be 'nationally' specified or 'locally' agreed. It is worthy of note that one of the new national enhanced services is for the care of patients with depression in primary care which has the potential to greatly improve the quality of service provision for patients in this important area of primary care.

Being an open, demand-led service means that patients present to primary care, with undifferentiated problems. These are often a mixture of physical and mental health problems. It is the role of the generalist to assess, investigate and treat these problems where possible and to refer on to specialist services where required. It is often challenging to deal with complex intertwined physical and mental health problems that frequently defy easy classification. PCTs therefore have a key role in both the commissioning and delivery of primary care services. They are responsible for the employment of a wide range of clinicians including health visitors, district nurses, school nurses, and other professions allied to medicine who work as part of the wider primary health care team (PHCT). The configuration, organisation and degree integration of PHCTs vary widely across the country.

MENTAL HEALTH POLICY: THE AGENDA FOR CHANGE

PCTs have the lead NHS role in commissioning the continuum of mental health services and integrating the effective components of care. The forces behind this agenda locally are local implementation teams (LITs) who are given the task of delivering change through a variety of milestones (see Box 6.1). LITs comprise key people from the local mental health community including service users and carers, specialist mental health trusts, social services and voluntary and other non-statutory agencies.

Box 6.1 A summary of key national milestones (DH 2002)

- The development of assertive outreach teams by December 2003
- The development of 24-hour crisis resolution and home treatment services by December 2005
- The development of early intervention services to reduce the amount of untreated psychosis by December 2004

The development of larger specialist mental health trusts (often known as secondary care) has meant that a number of PCTs may commission services from one large organisation. This provides some interesting challenges for PCTs and LITs in balancing local needs with wider imperatives and the need to work collaboratively. Primary care is the major provider of mental health services in the UK, with 90 per cent of patients with mental health problems treated solely in this sector (Goldberg and Huxley 1992). Up to 40 per cent of patients attending their general practitioner (GP) have an underlying mental health problem and in 20–25 per cent of those attending it is the sole reason for them seeing their GP (Goldberg 1991). (See Box 6.2.)

Box 6.2 A summary of mental health morbidity in primary care

- People with a serious mental illness consult their GP more than they consult any other professional. The majority of people experiencing common mental health problems who seek help will receive it from primary health care teams (Goldberg and Huxley 1992)
- Depression and anxiety are the most common mental heath problems presenting to the GP (Goldberg and Huxley 1992)
- Mental health problems are common; up to 40 per cent of patients consulting their GP for any reason have a mental health problem and for 20–25 per cent of patients a mental health problem will be the sole reason for attending (Goldberg 1991)
- Thirty to fifty per cent of presentations of depression are undetected by GPs (Goldberg and Bridges 1987)
- Practice nurses often treat common mental health problems or serious illnesses with little appropriate training or supervision (Mental Health Workforce Action Team 2001)

The *National Service Framework for Mental Health* (NSFMH) (DH 1999) outlines an ambitious programme of development incorporating seven national standards. PCTs have lead responsibility for standards 2 and 3 that relate to access and effective treatments around the clock (see Box 6.3). They are central, however, to the delivery of all seven standards.

Box 6.3 Key priorities from the NSFMH (DH 1999)

Any service user who contacts his/her primary health care team (PHCT) with a mental health problem should:

(Standard 2)
- have his/her mental health needs identified and assessed
- be offered effective treatments including referral to specialist services

(Standard 3)
- be able to use NHS Direct as it develops for first level advice or referral on
- be able to access services around the clock

To achieve these outcomes PCTs are required to work in partnership with specialist mental health services to undertake a number of actions (see Box 6.4).

Box 6.4 Key actions from the NSFMH (DH 1999)

- Develop the resources in each practice to assess mental health needs
- Develop the resources in each practice to work with diverse groups
- Agree arrangements for referral and assessment, advice, treatment or care
- Have the skills and necessary organisational systems to deliver high quality general medical services to service users with severe and enduring mental health problems

---

National milestones are challenging and require PCTs to develop and monitor in partnership with specialist services effective clinical pathways for a number of mental health problems. They are also required to develop local workforce strategies and implement audit programmes to monitor the prescribing of anti-depressants.

The NHS Plan (DH 2000) reinforces the key role that primary care plays in the overall delivery of mental health services and seeks to build capacity within the system. It outlines the requirement for three new types of workers to be integrated into existing systems of care. A new emphasis for the place of service users at all levels is also provided. The NHS Plan states clearly that service users need an identifiable person that they can turn to if they have a problem or need information about NHS services. The NHS patient advocacy and liaison service (PALS) was established in every trust in 2002. These developments provide an opportunity to strengthen the provision of high-quality information systems and care (see Box 6.5).

Box 6.5 Summary of NHS Plan roles

- Recruit and train 1000 primary care graduate workers by 2004
- Recruit and train 500 gateway workers to work at the interface between primary and secondary care by 2004
- Develop roles for service users and carers

PCTs will be required to consider local implementation plans in the context of existing and new mental health roles. There is therefore a challenging agenda for primary care. The Mental Health Workforce Action Team (DH 2001), in its Primary Care Key Group Report, acknowledges the scale of the work programme. It identifies four domains of action: organisational and leadership development, education and training which improves frontline clinical skills, the implementation of new types of workers and a focus on systems designed to improve the quality of care.

This challenging modernisation agenda has been recognised by the National Institute for Mental Health for England (NIMHE). NIMHE has a key role in supporting the wider agenda for mental health. Key issues in relation to implementing the primary care deliverables are identified in the National Primary Care Programme (see Box 6.6).

Box 6.6 NIMHE primary care programme aims

- To strengthen the commissioning function of PCTs to deliver on the broader mental health agenda
- To develop capacity in primary care, including the implementation of new workers such as primary care graduate mental health workers, gateway workers and support time and recovery workers
- To develop the primary care user perspective
- To support the implementation of evidence-based workforce development strategies, which build capability in the provision of primary care mental health services

---

MENTAL HEALTH AND PRIMARY CARE AS A SERVICE PROVIDER

Although there is no average practice, a typical GP with a list of 2000 patients will see around 200 people with a common mental health problem each year; around ten will have a severe depression; four people will harm themselves; and one person every five years will die by suicide (Fry 1993).

At the same time it is evident that the capacity in primary care to respond to this range of complexity is far from robust. Not only is the time of the average consultation limited to seven minutes, but only a minority of primary care team members (only 28% of GPs and 2% of practice nurses) have had further training in mental health (Mental Health Workforce Action Team 2001). It is therefore not surprising that a significant amount of mental health morbidity goes undetected.

Despite the high levels of mental health morbidity presenting in primary care there has historically been a lack of resources to support appropriate management and treatment of patients with mental health problems. To protect scarce resources for people suffering with severe and enduring mental illness, investment over the past decade has been directed to specialist mental health services. Given the historical underfunding of mental health services in the past this approach is understandable. The result, however, has led to service fragmentation and difficulties in managing care across the interface between primary and secondary care. In addition, a lack of specific funding and limited treatment options in primary care have resulted in an overemphasis on biomedical solutions, such as drug treatments. The majority of problems have a complex aetiology, in which social and relationship problems are often significant components and overreliance on drug therapy may be inappropriate. The presentation of mental health problems in primary care is common, but frequently complex in nature. Case Studies 6.1 to 6.5 outline the range of mental health issues that frequently present to GPs and other primary care clinicians.

CASE STUDY 6.1 ANXIETY

Mrs Benbow, aged 41 years, presents to her GP with feelings of 'panic'. She has breathlessness, palpitations and sweating. She feels that her anxiety is ruining her life. She feels unable to cope at work. She works for a bank, has two children and cares for her elderly mother. Her father died two years ago.

Questions for discussion

1. How might she present to other members of the primary care team?

2. What are the options for treatment?

Mrs Benbow is referred for assessment and anxiety management by the primary care mental health team (PCMHT). She has an individual assessment as there are a number of issues to look at before deciding on treatment. On the Hospital Anxiety and Depression Scale (HAD) (Zigmond and Snaith 1983), Mrs Benbow scores Depression = 6 and Anxiety = 6 (scores over 11 = moderate level of depression or anxiety). She is allocated to an anxiety management group. Mrs Benbow will be evaluated after six weeks to assess her need for further treatment.

Questions for discussion

3. What further treatment options exist?

4. When should they be used?

CASE STUDY 6.2 DEPRESSION

Mr Mahmood is a 52-year-old teacher. He is single. He presents to his GP with a six-week history of low mood, poor motivation, difficulty in concentration, disturbed sleep pattern and a poor appetite. He is tearful and appears distressed. He has had vague suicidal thoughts but dismissed them and denies real suicidal intent. He used to enjoy work but cannot cope now.

Question for discussion

1. What are the options for treatment?

Mr Mahmood is started on an anti-depressant but has made no real progress after six weeks of treatment. He is referred to the PCMHT for further full risk assessment, support and monitoring. His HAD scores are Depression = 18 and Anxiety = 12.

Questions for discussion

2.   Would cognitive behavioural therapy help this man?

3.   What other options are available to the GP and PCMHT?

4.   When should referral to specialist services be considered?

CASE STUDY 6.3
POST TRAUMATIC STRESS DISORDER

Mr Yang is aged 35 years and married with two children. He was a passenger in a car accident some eight months ago. He suffered only minor injuries but the driver sustained multiple injuries and a pedestrian was killed. He says he has been fine, but has become irritable, short-tempered and intolerant of family, friends and work colleagues recently. He has had nightmares and flashbacks to the accident over the past month.

Questions for discussion

1.   What are the options for treatment?

2.   Would an anti-depressant, be indicated?

Mr Yang is referred to the PCMHT for further assessment. He has HAD scores of Depression = 12 and Anxiety = 16.

Questions for discussion

3.   What further treatment options are available?

4.   When should specialist help be sought?

CASE STUDY 6.4
POSTNATAL DEPRESSION

Mrs Roberts is aged 34 years. She had her first child eight weeks ago. She has been seeing the health visitor who has become increasingly concerned about Mrs Robert's low mood. She is constantly tearful and feels she can't bond with the baby. She is a little suspicious of her family and feels immense guilt. She is struggling with breast-feeding.

Mrs Roberts' case is discussed at the PCMHT allocations meeting and the 'team leader' agrees to co-work with the health visitor to monitor her progress.

Questions for discussion

1. Should anti-depressant medication be considered?

2. What other therapies might be offered?

3. What risks should be assessed in relation to Mrs Roberts?

CASE STUDY 6.5 SCHIZOPHRENIA

Mrs Portman is a 56-year-old woman with schizophrenia. She is under the care of the CMHT, is on standard level CPA and has a key worker. She has not had a psychotic relapse for many years. There are some doubts as to her compliance with her anti-psychotic medication. She frequently asks to stop her treatment. Mrs Portman has non-insulin dependent diabetes mellitus and ischaemic heart disease, both of which are complex physical diseases. Front-line staff should have an understanding of both of these conditions. Mrs Portman attends her GP frequently with symptoms suggestive of physical illness. Mrs Portman does not comply with regular monitoring of her diabetes or heart disease.

Questions for discussion

1. What are the issues facing those involved with her care?

2. Who else should be involved?

3. What strategies could be used to optimise her care?

In primary care the distinction is often made between 'severe and enduring mental illness' (most often associated with schizophrenia and bipolar disorder) and 'common mental health problems' (most often associated with anxiety and depression). Increasingly, the care of severe and enduring mental illness is provided by specialist services whilst primary care is expected to be associated with the latter. In reality, however, primary care is the main point of contact for most of the continuum of mental health problems (Goldberg and Huxley 1992). Increasingly, both academics and clinicians agree that the distinction between severe and common is unhelpful as it is a poor predictor of complexity, severity and disability (Bower 2003).

A number of typologies, however, have emerged which provide differentiated descriptions of mental health problems. These are based on the type of problem and its severity and the availability of effective interventions to manage them (e.g. Goldberg and Gournay 1997). They are summarised in Table 6.1.

Goldberg and Gournay (1997) propose a general guideline that a patient should be treated in secondary care if the required skills are unavailable in primary care. They recognise that this particular definition is fluid and presents challenges, particularly in light of the range in both the scope and quality of services delivered in primary care. Table 6.1 highlights the fact that some mental health problems do not fit current service delivery criteria and may fall into a 'gap' between primary and secondary care, remaining untreated.

There is a lack of systematic development and evaluation of primary care models across the country. The traditional approach to the delivery of primary care mental health services has consisted of specialist mental health services providing a range of interventions. The different approaches have been summarised in Box 6.7. More recently, these types of delivery have been called 'replacement models'.

In the replacement model, the GP refers the patient to a specialist mental health professional who assumes responsibility for the patient's mental health problem and provides a specific intervention, thereby replacing GP interventions. This model relies on the expert, i.e. specialist mental health services, transporting models of secondary care into a primary care environment and is the predominant model of provision in the UK. The results of this have been demonstrated: a considerable number of mental health problems do not fit the criteria for specialist

Table 6.1 A summary of problems, severity and available interventions

Group	Description	Example disorders	Care
1	Severe mental disorders unlikely to remit spontaneously, which are associated with major disability	Schizophrenia, organic disorders, bi-polar disorder and life threatening cases of eating disorder	Involves both primary and secondary care
2	Well-defined disorders which are also associated with disability, for which there are effective pharmacological and psychological treatments. Even when these disorers remit, they are likely to relapse once more	Anxious depression, pure depresion, generalised anxiety, panic disorder, obsessive compulsive disorder	Can usually be managed entirely within primary care
3	Disorders where drugs have a more limited role, but where psychological therapies are available	Somatised or physical presentations of distress, panic disorders with agoraphobia and eating disorder	Rarely treated within primary care, and only a small proportion of cases are treated by CMHT
4	Disorders which resolve spontaneously	Bereavement, adjustment disorder	Supportive help, rather than a speific mental health skill, is required. This should be available in primary care or voluntary sector

---

Box 6.7 *A summary of four traditional models of primary care mental health provision*

- Liaison (where a specialist mental health worker is attached to a practice or groups of practices for communication purposes and provides differing levels of clinical support)
- Integrated 'consultation–liaison' (where primary care works with less severe mental health problems and the CMHT concentrates upon people with more severe mental health problems)
- Specialist primary care liaison teams within CMHTs
- Secondary care integrated within primary care

(Cohen and Paton 1999; Gask, Sibbald and Creed 1997)

---

mental health provision. Problems of poor access to appropriate and timely interventions for service users have abounded in primary care.

More recently, a distinction has been made between 'collaborative' and 'replacement' models of working (Bower 2003). In the collaborative care model the GP retains primary responsibility for the care of the patient but works in partnership with mental health professionals and the patient to increase the overall effectiveness of care. The degree to which these services are delivered within the two categories varies widely across the country.

Within primary care, the support, attention and investment that mental health has received has been patchy, meaning that mental health is often perceived to be on the 'too-difficult pile'. Issues of capacity and demand and the problems of access to specialist services are widespread. The development of GP fundholding in the 1990s saw a growth in the implementation of counselling and psychological therapy services. With the development of PCTs there is a move for these services to be more systematically organised across PCT areas rather than contracted on an individual practice basis.

Psychological therapies and counselling have a long history of working in primary care. The techniques and technologies, however, have often been developed in other contexts (Bower 2003). *The NHS Executive Review of Psychological Therapies* (NHSE 2000) described three different types of psychological therapy provision within the NHS (see Table 6.2). Types B and C represent the replacement model, which are the most common types of provision at present in primary care.

Table 6.2 Types of psychological therapy	
Type of psychological therapy	**Description**
Type A – Psychological treatment as an integral component of mental health care	This describes a wide range of psychological interventions offered within mental health services alongside other types of care, e.g. nursing, medical care. For example, a psychiatrist may offer a form of behavioural anxiety management whilst also attending to medication side-effects during an outpatient appointment
Type B – Eclectic psychological therapy and counselling	The characteristics of type B provision are that it is informed by more than one theoretical framework. It includes both non-directive counselling and psychotherapeutic work which uses a range of techniques to address different facets of a patient's problem
Type C – Formal psychotherapies	Formal psychotherapies are practised within particular models, well-developed bodies of theory and protocols for practice; for example, psychoanalytic, cognitive-beavioural, systemic. They are therefore undertaken by, or under the supervision of, a specialist practitioner, trained in a particular school of formal psychotherapeutic work, usually within a designated psychotherapy or psychology service

A number of PCTs across the country have attempted to develop more 'collaborative care models'. Models developed are far wider than psychological therapy alone and include interventions such as patient education, assistance with anti-depressant adherence, consultation with the GP about client progress and educational interventions aimed at the GP (Bower 2003). An example of this is described in Box 6.8.

Box 6.8 A collaborative model of primary care mental health provision

Chester City PCT/Cheshire West PCT – A first-wave NHS beacon site for primary care mental health services

- Implemented a multidisciplinary mental health team across the PCT
- Provided a single point of access in each practice for referrals
- Case-managed individual clients and coordinated packages of care with the GP
- Coordinated weekly liaison/supervision meetings with the PHCT and specialist mental health services
- Provided skills-based training packages for the PHCT
- Improved access to a range of psychological therapies

(Nixon, Saunders and Tanner 2000)

One of the major challenges facing primary care is access to services and the inherent capacity of primary care to provide treatment. The replacement model places an onus on GP referral and at this point the patient is likely to be placed on a waiting list for treatment.

It has long been recognised that traditional forms of therapy, for example an individual series of 50-minute sessions, are unlikely to meet the volume of demand in primary care. The collaborative model provides opportunities to increase the skills and capacity of GPs and the PHCT to provide effective interventions and improve equity of access to services. This will require organisations to search for less complex and intensive approaches (see Box 6.9).

Such interventions will be critical to enable existing professionals to work more effectively but are key to the modernisation of primary care and implementation of new roles and new ways of working.

> ## Box 6.9 A summary of evidence
> ## for low intensity interventions
>
> - Straightforward interventions, such as problem solving and self-help, have been shown to have as large an effect as usual care or formal psychological treatment in primary care (Lovell, Richards and Bower 2003)
> - Uncomplicated self-help or problem-solving treatments delivered within a case management framework can improve the care and outcomes of depression (NHS Centre for Reviews and Dissemination 2002)
> - Case management through telephone support improves outcomes in depression (Simon et al. 2000)

KEY CHALLENGES AND ISSUES

Progress in implementing the modernisation agenda for mental health has arguably been influenced by two factors. These are the commitment of primary care to build its capacity and capability in relation to mental health and the quality of partnership working with specialist mental health services. In many areas however the relationships between primary care and specialist mental health services have been fraught, characterised by hostility and stereotyped views of each other's role. Where the local context has been characterised by a history of positive joint working, or where it has been possible to overcome these difficulties (in some instances facilitated by the development of a PCT), it has been possible to make progress (Nixon et al. 2000). This has meant primary care being properly recognised as an equal partner in the provision of mental health services.

PCTs now have comprehensive commissioning responsibilities and, together with specialist trusts and other key partners, are responsible for delivering a range of service improvements and developments. They are also charged with developing primary and community services to improve the health of the populations they serve. These are major priorities and challenges for all PCTs and mental health must compete with other urgent and centrally driven imperatives. Given these demands it is therefore unsurprising that PCTs continue to show variation in the priority given to mental health services, and progress in delivering the modernisation programme. A major issue is the emphasis on the 'key deliverables' of the NSFMH with developments in primary care at risk of losing out to developments which focus on serious mental illness.

Primary care is challenged with developing its own capacity and capability and to address issues of access to effective treatments. Traditional replacement models delivered in primary care have resulted in an overreliance upon specialist mental health services and problems of matching service capacity to demand, resulting in long waiting lists for service users. Primary care, however, has some opportunities to review radically the current service delivery. An example of this relates to the implementation of primary care graduate mental health workers. It is proposed that these workers will fulfil three main roles: providing planning primary care low-intensity interventions; facilitating access to care by liaising across services; and networking within the primary health care team (Bower 2003).

One option is that these workers will provide an opportunity to improve access by working with large caseloads of patients with depression (between 50 and 100), adopting a case management approach (Richards 2002). *The New GMS Contract* (DoH 2003), with its new focus on the care of depression, also provides a significant opportunity to mainstream the mental health agenda in primary care and develop locally sensitive solutions. The key issues, therefore, for primary care and its partners to address in making further progress are summarised in Box 6.10.

Box 6.10 Key issues affecting successful implementation of primary mental health care

- Ensuring broad PCT commitment to the mental health agenda
- Building PCT capacity to commission mental health services, including the joint agenda with social care
- Assessing the workforce development needs within primary care and building the capability to respond to the range of mental health needs in line with the emerging evidence base

- Developing clarity around roles, responsibilities and resources within primary care and partner organisations
- Building positive partnerships with specialist mental health services and ensuring effective liaison on a range of issues, including communication, risk assessment and management of care across the interface

SUMMARY

Progress in delivering the modernisation agenda for primary care has been variable across the country and the reasons for this are outlined above. The development needs of PCTs have been recognised. The National Primary Care Programme, to be delivered by NIMHE over the next three years, aims to support implementation. A range of interventions and resources have been identified both locally and nationally to deliver this.

Opportunities presented by new roles and new ways of working outlined in *The NHS Plan* (DH 2000) need to be seized upon by PCTs and their partners. The challenge is for local mental health systems to integrate these roles effectively into local service delivery models. Local plans will need to consider the evidence base and best practice, workforce development strategies and models of delivery that reflect the needs and culture of primary care.

The quality of local partnerships will be a critical determinant of success. Partnerships are required at a strategic commissioning level to ensure a whole systems approach to service development and ensure that mental health continues to compete effectively for resources. At a service delivery level a collaborative approach will improve the overall effectiveness of service delivery addressing national imperatives for quality improvement.

REFERENCES

Bower, P. (2003) *Primary Care Mental Health Workers: Models of Working and Evidence of Effectiveness.* Manchester: National Primary Care Research and Development Centre, University of Manchester.

Cohen, A. and Paton, J. (1999) *A Workbook for Primary Care Groups.* London: Sainsbury Centre for Mental Health.

DH (Department of Health) (1999) *A National Service Framework for Mental Health. Modern Standards and Service Models.* London: DH.

DH (Department of Health) (2000) *The NHS Plan.* London: HMSO.

DH (Department of Health) (2001) *Shifting the Balance of Power*. London: DH.

DH (Department of Health) (2002) *Improvement, Expansion and Reform. The Next Three Years Planning and Priorities Framework 2003 to 2006*. London: DH.

DH (Department of Health) (2003) *The New GMS Contract*. London: DH.

Fry, J. (1993) *General Practice: The Facts*. Oxford: Radcliffe.

Gask, L., Sibbald, B. and Creed, F. (1997) 'Evaluating models of working at the interface between mental health services and primary care.' *British Journal of Psychiatry 170*, 6–11.

Goldberg, D. (1991) 'Filters to care: A model.' In R. Jenkins and S. Griffiths (eds) *Indicators for Mental Health in the Population*. London: HMSO.

Goldberg, D. and Bridges, K. (1987) 'Screening for psychiatric illness in general practice: The general practitioner versus the screening questionnaire.' *Journal of The Royal College of General Practitioners 37*, 5–18.

Goldberg, G. and Gournay, K. (1997) *The General Practitioner, the Psychiatrist and the Burden of Mental Health Care*. London: Institute of Psychiatry.

Goldberg, D. and Huxley, P. (1992) *Common Mental Disorders: A Bio-Social Model*. London: Routledge.

Lovell, K., Richards, D. and Bower, P. (2003) 'Improving access to primary care mental health: Uncontrolled evaluation of a pilot self help clinic.' *British Journal of General Practice 53*, 133–5.

Mental Health Workforce Action Team (2001) *The Primary Care Key Group Report to the Workforce Action Team*. London: DH.

NHS Centre for Reviews and Dissemination (2002) 'Improving the management of depression in primary care.' *Effective Health Care Bulletin 7*, 5.

NHSE (National Health Service Executive) (2000) *The NHS Executive Review of Psychological Therapies*. Unpublished internal report.

Nixon, D., Saunders, T. and Tanner, D. (2000) 'Managing mental health in primary care.' *Journal of Clinical Excellence 2*, 3, 175–7.

Richards, D. (2002) *The Clinical Case for Primary Care Graduate Mental Health Workers*. Tender for the Provision of Education and Training for Primary Care Graduate Mental Health Workers in the Northwest – unpublished.

Simon, G., VonKorff, M., Rutter, C. and Wagner, E. (2000) 'Randomised trial of monitoring, feedback and management of care by telephone to improve treatment of depression in primary care.' *British Medical Journal 320*, 550–4.

Zigmond, A. and Snaith, R.P. (1983) 'The Hospital Anxiety and Depression Scale.' *Acta Psychiatrica Scandinavica 67*, 361–70.

CHAPTER 7

MEDICAL DIAGNOSIS OF MENTAL ILLNESS

ROB POOLE

INTRODUCTION

Physicians have attempted to treat mental disorders since ancient times, but psychiatry as a medical speciality has its origins in the Victorian asylum-building programme. Victorian policymakers had a strong faith in the power of science and technology to solve problems, whether social, military or industrial. Consequently, the new asylums were placed under the control of the medical profession, in the belief that this would bring a scientific and humanitarian approach to the care of the mentally disordered, in contrast to the squalor and brutality which had been generally prevalent in their care hitherto.

Since that time medicine has remained the dominant profession in mental health care. This dominance has been vigorously challenged, though never broken, by the critics of psychiatry over the last forty years. There is a widespread unhappiness with the limitations of the 'medical model', though it is far from clear what the 'medical model' really is. Some critics regard it as a misapplication of the metaphor of disease to mental distress; other critics see it as the misuse of power by the profession to oppress the marginalised and to protect the established order; and some apologists see it as a holistic biopsychosocial approach to understanding the effect of complex illness processes in people's lives.

This chapter does not deal with these debates. Diagnosis is an intrinsically medical construct, and there is nothing to suggest that it is likely to go away or diminish in importance for the foreseeable future. The purpose of this chapter is to explain the concept of diagnosis, to show how diagnoses are made in modern psychiatric practice, and to illustrate some of the strengths and weaknesses of diagnosis in mental health care practice.

DIAGNOSIS IN GENERAL MEDICINE

The term *diagnosis* comes from the ancient Greek, meaning to *distinguish* or *discern* (*Shorter Oxford English Dictionary* 1973); in other words, to choose between two or more options. It is not synonymous with 'working out what's wrong', which might include making a diagnosis, but is a broader process that can be formulated in a number of different ways, some of which are essentially speculative and some of which are not mutually exclusive. 'Working out what's wrong' can be intensely subjective and is not easily subject to verification. In contrast, whilst a patient may have more than one diagnosis, a diagnosis corresponds to an objective reality and hence is either right or wrong (or, at least, this is the theory).

Diagnosis in general is most easily understood with respect to infectious diseases. When some micro-organisms infect humans they cause characteristic pathology in the body; in other words, changes in tissue structure and function. This pathology causes changes in the functioning of the body which are noticed by the patient (*symptoms*) and alterations which can be directly observed by a physician examining the patient (*signs*). As an infection develops the signs and symptoms alter, which is known as the *course* or *natural history* of the disease. The signs, symptoms and natural history of infection by a specific micro-organism often cluster together to form a *syndrome*. However, the various infectious disease syndromes have a good deal of overlap, and some signs and symptoms do not occur in all patients suffering from the same disease. In coming to a diagnosis the physician is trying to understand the signs, symptoms and course in order to decide which syndrome is affecting the patient. When physicians make accurate diagnoses of infectious diseases they correctly identify a syndrome and may be able to diagnose infection with a particular micro-organism. The diagnosis corresponds with a known pathology. It tells the physician what is likely to happen next to the patient (*prognosis*), and indicates what treatments are likely to be helpful. In some infectious diseases, diagnosis indicates that specific treatments are appropriate, for example particular antibiotics, either alone or in combination.

Many acute disorders of abdominal organs also generate predictable syndromes related to known pathologies; for example, acute appendicitis or peptic ulceration. However, in many physical illnesses the situation is more complex. Congestive cardiac failure, for example, is the situation where heart disease prevents the heart from working efficiently as a pump. Inadequate blood (and therefore oxygen) reaches organs via the arterial system, and they too stop working efficiently. Back pressure develops in the veins supplying the heart with blood, with the consequence that tissues become loaded with fluid (*oedema*). Congestive cardiac failure causes a syndrome (increasing breathlessness which is worse when lying flat, swollen ankles, visible congestion of the jugular vein in the neck and so forth), but it can be the consequence of a variety of different diseases. Investigations distinguish the different diseases, so that diagnosis may have two levels; for example:

1.   congestive cardiac failure (general syndrome) caused by

2.   ischaemic heart disease (specific disease).

THE PROCESS OF DIAGNOSIS IN GENERAL MEDICINE

Box 7.1 sets out the general schema for history taking and physical examination in general medicine which is taught to all doctors in training.

Some terms may be unfamiliar, but the process is clear. History taking starts by developing an understanding of the symptoms the patient has noticed and moves on to a systematic and general search for symptoms and factors that the patient may not have noticed or may not have understood to be of significance. Similarly, the search for physical signs moves from a careful search for signs likely to be related to the symptoms described to a systematic and general search for other signs which may or may not be related to the current problem. At the end of this process the doctor creates a *differential diagnosis*, which is to say a list of the possible diagnoses, ranked in order of significance and probability, which might account for the patient's signs and symptoms. The differential diagnosis may be as short as one certain diagnosis or it may be quite long. It may include coexistent illness and it may embrace the possibility that the current symptoms are caused by more than one underlying pathology. The diagnosis may or may not then become clear through the use of special investigations or observation of the patient in hospital over a length of time.

Box 7.1 The medical schema for history taking, examination, investigation and diagnosis

History of presenting complaint

- Patient's account of illness
- Clarification of patient's account
- Location (of symptom)
- Radiation (spread, especially of pain)
- Quality
- Quantity
- Duration
- Frequency
- Aggravating factors
- Relieving factors
- Associated symptoms
- Effect on function

Past medical history

- Previous medical illnesses and treatment
- Previous surgical problems
- Current medication
- Immunisations
- Allergies (especially to drugs)

Review of systems

- General/constitutional
- Cardiovascular
- Respiratory
- Gastro-intestinal
- Genito-urinary
- Musculoskeletal
- Neurological
- Skin/breast
- Endocrine
- Ears/eyes/nose/throat

Social history

- Smoking/alcohol/drugs
- Reproductive status
- Marital and family situation
- Occupational history

Physical examination

Specific examination of affected part of body.

Systematic examination including:

- Temperature
- General appearance (pallor?/jaundice?/rash? etc.)
- Clubbing of nails?/lymphadenopathy?
- Breasts: appearance/masses?/tenderness?
- Respiratory: appearance/trachea central?/percussion/ auscultation
- Cardiovascular: pulse/blood pressure/jugular venous pressure/cardiac apex/heart sounds/carotid bruit?/ peripheral pulses
- Abdomen: appearance (scars?)/tenderness?/masses?/rigidity?/ guarding?/bowel sounds/rectal examination
- Central nervous system: cranial nerves/power in limbs/deep reflexes/sensation/coordination

Scientific advance in physical medicine has tended to occur through doctors identifying syndromes, then trying to understand the physiology of the syndrome and searching for characteristic pathology, and eventually finding treatments which act on the fundamental cause of disease. A recent example of this process is Acquired Immune Deficiency Syndrome (AIDS). An epidemic of unusual infections in gay men and drug users was recognised in the USA in the early 1980s. A syndrome was identified, which was found to be related to the breakdown of a specific part of the body's immune defences. This in turn was found to be associated with infection by the Human Immunodeficiency Virus (HIV). Finally, drugs were developed to impede the reproduction of the virus and these treatments have proven effective in greatly slowing the progress of the disorder.

DIAGNOSIS APPLIED TO MENTAL HEALTH PROBLEMS

It is hardly surprising that physicians have applied an approach that has proven so powerful in general medicine to the understanding of mental disorders. The Victorian asylums contained many patients suffering from General Paralysis of the Insane (GPI), a syndrome with characteristic neurological and psychiatric manifestations. Advances in microscopy demonstrated that this was caused by syphilis infection in its late or tertiary stage. Treatments and preventative measures were developed, and as a consequence GPI is now rare in the UK.

This approach has been successful in understanding, and to a lesser extent treating, dementia and other coarse brain diseases. However, it has failed to reveal the nature of the commonest serious mental illnesses such as schizophrenia and bipolar affective disorder (manic depression). Psychiatrists have continued to develop and refine syndromic classifications of mental disorders. A lot of data have been published reporting structural and physiological changes in the brains of patients suffering serious mental illness, but so far no characteristic pathologies have been found. Earlier findings have been contradicted by later findings and there are several competing theories. The process of psychiatric diagnosis is largely concerned with the identification of syndromes whose true nature is poorly understood.

Thirty years ago it was found that psychiatrists in different countries had different criteria for the diagnosis of schizophrenia. At that time one could reasonably argue that, from the international perspective, the concept of 'schizophrenia' did not even amount to a syndrome. Since that time international psychiatry has made a major effort to agree criteria for the diagnosis of mental disorders. This effort is manifested in the tenth edition of the *International Classification of Disease (ICD-10)* (WHO 1992). We can now at least be reasonably confident that psychiatrists mean the same thing when they make diagnoses.

There are other problems associated with the use of psychiatric diagnoses. Whilst modern operationalised diagnostic manuals may allow psychiatrists to make reliable diagnoses, the predictive power of those diagnoses is limited. Patients given a diagnosis of 'schizophrenia' can experience a variety of symptoms, none of which are invariable. There is a wide range of outcomes in terms of long-term mental health. Treatment is mainly determined by the individual patient's symptoms and behaviour rather than being specific to a given diagnosis. Understanding a person from the social and psychological perspectives is usually at least as important as diagnosis in understanding his/her behaviour and symptoms. Diagnosis can be very unstable over time. Patients initially diagnosed as suffering from hallucinations and paranoid ideas due to the toxic effects of drug misuse ('drug-induced psychosis') frequently go on to be diagnosed as suffering from schizophrenia a few years later. Finally, and perhaps most important, patients feel stigmatised by some diagnoses and can suffer tangible psychological and social harm as a consequence of being so labelled.

These are all real difficulties with psychiatric diagnosis. Does diagnosis have any utility in helping people suffering from mental distress?

IN DEFENCE OF PSYCHIATRIC DIAGNOSIS

Most people in close contact with those suffering from mental distress come to feel that some disorders definitely are true illnesses, even if the causes are as yet obscure. Some patients develop mental states far beyond ordinary experience; for example, becoming so severely depressed that they believe that their organs are rotting inside them or so elated that they can go without sleep for days on end without tiring. Individual patients' disorders often follow predictable patterns and, untreated, have a momentum beyond their control.

Having said this, some mental disorders do not conform to a disease model at all. For example, people suffering from personality disorder have usually had emotionally damaging experiences in their childhood. This means that they fail to learn the full repertoire of adult behaviours. As a consequence, their responses to life's problems can be excessive or inappropriate and they can continue to show childlike behaviour, such as temper tantrums or reassurance seeking, far into adult life. These are developmental disorders.

Although terms such as 'schizophrenia' now have internationally agreed definitions, they are nonetheless very broad concepts. The concept of schizophrenia embraces illness characterised by brief episodes of bizarre and muddled thinking with emotional turmoil and fearfulness but, equally, includes lifelong illness where there are fixed paranoid beliefs but more prominently a lack of emotional response and a deterioration in daily living skills. The diagnosis probably reflects several different underlying pathologies.

Although imperfect, there is a degree of predictive power to these diagnoses, especially if an individual's life circumstances and personality are taken into account at the same time.

A large number of physical conditions, from drug intoxication and lack of oxygen to the brain to hormone imbalances and brain tumour, can mimic or complicate mental illness. We need a way of understanding mental disorder which can, in a straightforward way, take into account both the typical mental illness syndrome and physical disease.

Not all patients with serious mental illness need drug treatment, and drug treatment is rarely sufficient on its own to allow people to recover from mental illness. However, without drug treatment many patients suffering from mental illness would be ill for much longer, and some would not recover at all. Our present drug treatments are highly problematic. They can have unpleasant and occasionally dangerous side-effects. They interact with other medications and can worsen some physical conditions. A model of understanding that embraces the physical as well as the psychosocial is clearly necessary if we are going to deploy such therapies.

Psychiatric diagnosis is like a map reference. It tells you the general type of psychological terrain the patient is in; it tells you how this patient's disorder relates to other disorders, physical and mental. It conveys some limited predictive information, and a general indication of the types of intervention that might be helpful. However, just as a map reference cannot tell you the appearance of the landscape, similarly a psychiatric diagnosis does not tell you what the person is like, how s/he will behave and the nature of any risks s/he faces. These matters have to be assessed individually on the basis of knowledge of the person.

Although the general public, politicians and some health professionals may have stigmatising attitudes to psychiatric diagnoses, most people want to know what is wrong with them. A lot is known about mental illness: what makes it worse, what helps and what the patient, families and friends can do to improve their condition. Without a diagnosis it is very difficult to obtain or explore this information. Understanding the illness can help people take back control of their lives.

Diagnosis is essential in multidisciplinary care planning for individuals. Administratively it is important to understand the types of problems from which patients suffer in order to plan and develop services, and the collection of diagnostic information is an important way of achieving this.

For all of these reasons, psychiatric diagnosis remains important. The diagnostic process does not belong solely to physicians; indeed it can be appropriately carried out without involving a psychiatrist. However, it always involves the awareness of biomedical factors as well as the psychosocial.

THE DIAGNOSTIC SCHEMA IN PSYCHIATRY

Psychiatry, like all of Western medicine, aspires to the status of an applied science. This is both its major strength and its major weakness. In following the scientific tradition it makes some implicit assumptions which transcend the personal beliefs of individual practitioners. Its approach is intrinsically *materialistic*, which is to say it recognises only factors in the material world and rejects the metaphysical. For example, no psychiatrist could conscientiously treat a mental disorder as if it were literally due to demonic possession. Individual psychiatrists might believe in the reality of demonic possession, but this belief could not ethically be part of their professional approach to treating patients.

Underlying scientific materialism explains why psychiatry is attached to those aspects of mental disorder that can be measured and quantified. Psychiatrists like evidence in support of theories and treatments to be verifiable and reproducible. This attachment to objectivity has led to the abandonment of treatments that do not work and the rejection of dubious diagnostic entities such as multiple personality. Conversely, it has sometimes given the impression that psychiatrists are indifferent to patients' subjective experiences and feelings.

Psychiatry, like much of natural science, is fundamentally *reductionist*, which is to say it tends to try to understand complex phenomena by breaking them down to smaller, simpler processes. Reductionism tends to understand the properties of large and complex systems by reference to the properties of their component parts. Hence the way a car works can be understood in terms of the interaction of individual engine parts and the properties of a diamond can be understood in terms of the nature of the bonds between individual carbon atoms.

Although the reductionist approach has led to major advances in the understanding of mental illness, it has limitations. For example, a football crowd is different to the aggregated qualities of the individuals within it. It has characteristics that could not be predicted from knowledge of individuals. Being in a football crowd induces behaviour in individuals that they do not display in any other setting. Psychiatry does use some non-reductionist approaches; for example, systems theory in some types of family therapy. Nonetheless, reductionism is pervasive throughout psychiatry, not least in its approach to diagnosis.

In keeping with materialism and reductionism, psychiatrists understand thoughts and feelings as brain activity, leading to tangible consequences in the form of behaviour. By analogy, the kidney's activity is the transfer of salts and other chemicals in and out of the blood, leading to tangible consequences in the production of urine and stability of the chemical composition of blood. In both cases, the organ's activity (thought and feelings, chemical transfer) cannot be directly observed. The consequence of the activity is directly observable, and from this one can infer what is happening to the organ's functioning. Although the analogy is flawed, this is the fundamental model through which psychiatrists think about mental disorder.

Psychiatrists recognise the *diagnostic hierarchy* that is set out in Box 7.2.

Box 7.2 The hierarchy of psychiatric diagnoses

1. Coarse physical brain disorder
2. Psychotic disorders (schizophrenia, bipolar affective disorder, persistent delusional disorder, severe depression with delusions)
3. Personality disorder
4. Non psychotic depression (depression without delusions)
5. Anxiety states

In each case, disorders can cause symptoms of all the disorders lower in the hierarchy. Hence, if two disorders are present, the disorder higher in the hierarchy becomes the overarching diagnosis and the lower diagnosis is dismissed. A physical disorder such as infection of the brain tissue (encephalitis) can generate psychiatric symptoms of almost any type. This is more of a rule of thumb than an invariable truth. For example, it is difficult to place anorexia nervosa in this hierarchy, where the self-starvation has its origins in physical, developmental, family and social factors. Nonetheless the hierarchy is important in avoiding diagnostic errors and it demonstrates the way that psychiatrists attempt to organise their ideas in the absence of known underlying pathologies.

BEYOND DIAGNOSIS

It would be easy to suppose that dissatisfaction with the limitations of psychiatric diagnosis originated in the anti-psychiatry movement of the 1960s and 1970s. In fact, long before this, psychiatrists themselves recognised that a more sophisticated understanding was necessary. Traditional British psychiatric teaching stated that the outcome of assessment should be a *formulation* of the case. A formulation includes a differential diagnosis, but is also intended to draw together all the relevant physical, social and psychological dimensions needed to answer the question: 'Why has this patient presented with these symptoms at this time?' There are numerous different ways of constructing a formulation, with no general agreement as to which is the best. As a consequence, the term has tended to fall from use, although all competent psychiatric assessment leads to this type of broad understanding. Some psychiatrists generate a problem list, which includes items related to diagnosis (such as hallucinations or paranoid ideas), but might include items such as problems in claiming benefits or problems with noisy neighbours. Reflecting this, ICD-10 is not a simple list of possible diagnoses. It is a multi-axial system with five axes, as shown in Box 7.3.

This recognises that a simple classification of the patient's signs and symptoms into a mental illness diagnosis is insufficient to understand his/her mental health problem. In each case the possibility of developmental problems and intellectual impairment must be assessed independently of mental illness. All of this is then placed against the background of physical factors and problems of living day to day (psychosocial factors). The term *axis* really reflects dimensions of people's lives rather than a graph (as no graph can have five axes).

Box 7.3 ICD-10 axes

Axis I: Mental disorder (e.g. mental illness)

Axis II: Developmental disorder (e.g. personality disorder)

Axis III: Intellectual impairment (e.g. learning disability)

Axis IV: Physical disorder

Axis V: Psychosocial problems

THE PROCESS OF MAKING A PSYCHIATRIC DIAGNOSIS

Box 7.4 shows the general schema for history taking and mental state examination in psychiatry, analogous to the schema for general medicine in Box 7.1.

Assessment should also include physical examination, discussion with informants (usually family and friends) and special investigations as appropriate (e.g. blood tests to exclude undetected physical problems; blood tests or urine tests to detect psychologically active drugs). Like the general medical schema it divides history (what the patient tells you) from examination (what the clinician observes). It follows the pattern of moving from what the patient says spontaneously to a wide-ranging and systematic exploration of other potentially relevant areas of their life. However, it differs from the general medical schema in the degree to which it explores psychological and social context, both current and historical.

The study of abnormalities of thought, belief, perception and cognitive functioning is known as *descriptive psychopathology*. Psychopathology is concerned with the delineation and classification of signs and symptoms in the mind, with the presumed actual pathology located physically in the brain. Physical pathology, for example inflammation, is objectively abnormal if present. Psychopathology, on the other hand, is usually only abnormal when set in a psychological and social context and when a range of the patient's other ideas, beliefs and emotions are taken into account. For example, many patients describe hearing voices. These experiences can be normal (for example, the recently bereaved often fleetingly hear the dead relative's voice), or they can be due to anxious repetitive (obsessional) thinking, confusion due to physical illness (delirium), schizophrenia and a range of other conditions.

Box 7.4 The schema for psychiatric history taking and mental state examination

History

- Reason for referral (patient's and referrer's). How and why did this patient come for assessment at this time? What events provoked referral?
- History of presenting problem (what symptoms/for how long/precipitants/effect on functioning/treatment so far and its effect)
- Past psychiatric history (previous problems/previous treatment/outcome)
- Family history (structure/quality of relationships with family members in past and now/family history of mental illness)
- Childhood history (developmental milestones/ problems/ losses/separations/abuse)
- Educational history (academic attainment/peer relationships/ attendance/changes of school)
- Occupational history (dates/job changes and why/promotions/ peer relationships)
- Psychosexual and reproductive history (age of puberty/ menopause/sexual relationships/unwanted sexual experiences/ pregnancies/current sexual problems)
- Medical history, including present medication and allergies
- Social history (current circumstances/housing/friends/ interests/financial problems/daily routines)
- Substance misuse (tobacco, alcohol, illegal drugs, misuse of prescription drugs)
- Forensic history
- Premorbid personality

Mental state examination

- Appearance
- Behaviour
- Mood (what patient says and what is observed)
- Speech and thought
- Formal disorders of thought
- Abnormal beliefs (delusions)
- Abnormal perceptions (hallucinations, passivity experiences)
- Phobic symptoms

- Obsessive-compulsive symptoms
- Suicidal ideas
- Homicidal ideas
- Cognitive testing
- Insight (what the patient thinks is wrong)

One can only choose between these possibilities by exploring the person's life and emotional state more widely. Novices who carefully explore psychopathology but do not understand the psychological and social context of the patient make errors, often by overemphasising the diagnostic importance of isolated abnormalities on mental state examination.

Trainees in psychiatry at the start of their career use the general schema as an *aide-mémoire* and tend to interview by rigidly working through all the headings. At the end of the process they construct a differential diagnosis. The process is not only laborious, it is also inefficient. Many beginners collect comprehensive information and yet are unable to organise and understand the information. Experienced and skilled psychiatrists tend to interview quickly in a conversational style. They tend not to construct differential diagnoses so much as multifaceted formulations including one or two diagnostic possibilities. The beginner unavoidably starts with a rule-based approach to diagnostic interviewing. The expert, however, is following a number of different processes that require a depth of understanding of mental disorder combined with clinical skills in the interview situation.

Expert diagnostic interviewing is a process of hypothesis formation and testing, working 'backwards' from diagnosis. Psychiatrists quite quickly form an impression of the likely nature of the problem, and spend a good deal of the interview looking for confirmation or refutation of the initial hypothesis. If further exploration refutes the hypothesis the psychiatrist forms a new hypothesis and tests it. Case Study 7.1 briefly describes this process in action.

CASE STUDY 7.1

A is a 23-year-old man seen by Dr Z at the request of his general practitioner (GP) after complaining of hearing voices telling him to attack people. He is friendly and cooperative at interview. He confirms a three-month history of hearing frightening voices suggesting that he should harm people. As a consequence he has been avoiding contact with others, fearing that he may act on the instructions.

Dr Z must first test the hypothesis that A is experiencing hallucinations and that he has fixed false beliefs (delusions), suggesting that he is suffering from schizophrenia. This is important because there is a relatively high risk that people suffering from hallucinations which give commands will eventually act upon the instructions. Dr Z therefore asks A where the voices seem to be coming from and what he thinks is causing the voices. Patients suffering from schizophrenia are likely to feel that the voices are arising completely externally and that they are true perceptions. They are likely to have delusions related to the voices.

A says that although the voices are vivid, they must really be his own thoughts. He does not want to harm anybody, so they seem alien and frightening. He does not know what is causing him to have these experiences. Although he is sure that he will not lose control and attack someone, he still needs to reassure himself through isolation (which has, in the long run, tended to make him feel worse).

It is clear to Dr Z that A is not suffering from schizophrenia and that these are not command hallucinations. His second hypothesis is that they are *obsessional ruminations*. These are anxious, repetitive thoughts reflecting the person's fears. They are resisted by the patient, who understands that they arise from within himself. They can be the main symptom of obsessive-compulsive disorder, but more commonly arise in people with certain personality traits when they become depressed. It is very rare for anyone to act upon obsessional ruminations.

Dr Z therefore has a two-stage hypothesis. He is already fairly certain that the voices are obsessional ruminations, and can test this by further exploring what happens if A resists them and what else he does to control them. To test the underlying diagnostic hypothesis (depression in a man with obsessional traits) he must search for convincing depressive symptoms including low mood (worse in the morning), pessimistic thinking, sleep disturbance, etc. Obsessional traits are evident both on direct

> questioning and by exploration of life history, which slowly reveals patterns of behaviour associated with obsessionality (love of routine, difficulty with uncertainty and risk taking, conscientiousness, pedantic interest in detail, tendency to emotional over-control). Dr Z confirms his diagnostic hypothesis, whilst simultaneously looking for and testing hypotheses as to why A has become depressed at this particular time in his life.

Expert diagnostic interviewing is inquisitive. The interviewer is curious and constantly attentive for clues and hints to help explore the patient's world. Inconsistencies and gaps in chronology often indicate that important information is being withheld, either deliberately or unwittingly. Pursuing clues, hints and gaps helps the psychiatrist to obtain all the relevant information to properly understand the person's context and to make an accurate diagnosis. In order to develop this kind of inquisitive interviewing psychiatrists have to understand lifestyles very different to their own. Case Study 7.2 illustrates how inquisitive interviewing can help form a diagnosis.

CASE STUDY 7.2

Dr X assesses B, a 53-year-old man, in an outpatient clinic. B has developed severe panic disorder over the past six months without any identifiable precipitants. On taking the background history, Dr X records dates for all the main events. It becomes obvious that there is a gap of one year when B was aged 20. Dr X presses B who initially denies that there is a gap in his chronology. Dr X persists in trying to make the dates join up, and eventually B tearfully tells Dr X that he was in prison for a year for having sex with an underage girl. Although he denies any present paedophilic sexual interest, he has been alarmed at recent publicity about sexual offenders. Dr X, having uncovered a secret, must now sensitively explore both B's sexual life but also the consequences of the offence and punishment on him psychologically, as both are bound to be important.

In modern psychiatric practice only a minority of patients are seen by psychiatrists working alone in a clinic. Many patients are assessed in their own home by multidisciplinary teams. This form of assessment is complex, but provides a richer quality of assessment. Seeing a patient's home tells the clinician a great deal about their personality, attitudes, abilities and lifestyle. Different professions conduct assessments in different ways and the involvement of more than one profession provides a type of 'stereoscopic' assessment. It does, however, create some problems in collating information and in ensuring that assessment is comprehensive. Case Study 7.3 illustrates multidisciplinary assessment at home.

Although expert diagnosticians, working in multidisciplinary teams in the community, tend not to work through the standard interview schema in a rigid fashion, they are aware of the need to explore each category, no matter how tangentially. The conversational nature of the interview belies a high level of underlying structure that is essential to ensure that history taking and mental state examination are comprehensive in their scope.

CASE STUDY 7.3

C is a 63-year-old woman who is referred by her GP eight weeks after the death of her husband. M, a community psychiatric nurse, sees her at home with Dr Y. C is agitated, depressed and full of thoughts of self-reproach. Dr Y feels she is suffering from severe agitated depression and that she might need electro-convulsive treatment (ECT). M notices that there are symbols of Roman Catholicism around the house and asks her about her faith. It emerges that C is a devout Catholic; M asks about her husband's faith, at which C becomes even more distressed. It slowly emerges that he was an atheist who refused the attentions of the priest in his final illness. He insisted on a secular funeral. C now fears that she and her husband will be separated for eternity. C is admitted to hospital, and the Catholic chaplain is involved in her care.

CONCLUSION

Recurrent announcements of the death of the medical model and of diagnosis in mental health care have proven premature. Medical diagnosis does have real flaws, but it remains one of a number of important ways of understanding what is wrong with people suffering from mental disorders. It is no substitute for understanding the patient as an individual, but it conveys sufficient information to be useful. All mental health professionals need to understand the process of diagnosis.

REFERENCE

Shorter Oxford English Dictionary (1973). Oxford: Oxford University Press.
WHO (World Health Organisation) (1992) *Classification of Mental and Behavioural Disorders: Clinical Descriptions and Diagnostic Guidelines*. Tenth Edition. Geneva: WHO.

CHAPTER 8

MULTIDISCIPLINARY TEAMWORKING AND THE ROLES OF MEMBERS

KAREN NEWBIGGING

INTRODUCTION

Multidisciplinary teamworking is now widely accepted in mental health, and the health care field more generally, as being the most effective way of using the different skills and experiences of professionals and others to improve the health status of individuals. Teamworking is therefore an expectation in the modernisation of mental health care and is enshrined in guidance for new service models (DH 2001a). The opportunities which effective teamworking brings are therefore well understood. The realities of working in multidisciplinary teams can, however, mean that there is a failure to satisfy these aspirations and there is an extensive literature describing the difficulties of multidisciplinary teamworking in mental health, particularly within community mental health teams (CMHTs) (e.g. Onyett and Ford 1996; Peck and Norman 1999). These difficulties may in part reflect the complexities – indeed, some might say, impossibilities (Willshire 1999) – of organising mental health care. However, it is equally likely that they also reflect the lack of attention to the clarity and detail that is needed in the development of multidisciplinary teams and that merely bringing together a group of different professionals and, more recently, non-professionally aligned staff, in the hope that they can work it out together, leaves much to chance.

The key question then becomes, what needs to happen for multidisciplinary teams to deliver the best outcomes for people using mental health services? This chapter looks at what multidisciplinary working means, the inherent difficulties and, drawing on both the work of the Centre for Mental Health Services Development and recent seminal research (Borrill *et al.* 2000), explores what needs to happen to secure the benefits of bringing together diverse perspectives, skills and experience for people using mental health services.

WHAT IS A MULTIDISCIPLINARY TEAM?

A multidisciplinary team is typically conceived of as a mixed group of professionals working together in the same place to achieve the same end; that is, improved health and social care status of an individual. In mental health services this has typically been mental health nurses, psychiatric social workers, occupational therapists, clinical psychologists and psychiatrists. More recently, teams have begun to include non-professionally aligned staff such as community support workers, and service users as survivor workers are beginning to be introduced (Relton 2002). However, the term has been used loosely and in practice a significant majority of teams have consisted of two professional groups, social work and nursing. Indeed, a survey of 113 CMHTs found only 12 per cent of teams included members from all of the disciplines listed above (Borrill *et al.* 2000). Not surprisingly, the term has been criticised for being ambiguous and misleading (Cott 1997) and it has been referred to as an umbrella term used to describe a wide range of patterns of working, rather than a discrete and measurable concept (Whyte and Brooker 2001).

The concepts of shared objectives, interdependency and shared accountability for outcomes are central to the definition of multidisciplinary teamworking (Mohrman, Cohen and Mohrman 1995). These characteristics are what distinguish teams from a group of people who are co-located (Brooks 1999 as cited in Peck 2003). Ovretveit (1996) identified five dimensions of teamwork, each of which can be viewed as a continuum and help describe the ways in which teams differ. They are:

- the degree of integration among the members of the team
- the extent to which a team collectively manages its resources in response to service user needs as opposed to managing resources by professional discipline
- membership

- team processes including decision-making processes about who does what
- management of the team.

Each of these dimensions can be viewed as a continuum and they are key considerations in developing teams. Clarity on these is helpful in addressing the ambiguity about role and function that beleaguers many mental health teams.

THE RATIONALE FOR MULTIDISCIPLINARY TEAMWORKING

Senge (1990) has drawn attention to the way in which teams help organisations to learn more effectively and to enable the organisation to be more innovative because of the cross-fertilisation of ideas which can take place. The underlying rationale for emphasis on multidisciplinary working is summarised in relation to community mental health teams in reviews by Chalk (1999) and Onyett (2002) and includes:

- better-informed holistic care: multidisciplinary working giving access to a wide range of skills across health and social care
- a single point of access to these skills, avoiding unnecessary delays, duplication of effort and fragmentation of care
- access to practical local information about services and contacts
- coordination of care and cases allocated according to needs
- direct and regular contact between those providing care, creating opportunities to share information, delegate work, develop joint initiatives and enhance decision making
- a better use of resources and therefore the potential to be more cost effective
- mutual support for team members and a positive impact on morale.

Chalk (1999) found support for some of the above in the literature (e.g. Onyett and Ford 1996) including positive evaluations made by service users and carers. This is echoed by the recent Cochrane Review of CMHTs which found that they were superior than standard care in promoting acceptance of treatment as well as indications that it is superior in reducing hospital admissions and avoiding death by suicide (Tyrer et al. 2003). There is as yet relatively little evidence comparing the emerging functionalised models of multidisciplinary working to generic

CMHTs in the UK (NIMHE 2003). However, the confusion about terminology and heterogeneity of multidisciplinary working referred to above has also raised questions about the validity of evaluating different models of team-based care (NIMHE 2003).

The policy context builds on the perceived benefits of teamworking and emerging evidence. New service models are now, without exception, conceived as relying on a pool of expertise drawn from a broad range of individuals both professionally and non-professionally qualified (see DH 2001a, 2001b and 2002 for example). The importance of partnerships and the integration of care provided by health and social services is an important theme running through wider health policy, not only mental health policy. *The NHS Plan* (DH 2000) and the *National Service Framework for Mental Health* (NSFMH) (DH 1999) sets the framework for new ways of working and new models of service delivery for people with mental health problems. One of the guiding principles of the NSFMH is that 'care will be coordinated between all staff and agencies' (p.4). It makes it clear that this means care planning, and the delivery and review of services for people diagnosed with a serious mental illness is not only a multidisciplinary but also a multi-agency endeavour and that the processes of care management[1] and the Care Programme Approach[2] must be fully integrated.

WORKING IN TEAMS

As Robbins and Finley (2000) make clear, teamwork has a number of inherent difficulties. They outline these as:

- defining the task
- keeping the focus on the client/customer/service user
- balancing individual needs with team needs
- different personal styles and approaches to work of team members
- quality of decision making

---

1   Typically undertaken by Social Services.
2   Introduced in 1991 for people receiving the specialist mental health services.

- leadership style and the relationship to the task
- organisational context for teamworking
- insufficient feedback and information
- resistance to change.

In mental health these difficulties are compounded by two issues: first, the complexity of mental health and the differing and often opposing perspectives on mental health and mental illness, and second, the professional allegiance developed through professional socialisation of individual team members providing a more easily available source of consensus and support. The difficulties which have been identified in multidisciplinary mental health teams, mainly in respect of CMHTs, are both internally generated and external to the team. There is:

- insufficient planning and consideration as to what type of team, what is the best composition, what skill mix is required (Chalk 1999), what level of resources is required and what is the 'fit' within the whole system of care
- lack of a coherent and shared vision (Ansoff 1990) and absence of a strong philosophy of community mental health services (Norman, Peck and Richards 1999)
- lack of clarity about the remit of the team (Onyett 1997)
- little, if any, preparation for multidisciplinary working as part of prequalification training combined with professional socialisation (Stark *et al.* 2002) and strong adherence to uniprofessional cultures (Norman *et al.* 1999)
- lack of agreement about what working together means and an incomplete understanding or appreciation of the roles of others (Norman et al. 1999; Peck and Norman 1999)
- a high number of caseloads combined with an increase in administrative work associated with the CPA (SCMH 1998)
- a failure to integrate processes in respect of case management and record keeping
- a lack of clarity in the accountability arrangements with tensions arising between professional accountability and team accountability (CMHSDE 2003)
- absence of a clear leader, conflict over leadership or poorly developed leadership skills with an over-emphasis on management (transactional) as opposed to transformational leadership (Onyett 2002)

- a loss of the faith of mental health professionals in the system in which they work and a mistrust of managerial solutions to the problems of interprofessional working (Peck and Norman 1999).

The manifestation of these difficulties have led a number of researchers and practitioners to pose the question of whether teamwork in mental health is achievable in practice (Stark *et al.* 2002). Indeed, they impact on both team functioning and the morale of individual members and therefore ultimately on the outcomes for people using mental health services. From work undertaken by the Centre for Mental Health Services Development with a large number of teams (predominantly CMHTs) it is possible to describe a process of demoralisation and loss of confidence in the system and self, resulting in loss of staff, burn-out among staff and, eventually, negative outcomes for service users, as illustrated in Figure 8.1.

ROLES OF TEAM MEMBERS

Both Onyett (2002) and Peck (2003) provide an overview of the history of the development of multidisciplinary working in the UK. Central to the development of multidisciplinary working was the hope that there would be a fundamental shift in the nature of professional relationships (Tyrer 2000); in particular, a hope that there would be a shift from medical dominance to a more consensual and democratic style of working. Whilst it is not clear the extent to which this hope has been realised it is clear that the blurring of roles and the associated 'role confusion' has been a source of difficulty for many teams (Moller and Harber 1996). It has led to a widespread call for the clarification of roles and responsibilities (Peck and Norman 1999) and a need to develop a good understanding and respect for the differing roles of the contributors to the multidisciplinary effort (Onyett 1999).

The concept of role is a multidimensional one and, in multidisciplinary teams, team members can take up a number of different roles. These include generic roles, roles that reflect professional training and/or experience, team roles and social roles. Specific roles include professional roles and non-professionally aligned roles, community support workers and service user roles. These are relatively new roles which are recognised as bringing an important and often missing perspective to teamwork. Mental health professionals will have some knowledge, attitudes and skills that overlap with those of other professional groups,

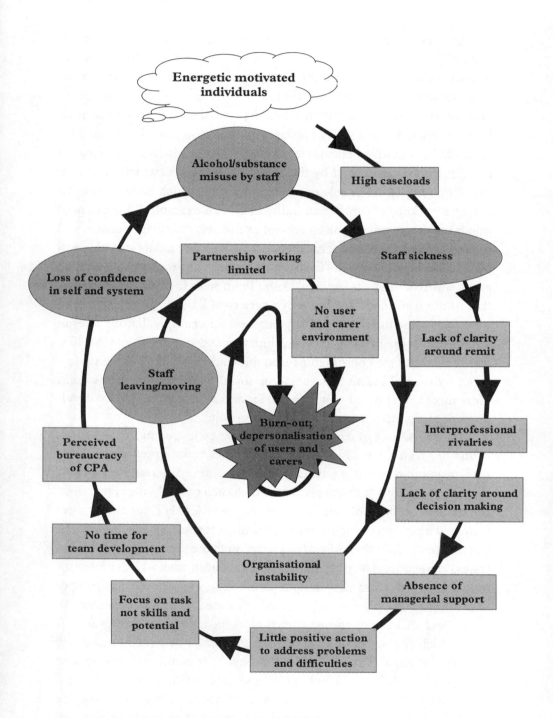

Figure 8.1 A negative experience of multidisciplinary working

usually described as core competencies. The Sainsbury Centre for Mental Health (SCMH 1997), for example, identified 27 competencies in four areas: management and administration; assessment; treatment and care management; and collaborative working. In addition to shared areas of competence many mental health professionals pursue post-qualification training that is increasingly multidisciplinary in nature, for example in cognitive behavioural therapy. This leads to a 'blurring' of roles, further complicated by the generic roles that exist within multidisciplinary teams. The role of care coordinator, which involves coordinating a package of care for an individual, is an example. This essential role is taken up typically, although not exclusively, by social workers and mental health nurses and some mental health professionals view this and other generic roles, such as that of duty worker, negatively as de-skilling and a waste of their professional skills. Team roles include those such as that of the team manager but also a variety of liaison roles designed to work across the interface with key services; for example, liaison roles in relation to primary care or acute inpatient services within CMHTs. Again, as with care coordinator roles, these are most likely to be undertaken by mental health nurses and/or social workers. The consequent blurring of roles has led to both a call for and a concern about the development of a generic mental health worker role.

Another source of tension, largely unacknowledged in the literature, is that of social roles. There will be differences between team members, particularly in terms of gender and ethnicity. These differences can affect behaviour and how team members relate to each other. In the research by Borrill et al. (2000) 67 per cent of the 1443 CMHT members were women whilst men predominated in the highest status group, psychiatry. Borrill et al. (2000) therefore draw attention to the literature, which illustrates how gender is an important influence within teams. Different communication styles and expectations, combining with sex role stereotypes and compounded by status, influence both the perception of women in teams and their willingness to participate in team communication. A team which enables both male and female staff to be equally heard will reap the benefits of the different approaches to work and ensure that attention is paid to both processes and relationships, and tasks and outcomes (Alexander, Lichenstein and D'Aunno 1996). Diversity in terms of ethnicity and life experience of team members, including experience of mental health problems, are equally important and should be regarded as valuable assets to support the team in developing its repertoire of knowledge, skills, values and networks. Whilst little research has been undertaken on the emerging service user roles there is a widespread concern amongst survivor workers that these roles are the lowest status roles within teams and that an absence of management and support combined with bullying and discrimination is reflected in 'epidemic' levels of stress for these workers (Snow 2002, p.6). Given that these workers, and indeed some staff from black and ethnic minorities, may be the lone worker and yet expected to carry the mantle of challenge, the isolation of these positions should not be underestimated.

MAKING TEAMS WORK

The difficulties highlighted above are well recognised and have been articulated as a reason for individual professional groups to steer clear of multidisciplinary working. Arguably, this serves the interest of the individual professional group at the expense of the interest of the person experiencing mental health difficulties. Keeping these interests central the question becomes not *whether* multidisciplinary teamworking in mental health is achievable but *how*. A number of writers have proposed the conditions for effective teamworking, particularly for CMHTs (e.g. Onyett and Ford 1996). There are a number of consistent themes in the recommendations:

- clarity of focus
- shared aims and objectives
- appreciation of and clarity of roles and responsibilities
- clarity of accountability arrangements
- integration of management
- effective management and leadership
- review and evaluation.

More recently, the Department of Health (DH) commissioned research to identify whether and how multidisciplinary teamworking contributes to quality, efficiency and innovation in health care in the NHS. The research, known as the Health Care Team Effectiveness Project (Borrill *et al*. 2000), was an in-depth study of over 400 teams which included 113 CMHTs. This study found that the quality of teamworking is powerfully related to the effectiveness of the health care team and its ability to be innovative. The research enabled the characteristics of an effective team to be identified, as summarised in Table 8.1.

The study found that the higher the quality of teamworking the more effective it was, i.e. the clearer the objectives, the higher the levels of participation, and the greater the commitment to quality and support for innovation, then the more effective the team was in delivering good quality care. Team members also benefited, with those working in teams having much better mental health than those working in looser groups or working individually. The benefits appear to be due to greater role clarity, better peer support and being buffered from the effects of organisational climate and conflict. Those teams characterised by clear leadership, high levels of integration, good communication and effective team processes have team members with good mental health and low stress levels. Further, in secondary health care settings the retention rates are higher in those teams characterised by good team processes, in sharp contrast to the process previously outlined in Figure 8.1. This research provides a basis for the informed development of multidisciplinary teams.

Table 8.1 Characteristics of an effective team	
Clear objectives	The objectives of the team are clear and shared by team members. Each member has a well-defined role and clear understanding of how they contribute to achieving these objectives
High level of participation in the team	Team members regularly interact with each other in order to achieve the team's shared objectives. They are able to contribute their knowledge and expertise to decision-making in the team and therefore feel part of the team. The opportunity for the team to regularly reflect is important and also crucial
Commitment to and focus on quality	Team members have a shared commitment to achieving the best possible for people using their services
Support for innovation	Team members support innovation by providing each other with practical and social support. Examples of innovation include measures to improve the quality of care, novel use of resources and collaboration with external organisations

SECURING THE BENEFITS OF MULTIDISCIPLINARY WORKING

It is evident that a systemic approach to teamworking is needed, addressing both the context within which the team works and the way in which the team brings together different professionals to work together. Adopting a systemic approach to multidisciplinary teamworking means:

1. Developing multidisciplinary teamworking within a whole-system approach

A 'whole system' approach means that all the elements of the system complement each other, in total are able to meet the needs of a particular individual. For this to happen in practice clarity about the role, function, skill mix and interventions that the multidisciplinary team will deliver and its 'fit' within the whole system needs to be developed during the process of establishing the team. Clarifying the membership and the roles of different team members within the team is an important part of this. Where more than one multidisciplinary team is being developed, as is typically the case with CMHTs, attention needs to be paid to the equity of resourcing and consistency of team processes, taking account of important differences in the populations being served.

A further key consideration is the interface between the team and the other elements of the system. For example, some of the difficulties experienced by CMHTs reflected an ambiguity about their role in relationship to primary care. Further, the difficulties encountered by people who have complex needs, such as those with a dual diagnosis either of substance misuse or learning disability, in accessing appropriate support often illustrate dramatically the failure of the whole system to work together effectively. Working out the respective roles and the way in which the different elements will communicate and work together to meet needs, alongside building constructive working relationships, will go a long way to addressing these difficulties.

2. Preparing staff for multidisciplinary teamworking

Preparation for multidisciplinary teamwork needs to be integral to pre-qualification training. This is currently largely absent and needs to be addressed by organisations responsible for commissioning and providing training. Post-qualification preparation and development can be provided locally and a development programme is an essential part of establishing teams. A development programme should focus on:

- developing an agreed philosophy of care through developing shared aims, objectives, values and ways of working. This will include clarifying the range of interventions to be provided by the team and the implications for the organisation of the team as a consequence
- team building and developing positive working relationships through clarifying and developing an appreciation of the roles and responsibilities of different team members
- providing grounding in the nature of working in groups and teamwork, the inherent difficulties and tensions and how these may be addressed
- addressing diversity through sensitising members to the issue of social roles and their potential impact on individual behaviour and team dynamics.

Box 8.1 provides an outline of a team development programme. Such a programme will need to be supported by and engage senior managers. It could usefully be run in parallel with a leadership programme aimed at team managers. Peck and Norman (1999) have also drawn attention to the importance of uniprofessional development and suggest a process for this in the context of developing an understanding of the roles of the different team members.

3. Securing organisational support for teamworking

Senior management teams also need to reflect on how the organisation can sustain multidisciplinary teamworking. Peck (2003) has observed that 'inter-professional dialogue may result in more creative tension and less destructive conflict, but only if the professionals involved are nurtured from being groups into becoming teams' (p.76).

This implies that organisations need to foster a climate within which teamworking and team performance are developed. Figure 8.1 illustrates how organisational factors interweave with team factors to impact on the morale of staff and the quality of experience for service users and carers.

Box 8.1 An Outline Development Programme

- Understanding the agenda
    - ∘ scene setting
    - ∘ context for change: national and local
    - ∘ identification of issues, problems and assessment of team effectiveness
- Developing a shared vision
    - ∘ outcome for service users and their families and/or carers
    - ∘ values and philosophy of care
- Clarifying roles and responsibilities
    - ∘ the service user group
    - ∘ the care process
    - ∘ management and supervision
    - ∘ information sharing
    - ∘ decision-making
- Understanding team functions, processes and ways of working
    - ∘ assessment
    - ∘ therapeutic interventions
    - ∘ acute interventions
    - ∘ social care
    - ∘ long-term support
- Understanding different professional roles and responsibilities
- Working with diverse needs
- User and carer involvement
- Effective teamworking and evaluating how we are doing
- Interface with other services

In summary, the organisation should:

- demonstrate that commitment to multidisciplinary working is reflected throughout the organisation and not only at an operational level

- ensure that management, accountability arrangements and service governance are consistent with teamworking
- delegate resources and authority for the use of these to the team to support them in their role
- develop performance management systems and management information systems that have a team focus.

4. Integrated management and accountability arrangements

Recent policy initiatives have focused on the integration of health and social care with the expectation that there will be a single management structure and a multidisciplinary team manager with staff co-located (DH 1999). These arrangements have as yet not been comprehensively evaluated. However, an evaluation of the first combined mental health and social care provider in the UK (Peck, Gulliver and Towell 2002) indicates that the process of achieving this requires some care. The study tentatively indicates benefits to service users in terms of improved coordination of services and to staff in terms of improvements in team environment and communication. Peck *et al.* (2002) draw attention to the concerns that staff had during this process, particularly in relation to workload demands, bureaucracy and loss of professional autonomy. Other writers (notably Brown, Crawford and Darongkamas 2000) have highlighted that when professional identity is perceived as being under threat through attempts to promote multidisciplinary working there is the possibility of entrenchment and policing of professional boundaries rather than more flexibility. Working with this whilst achieving integration is a complex but necessary task if a retreat into professional camps is to be avoided.

In introducing single line management, arrangements for supervision need to be clear. They should include professional, line management and practice supervision and should provide a structure to support professionals in their unique roles and allay fears about losing identity and becoming a 'generic' worker. Ensuring that there is adequate professional development where individuals can receive consultation and support from a more senior member of their own profession and/or access to a professional network can help to address the threats to teamworking posed by professional identity.

5. Developing the team culture

Borrill *et al.* (2000) have demonstrated that, in addition to being clear about shared objectives and individual roles, the ways in which teams work has a significant bearing on how effective they are and on the outcomes for people who use the service and the mental health of those working in them. There are therefore a number of things which teams need to do which will support the delivery of these outcomes and their ability to be innovative. These are:

- Develop a shared vision and philosophy of care – focusing on the outcomes for service users is the best way of doing this. In doing so the differences in perspectives and what really matters to individuals can be shared. Developing a shared philosophy should underpin different contributions team members can make and together with shared objectives replace traditional ways of working. The recovery model provides a good example of a model for teams to unite around.

- Interact regularly – whilst multidisciplinary meetings can be criticised as a waste of resources and an ineffective way of allocating referrals, it is clear that they *do* serve an important function in enabling members to understand and explore each other's roles and to develop the 'team culture'. Clarity about decision-making processes as well as explicit time for development will support positive collaboration. Indeed, the extent to which team members participate in decision making is another key feature of effective teams (Borrill *et al.* 2000).

- Regularly reflect on how the team is working and how well it is achieving its objectives has been identified as critical to the team's success. Facilitated team 'away' days or more formal development programmes are useful methods of doing this. Using an external facilitator who is not part of the team is invaluable as it provides an external perspective and means that attention is paid not only to the *what* but also the *how* of team activity.

In addition to formal development programmes, the implementation of new approaches, for example psychosocial approaches, will be facilitated through being introduced in a team context. Focusing on the team's competencies, as opposed to the individual practitioner's, will support the development of the team culture.

6. Ensuring positive leadership

The majority of staff who are team managers or team leaders have been clinicians or practitioners working with people with mental health problems. This can be both a strength and a source of difficulty. It means that the individual understands and is connected to the primary task of producing an effective response to individual needs. However, many individuals are ill prepared for the task of leading and managing a team. Attention needs to be paid to supporting the individual in this transition from team member to team manager to enable him/her to direct effectively the work of the team and engage with senior management and the external organisations. The development of team leaders should focus on:

- role
- personal development and leadership skills
- management of change
- organisational learning.

It should be designed and delivered in a way which promotes peer support and action learning. As teams become more sophisticated in their ability to work together then shared leadership or distributed leadership across different functions can be developed. This is associated with higher levels of effectiveness, innovation and better-quality teamwork (Borrill *et al.* 2000).

7. User and carer involvement

For user and carer involvement to be meaningful they need to be integral to the activity of the team. The ways this can be achieved include:

- employing people with current experience of using mental health services as part of the team and ensuring appropriate support. There are many examples of this emerging, with the service user development worker post within the Bradford Home Treatment Team being possibly one of the best known (Relton 2002)
- establishing a reference group for the team, which draws together people who are involved with the team as service users and/or carers. This group is a vital source of feedback, evaluation and source of ideas about service improvement and development

- the user and carer contributing to team training and development
- providing good information for service users in appropriate formats and languages on mental heath issues and the role of the team
- ensuring that service user activity is appropriately resourced and that service users are paid for their time and funding is available for training opportunities. Chapter 10 of this book provides good practice guidance on this.

CONCLUSION

High-quality multidisciplinary working can deliver more effective outcomes for people who use mental health services. The centrality of teamworking to positive practice now needs to be recognised as a feature of professional and organisational life. Its development needs to be supported by changes in organisations and their approach to team-based working, in education and training for professional groups and in the active development of teams to ensure that the diverse skills and experiences of team members are put to best effect.

REFERENCES

Alexander, J.A., Lichenstein, R. and D'Aunno, T.A. (1996) 'The effects of treatment team diversity and size on assessments of team functioning.' *Hospital and Health Services Administration 41*, 37–53.

Ansoff, I. (1990) *Implanting Corporate Strategy*. London: Prentice Hall.

Borrill, C.S., Carleta, J., Carter, A., Dawson, J., Garrod, S., Rees, A., Richards, A., Shapiro, D. and West, M. (2000) *The Effectiveness of Health Care Teams in the National Health Service*. Birmingham: Aston University.

Brooks, I. (1999) *Organisational Behaviour: Individuals, Groups and the Organisation*. London: Financial Times/Pitman.

Brown, B., Crawford, P. and Darongkamas, J. (2000) 'Blurred roles and permeable boundaries: The experience of multidisciplinary working in community mental health.' *Health and Social Care in the Community 8*, 6, 425–35.

Chalk, A. (1999) 'Community mental health teams: Reviewing the debate.' *Mental Health Nursing 19*, 2, 12–15.

CMHSDE (Centre for Mental Health Services Development England) (2003) *An Evaluation of Community Mental Health Teams*. Unpublished report.

Cott, C. (1997) 'We decide, you carry it out: A social network analysis of long term care teams.' *Social Sciences and Medicine 45*, 1411–21.

DH (Department of Health) (1999) *The National Service Framework for Mental Health*. London: DH.

DH (Department of Health) (2000) *National Health Service Plan*. London: DH.

DH (Department of Health) (2001a) *The Mental Health Policy Implementation Guide*. London: DH.

DH (Department of Health) (2001b) *Mental Health National Service Framework (and the NHS Plan) Workforce Planning, Education and Training Underpinning Programmes: Adult Mental Health Services: Final Report by the Workforce Action Team Report.* London: DH.

DH (Department of Health) (2002) *Mental Heath Policy Implementation Guide: Community Mental Health Teams.* London: DH.

Mohrman, S.A., Cohen, S.G. and Mohrman, A.M. (1995) *Designing Team-Based Organisations.* San Francisco, CA: Jossey-Bass.

Moller, M.D. and Harber, J. (1996) 'Advanced practice in psychiatric nursing: The need for a blended role.' *Online Journal of Issues in Nursing. http://www.nursingworld.org/ojin/tpc17htm*

NIMHE (National Institute for Mental Health England) (2003) *Cases for Change: Community Services.* London: Department of Health.

Norman, I.J., Peck, E. and Richards, H.L. (1999) 'Interprofessional working in adult community mental health teams: an interprofessional dialogue.' *Journal of Mental Health 8,* 217–30.

Onyett, S. (1997) 'Collaboration and the community mental health team.' *Journal of Interprofessional Care 11,* 3, 257–67.

Onyett, S. (1999) 'Community mental health team working as a socially valued enterprise.' *Journal of Mental Health 8,* 3, 245–51.

Onyett, S. (2002) *Teamworking in Mental Health.* Basingstoke: Palgrave Macmillan.

Onyett, S. and Ford, R. (1996) 'Multi-disciplinary community team: Where is the wreckage?' *Journal of Mental Health 5,* 47–55.

Onyett, S. and Malone, S. (1990) 'Making the teamwork.' *Clinical Psychology Forum 28,* 16–18.

Ovretveit, J. (1996) 'Five ways to describe a multidisciplinary team.' *Journal of Interprofessional Care 10,* 163–71.

Peck, E. (2003) 'Working in multidisciplinary community teams.' In B. Hannigan and M. Coffey (eds) *The Handbook of Community Mental Health Nursing.* London: Routledge.

Peck, E. and Norman, I. (1999) 'Working together in adult community mental health services: Exploring inter-professional role relations.' *Journal of Mental Health 8,* 3, 231–44.

Peck, E., Gulliver, P. and Towell, D. (2002) *Modernising Partnerships: An Evaluation of Somerset's Innovations in the Commissioning and Organisation of Mental Health Services.* London: Institute for Applied Health and Social Policy, King's College.

Relton, P. (2002) 'Revolutionary agents of change.' in Snow, R. *Stronger than Ever: Report of the First National Conference of Survivor Workers UK.* Manchester: Asylum Publishing.

Robbins, H. and Finley, M. (2000) *Why Teams Don't Work: What Went Wrong and How to Make it Right.* London: Texere.

SCMH (Sainsbury Centre for Mental Health) (1997) *Pulling Together: The Future Roles and Training of Mental Health Staff.* London: SCMH.

SCMH (Sainsbury Centre for Mental Health) (1998) *Keys to Engagement: Review of Care for People who are Hard to Engage with Services.* London: SCMH.

Senge, P. (1990) *The Fifth Discipline: The Art and Practice of the Learning Organisation.* New York: Doubleday.

Snow, R. (2002) *Stronger than Ever: Report of the First National Conference of Survivor Workers UK.* Manchester: Asylum Publishing.

Stark, S., Skidmore, D., Warne, T. and Stronach, I. (2002) 'A survey of "teamwork" in mental health: Is it achievable in practice?' *British Journal of Nursing 11,* 3, 178–86.

Tyrer, P. (2000) 'The future of the community mental health team.' *International Review of Psychiatry 12,* 3, 219–26.

Tyrer, P., Coid, J., Simmonds, S., Joseph, P. and Marriott, S. (2003) 'Community mental health teams (CMHTs) for people with severe mental illnesses and disordered personality (Cochrane Review)'. *The Cochrane Library, Issue 3.* Oxford: Update Software.

Whyte, L. and Brooker, C. (2001) 'Working with a multidisciplinary team: In secure psychiatric environments.' *Journal of Psychosocial Nursing and Mental Health Services 39,* 26–35.

Willshire, L. (1999) 'Psychiatric services: Organising impossibility.' *Human Relations 52,* 6, 775–804.

FURTHER READING

Assessment tools that help teams identify their areas of strength and areas for development:

Onyett, S. (2002) *Teamworking in Mental Health*. Basingstoke: Palgrave Macmillan.

Borrill, C. and West, M. (2000) *Developing Team Working Health Care: A Guide for Managers*. Birmingham: Aston Centre for Health Service Organisation Research.

Borrill, C. and West, M. (2000) *How Good is your Team? A Guide for Team Memebers*. Birmingham: Aston Centre for Health Service Organisation Research.

USEFUL CONTACTS

Aston Centre of Health Organisation Research

Aston Business School

Aston University

Aston Triangle

Birmingham B4 7ET

Tel: 0121-359-3611

Web: www.wandop.abs.aston.ac.uk

Centre for Mental Health Services Development at the Health and Social Care Advisory Service

Kings Fund

11–13 Cavendish Square

London W16 0AN

Tel: 0207-307-2892

Fax: 0207-307-2890

Web: www.hascas.org

Emerson Business Centre

5th Floor

St James's House

Pendleton Way

Pendleton

Manchester M6 5FW

Tel: 0161-743-2044

Fax: 0161-743-2067

National Institute for Mental Health in England

Blenheim House

West One

Dunscombe Street

Leeds LS1 4PL

Tel: 0113-254-5000

Details on national programmes and regional development centres available at www.nimhe.org.uk

Sainsbury Centre for Mental Health

134–138 Borough High Street

London SE1 1LB

Tel: 0207-403-8790

Fax: 0207-403-9482

Web: www.scmh.org.uk

CHAPTER 9

SUPPORTING STAFF

JANE GILBERT

INTRODUCTION

Mental health services are *human* services – services are provided and received by people in relationship with one another, and those who provide care for people in emotional distress each have their own vulnerabilities and strengths. Receiving support and feeling supported makes the difference between thriving and surviving in work that is often intensely personally demanding. Failure to provide appropriate support for staff also has financial implications. Sickness rates of 5 per cent currently cost the National Health Service (NHS) £700 million each year (Williams, Michie and Pattani 1998), and more than 30,000 nurses left the profession in 1996 (Ward 2000).

The *Pocket Oxford Dictionary* (1982) defines *support* as: 'to keep from falling, sinking, or failing, to strengthen, encourage or give corroboration to'. Supporting staff is therefore not necessarily 'supervision', but supervision can be *part of* staff support. This chapter focuses on the provision of the strengthening and encouragement necessary for staff to be sustained in emotionally demanding work. Some of the potentially damaging effects of lack of staff support are outlined, the differences and overlap between support and supervision are identified, and some of the difficulties and obstacles in receiving and providing support, both at individual and organisational levels, are discussed. Some guiding principles and specific suggestions as to how staff support can become an integral part of services at all levels are put forward.

STRESS FACTORS IN MENTAL HEALTH SERVICES

Working within mental health services is recognised as a demanding, stressful occupation within both community and residential settings. Changes in service structure, the development of integrated teams and the increased demands for accountability and the meeting of targets, objectives and budgets have affected all front-line practitioners. As mental health care has moved further and further away from an alliance with the traditional medically based model of care, the psychological protection historically afforded by such a system has diminished, and all individual practitioners carry a greater degree of personal responsibility than in the past. The development of community rather than institutionally based services means that an ever increasing number of practitioners is working alone and mental health workers in the community can feel lonely and unsupported. The demands of working alone can also be exacerbated if one is the sole representative of a profession, for example the only social worker, occupational therapist or psychologist within a team, and carrying a caseload for which one is responsible can leave insufficient time for camaraderie, friendship or appropriate professional support.

Practitioners stepping into community work for the first time can be particularly vulnerable, often fearful of their own professional autonomy and responsibility, and the autonomy of their patients. The higher expectations of service users compared with earlier times can also engender feelings of insecurity and frustration. Personal responsibility is often pushed to the 'edges' in large organisations, and individual practitioners can be left with the full emotional impact of service users' problems, frustrated that 'they' – meaning managers – do not seem to care. Managers in all settings have to respond to the seemingly never-ending demands made upon them by the organisation – managing budgets, meeting targets, implementing policies and procedures – so they can be unaware when a practitioner's personal limits have been reached or when a practitioner has begun to carry an excessive and potentially damaging sense of personal responsibility.

In a study of community mental health nurses in Wales, half the respondents were found to be over-extended and highly emotionally exhausted, and therefore unable to give of themselves in their everyday work with their service users. One in seven experienced little or no satisfaction or sense of achievement in their work, whilst one in four admitted to negative attitudes towards those in their care (Hannigan *et al.* 2000).

These feelings can be common for all front-line practitioners in mental health, whether working in community or hospital settings, as working in this field is, by its very nature, inherently stressful (Carson, Fagin and Ritters1995; Moore and Cooper 1996). If levels of stress and overload go beyond the capacity of personal coping mechanisms, and staff are insufficiently supported, they will become emotionally exhausted and the symptoms of 'burn-out' will appear.

Symptoms of 'burn-out' – warning signs

Common early warning signs that staff are not receiving sufficient levels of support and may be becoming overwhelmed are occasional episodes of 'not coping', increasing cynicism towards the work in which they are engaged, and increased sickness rates. If this growing emotional exhaustion is not recognised by the individual, colleagues or manager and the necessary supportive actions taken, staff will become increasingly less effective and eventually be unable to work.

Feelings, behaviour and thinking

The experience of burn-out or acute emotional exhaustion can be described in terms of feelings, behaviour and thinking.

Feelings can include:

- loss of a sense of humour
- persistent sense of failure
- anger/resentment
- an increase in cynicism
- fear and loneliness
- sensitivity to criticism
- feeling that one cannot be bothered
- depression
- a sense of panic.

Behaviour can include:

- resistance to service user contact and going to work
- working harder to achieve less
- increasing social isolation
- avoidance of contact with colleagues

- clumsiness
- aggressive driving
- inability to sit still or settle
- eating too much or too little
- nervous laughter.

Negative thinking can include:

- thoughts about leaving the job
- loss of creative problem solving
- inability to concentrate or listen
- tendency to dehumanise service users
- suspicion and mistrust of others
- inability to make decisions
- forgetfulness
- inability to make plans
- thinking about the past

The signs of burn-out are usually much easier to recognise in others than in oneself.

CASE STUDY 9.1

Gina is a conscientious and highly experienced G grade (senior clinical professional grade) community psychiatric nurse. She has worked in the same community mental health team (CMHT) for many years, gradually becoming the most highly regarded and most experienced member of the team, someone to whom others turn for help and advice, and who is seen as courageous in terms of dealing with a difficult psychiatrist. Gina herself had come through a painful divorce a number of years ago and her children left home two years ago to attend university. She has gradually become increasingly isolated both personally and professionally. She has lost her enthusiasm for work, begun to avoid service users, is increasingly bitter and cynical about the NHS and cannot see 'the point of it all'. After many years of never taking sickness absence, Gina has become more frequently physically ill with minor somatic complaints, and her thoughts have become increasingly negative, about both her own social isolation and the 'pointlessness' of coming to work.

> Because other members of the team needed her for their own sup-
> port and she has always been perceived as 'strong', it took some time
> before other team members and Gina herself recognised the seriousness
> of the situation and that action needed to be taken.
>
> ## Questions for discussion
>
> 1. What could have been done to help Gina before her symptoms of burn-out became acute?
>
> 2. How can a community team provide support for its members?
>
> 3. How do you know when you are reaching your own limits?

Sometimes practitioners may resist expressions of concern from their colleagues, and may even be aware themselves that they are not functioning well but insist that they cannot take any time off because of felt obligations to service users or colleagues. Lone community practitioners have the additional stress of knowing that if they themselves take time off, one of their colleagues who may be already overworked will have to take on the additional work of the absent practitioner's caseload, and those working in hospital settings know that managing a ward with insufficient staff causes additional demands on all concerned.

INFORMAL STAFF SUPPORT

Processes of informal support are fundamentally similar regardless of the occupational group or status. They include individual friendships between those of equivalent status, informal networks which come together on an *ad hoc* basis (for example, over cups of tea after meetings), particular staff groups who decide amongst themselves to meet up informally on a regular basis (such as on 'nights out' organised by ward staff or teams on a regular basis) or an informal 'mentoring' relationship where an individual has an established relationship with a more senior member of staff who can be relied upon for support and encouragement when necessary. These informal support networks are sometimes considered to be optional extras, but for many working in mental health services such networks can be personal 'lifelines' during times of stress, and an extremely valued part of working life.

It could be assumed that these informal groupings might provide sufficient emotional support for staff. However, when a group of practitioners or managers come together for informal support, those present will not necessarily *feel* strengthened and encouraged unless the following factors have been present to some degree. Each person needs:

- to feel emotionally safe
- to be understood and accepted
- to be able to admit some of his/her own vulnerability
- to be able to express feelings without criticism from others
- to feel that those present share common difficulties and problems
- to have a sense of humour and perspective restored.

However, if a person is shy or feels unable to admit vulnerability, if there are any interpersonal personal difficulties which inhibit the closeness of the group or if there are other organisational and interpersonal constraints, informal meetings will not necessarily provide the staff support required. It is thus not sufficient for organisations simply to facilitate informal social contact.

CLINICAL SUPERVISION: SUPPORT OR SCRUTINY?

Formal support for practitioners and clinicians is most often provided through the medium of supervision but, as Cottrell and Smith (2000) comment, clinical supervision, while accepted conceptually, is not yet well established in practice. A detailed review of the many definitions of clinical supervision is outside the scope of this chapter, but it has to be recognised that, despite the extensive literature now available, there is little consensus (Todd and Freshwater 1999). The variety of broad-based definitions contributes to confusion, but all definitions contain the following common elements:

- a process of support and learning
- discussion and reflection with a colleague in a safe environment with the purpose of developing competence
- ensuring quality (service) user services.

Regular supervision is advocated for all mental health and social services staff, and it is increasingly recognised that such formal support for staff needs to be 'built in'. Why is it that efforts to implement and maintain clinical supervision often fail in practice?

Role conflict and role confusion

No matter how strong the organisation's commitment to ensuring clinical supervision, provision of supervision alone does not necessarily make the practitioner feel supported, and supervision may be given by the 'wrong' person. If supervision is felt to have elements of scrutiny practitioners are likely to be concerned that in some way they might not 'measure up' to the standards which they think are expected of them. They may be therefore very reluctant to acknowledge their own difficulties or emotional vulnerability, and will be far more concerned that they are not 'found out' in some way, as either not being sufficiently competent or not fulfilling the demands of the job.

This is most likely to occur if the supervisor is also a manager or is of significantly higher status, or if the role of the supervisor is unclear. If the roles of manager and supervisor are insufficiently clarified or overlap, there will be resistance to supervision and any potential benefits are likely to be nullified (Grant 2000). Lack of clarity between managerial and clinical supervision will create anxiety and mistrust in the supervisee and a conflict of interests and role confusion in the supervisor/manager.

Usually when there has been a decision made to implement supervision and supervision is seen as desirable, there is considerable discussion as to how much time may be appropriate. Any time taken for supervision can be seen as time taken away from that given to service users and other work responsibilities. The frequency of time allocated usually varies depending on level of experience, less experienced staff being considered to need more time, for example one meeting per week/fortnight; more experienced staff meet less frequently. However, even if agreement is reached regarding the allocation of time, role conflict and role confusion can create difficulties for both parties and this allocated time is less likely to provide the support for staff that is needed.

CASE STUDY 9.2

When supervision had to be introduced into the CMHT it was decided by management that supervision be given by the person who is next above in grade. Therefore, a G grade CPN had to be supervised by an H grade who was also the team manager. The G grade's comments were:

> You should be honest about what you are struggling with but if it's your manager you can't admit anything because there is not enough trust. She says it's OK, but if you admit you're struggling it will be seen as not being up to scratch. I had to be supervised by the grade above and it had to be H grade, I could not choose who it was. I don't particularly like her and do not trust her not to use things against me.
>
> I myself have to supervise an E grade who is also my friend. Because she is my friend we have respect and trust, but it is mixed. If things are running well it's good, but it is hard when there are any disciplinary issues.

Questions for discussion

1. From whom do you receive supervision?

2. Are there elements of role confusion? (If so, why do you think this is?)

3. Is it possible for supervision to include both the monitoring of casework and accountability *and* personal support?

Psychological proximity

Degrees of perceived 'psychological proximity' between participants may also impact on the implementation and operation of clinical supervision. *Proximity* describes the perceived or real collusive interpersonal relationship between two or more participants who, without awareness, foster closeness through the exclusion of another. Collusion only has to be perceived to have an impact on supervision. Some examples of these potential difficulties are outlined briefly below. For a more detailed discussion see Cottrell and Smith (2000).

If supervisors are perceived as agents of the organisation, and if those receiving supervision have not been sufficiently involved in its implementation, suspicion is immediately engendered. Without clear prior discussion relating to what subjects may be discussed and what will happen to the information, participants will be guarded and hostile and will not participate in the process of supervision with openness and commitment.

Supervisees and supervisors may also sometimes be perceived as being 'in league' with one another and may meet and form a sub-group within an established system. Typically, they may wish to provide peer supervision for one another, or start a process of supervision for others. Unfortunately, this can result in envy and hostility from other practitioners, and sometimes the needs of the organisation for information and the needs of the manager for control and authority can be neglected. The supervisee/supervisor dyad practise as though they were in an organisational vacuum and, without awareness, may fail to make sufficiently close contact with other team members, and fail to sufficiently recognise and appreciate their needs and abilities.

CASE STUDY 9.3

A group of six practitioners, committed to utilising psychosocial intervention approaches in their own caseloads, continued to meet as a group for mutual support and peer supervision, even when their training was not sufficiently recognised or valued by the trust for which they worked. Meetings took place monthly, sometimes covertly without the support of management. These meetings did enable those present to share their frustrations, maintain their commitment, sense of humour and perspective, and further develop their knowledge base, but other colleagues felt excluded and perceived the group as separate and elitist.

Questions for discussion

1.   How could these difficulties have been avoided?

2.   In what circumstances would group supervision be beneficial?

Qualities of good supervision

Supervision will not be perceived or experienced as a form of professional clinical support without the following qualities:

- The roles, responsibilities and expectations of all parties –
  supervisors, supervisees, managers, the organisation as a
  whole – must be clearly elucidated before attempting to
  introduce supervision. It is essential to ensure that none of the

stakeholders is unwittingly excluded, whether supervision is to be implemented within hospital or community settings.

- The time and energy spent addressing core issues of roles, responsibilities and expectations are more likely to lead to the successful adoption of clinical supervision, and allow anticipated problematic factors in the process of implementation to be identified and addressed in advance.

- Those providing supervision must be trustworthy and professional, able to provide an emotional 'safe space' where difficulties and vulnerabilities can be addressed openly.

- The supervisor needs to be accessible, emotionally responsive and attuned to the needs of the supervisee.

- Supervision needs to balance caseload with professional development and personal support. If supervision is focused only on the management of casework it is likely to be experienced as scrutiny.

- Supervision should develop confidence to deal with difficult cases, provide reassurances that feelings are normal and help set limits for individual responsibility.

Supervision allows organisationally sanctioned time for participants to communicate, and fosters alliances which provide a form of social support, develop clinical skills, and mitigates against isolation and detachment.

There are many difficulties in the provision of supervision, and the evaluation of clinical supervision in terms of service user or staff outcomes in the longer term is methodologically complex (Burrow 1995; Fowler 1996), but there is significant evidence regarding the beneficial effects on staff well-being (Butterworth, Carson and White 1997). The provision of time to reflect upon practice demonstrates an organisation's commitment to an endorsed process whereby staff may address practice and personal issues as an integral part of their working day. *Genuine* commitment, rather than the appearance of commitment (Grant 2000), by organisations to the provision of personal time for staff is essential and it is the responsibility of all parties to ensure that personal support for staff is an integral part of the supervision process.

STRESS FACTORS FOR MANAGERS

While it is now well recognised that support and supervision are essential for *practitioners* providing clinical services, appropriate and relevant support specifically for *managers* in mental health and social services is often neglected. The role of manager has undergone, and is still undergoing, immense change, and many are now more isolated and carrying more individual responsibility for targets and budgets.

Ongoing changes in mental health services have resulted in greater potential confusion regarding a manager's role. Is s/he a leader or a manager? Who is actually responsible for the team's performance and the meeting of targets and deadlines – the manager or the senior clinician? Who is the team leader? Role confusion can be exacerbated when managers are expected to manage practitioners from a different professional background – for example a manager with a social work background having to manage nurses, a psychologist and occupational therapists – and lack of clear lines of accountability and responsibility can also be significant contributory stress factors.

Managers are also regularly expected to implement and be accountable for changes demanded by the organisation, but often without any training or support in understanding the complex *processes* involved in initiating, implementing and sustaining change. Because managers are judged and held accountable, it can be a source of great anxiety that staff are not changing in the ways that are required, or within the expected time scales. These stresses can be exacerbated by managers having to spend so much of their time reacting to demands/crises that they are left with insufficient opportunity for proactive contributions or creativity.

Many managers have been appointed as a promotion from direct face-to-face service user work. For many it is a shock to discover that those people alongside whom they have previously worked as friends and colleagues view them very differently once they become managers. They may no longer be considered trustworthy, and may also be 'blamed' by front-line practitioners for difficulties within the organisation. Managers' experience of 'divided loyalties' can be very stressful. Their prior experience as a practitioner means that they have sympathy and understanding for their colleagues but they are now representing the organisation and have to implement organisational demands from their own higher-level managers. Thus, if specific support is not provided, managers can feel far more alone.

CASE STUDY 9.4

During a personal development day facilitated by the author, middle managers from different services listed the following factors as major difficulties:

1. differences in priorities between managers and different team members

2. the expectation by team members that all requests can be met

3. the 'gap' between statutory requirements and what individual practitioners think they should do

4. tensions between clinical and managerial responsibility, particularly in relation to consultant psychiatrists

5. little feedback about 'good' things

6. being perceived as 'an inanimate problem solver'

7. receiving no acknowledgement of work done

8. a lack of clarity of outcomes

9. 'never able to finish'

10. receiving too much irrelevant information

11. a lack of involvement in budget setting but being responsible for managing and monitoring

12. a lack of role clarity at senior and middle management levels

13. inadequate recognition of skills and experience

14. the impact of significant organisational changes on managerial roles and inter-professional relationships.

As can be seen from the following comments, the personal development day was the first time the managers had met together for mutual support without the scrutiny of higher management:

It provided a chance to look at myself in terms of my position in relation to my role within the team I manage and my role within the trust as a whole.

It was an opportunity to reflect and to share other managers' ideas and thoughts.

> The day gave me the opportunity to get to know my colleagues personally, and gave me time to share experience and to realise that many have the same problems.
>
> ## Questions for discussion
>
> 1.   What are the implications for recognising the unique role of middle managers within your organisation?
>
> 2.   What kind of support do they need?

SUPPORT FOR MANAGERS

Providing opportunities for informally supporting managers can be difficult. A group of staff based within the same building or ward will be able to provide much informal support for its members. However, although the manager may provide considerable formal and informal support to team members and is the person that staff turn to when problems arise, s/he is much more restricted in being able to use colleagues for his/her own personal support because of differences in status.

Thus, support for managers must be addressed at an organisational level and seen as an integral part of the job in the same way as clinical supervision (Gilbert 2003).

Formal support for managers needs to include:

- the provision of a safe space, either in groups or individual mentoring, where difficulties and vulnerabilities can be acknowledged openly. Due to concerns about being seen as 'failing', support for managers could usefully be provided by an outside facilitator

- open discussion of and support for the reality and difficulties involved in managing a diverse group of people

- greater clarification of role, responsibilities and the setting of boundaries

- acknowledgement that managers do not necessarily have the skills to manage change. Specific training in understanding the factors that enhance or inhibit the change process, the effects of organisational change upon individuals and how to facilitate change by the use of positive strategies may need to be provided

- acknowledgement and support for the inevitable 'in-between' position of middle management and the resulting struggles when having to respond to both the concerns of practitioners and the demands of the organisation.

MANAGING CHANGE: A SPECIAL CASE OF STAFF SUPPORT

There is now a myriad of books and articles about the management of change. This section focuses on what is often forgotten – change cannot occur without loss. In the push to implement the change agenda in mental health – policies, services, working practices – the psychological effects of loss are often given insufficient attention, and this often lies at the root of many of the difficulties associated with implementing change.

Everyone experiences sadness at the loss of familiar places, ways of living/working that 'used to be', and to which they were emotionally attached. According to Marris (1996) loss fundamentally disrupts the ability to find meaning, and therefore feelings of loss can be evoked by any situation where the ability to make sense of life is disrupted. This process will occur no matter how 'rational' or 'beneficial' changes may seem to be to another person who does not have the same intensity of attachment. Thus, for example, even if it 'makes sense' to close a hospital and even if staff who have worked there also agree that it is the best option, those who have worked in that environment for many years will experience feelings of sadness and loss at the change. The severity of this reaction will be directly dependent upon the *intensity* of that member of staff's earlier emotional attachment, and will vary from person to person. Acute feelings of loss will also not necessarily be shared by younger members of staff whose attachment to the old hospital is less, and whose professional identity has not been established in that working environment. Adapting to any loss requires psychological reintegration – i.e. a recognition that previous meanings by which one made sense of life are no longer valid, and that new meanings, to make sense of a new situation, have to be reconstituted.

Reactions to loss/change

The process of loss of meaning through change means that events have become unpredictable. To readjust, some continuity of meaning has to be restored before life will feel manageable again. A person will automatically actively search out for 'threads of continuity' in his/her experience to join the past to the new present, and find ways to restore a sense that what has been lost can still give meaning to the present. For example, staff who have spent many years working in a particular place in particular ways who are then required to work in a different place and in different ways have to adapt knowledge and skills acquired within one setting to the very different demands of another setting. Somehow, the past has to be reformulated so as to make sense in the present and the future. This process will be more difficult when change is enforced rather than freely chosen, and when past contributions of staff are not specifically validated and valued. Many difficulties in implementing and sustaining change in organisations arise from an inadequate understanding of these natural human processes in reaction to change.

In supporting staff through change an essential question to be addressed is: Can staff make sense of what is happening? All too often there is insufficient consultation and lack of information as to how new services, policies and procedures connect with each other and/or will operate in practice; and also, even more important, how proposed changes will connect with the experience and skills staff gained in different settings and circumstances. Imposed changes often result in feelings of powerlessness, disorientation, anger and resentment. These feelings need to be understood and accepted so that appropriate ways of supporting staff through change can be provided. If staff cannot make sense of changes in terms of their own experience and professional background and are not able or helped to react in articulate ways to the threats posed by change, their sense of loss is more likely to result in apathy, depression, aimlessness or cynicism, even when changes may be intelligent and necessary. Many managers and organisations become frustrated and anxious when staff do not embrace changes enthusiastically but, if these issues could be addressed openly, many of the difficulties in implementing and sustaining change could be minimised.

Support for staff during periods of significant change needs to incorporate the good practice points on the following page.

The pace of change in mental health services shows no sign of abating, and often organizations find themselves reacting to rapidly changing political and social agendas, rather than being able to reflect upon, plan for, implement and review change in ways that are effective and meaningful to staff. Ongoing change adds to the stress already experienced by both practitioners and managers in mental health services and is a major contributor to increasing cynicism and difficulties in retaining trained staff. It is essential that organisations acknowledge the human costs of change and provide the necessary support for staff through the process.

Good Practice Points

- Each person has a profound need to maintain consistency and to sustain the familiar attachments and understandings which make life meaningful. This includes the environment in which staff spend their working lives
- Some changes, at both personal and professional levels, involve the loss of important attachments, and thus the process of grieving will occur
- Too many changes break down emotional resilience. It is essential to recognise the human need for continuity between past and present. If changes are disruptive and frequent, staff will lose confidence that their professional lives have a meaningful continuity of purpose
- It is essential to make explicit what will be lost and threatened by change. If this is not done the process of systematically exploring what can be retrieved and reformulated from the past into different contexts for the future cannot take place
- During the process of change conflict must be expected and even encouraged. Staff need to be explicitly given the opportunity to react, to have past contributions, experience and skills validated, to contribute their own suggestions in terms of implementing any planned changes, and to articulate their own ambivalent feelings
- It must be accepted that individuals and groups will react to change differently. Every individual and each staff group has to find its own sense of continuity
- It must be acknowledged that all individuals love particular environments, people and ways of working, and these cannot be readily substituted simply because there are rational/financial reasons for change
- Change requires time and patience

GOOD PRACTICE POINTS FOR STAFF SUPPORT

Stress is a very imprecise term for what is in essence a complex, multivariate and multilevel phenomenon, but it is usual when considering support for staff to focus on individuals – their workloads, coping strategies – and the provision of supervision. However, focusing solely on supporting staff as individuals can mean that stresses resulting directly from the organisation's ethos and practices can be ignored. Even within individual supervision there can be a tacit agreement that organisational practices are not acknowledged or their implications for individuals discussed (Duncan-Grant 2001). Most organisations now provide individual staff support through the provision of supervision time and staff counselling services, but this does not necessarily mean that the ethos of the organisation is humane. Providing staff support on a purely individual level will not succeed over time if there are working practices within the organisation which are actively harmful for staff. Some organisations implicitly maintain a 'macho' image such that a manager or practitioner who takes time off, utilises staff counselling services or requires support is somehow seen as a 'failure' and not up to the job. In such organisations individual vulnerability cannot be acknowledged.

The following good practice points are relevant to all staff in mental health services – front-line practitioners, managers who manage and support practitioners on a daily basis and higher-level management who set the culture, ambience and ethos of an organisation.

Good Practice Points

- Some levels of stress are essential for growth and development, but perception of stressors is mediated by individual personality. What is stressful for one person may not be for another and vice versa; therefore staff support and supervision need to be tailored to individual needs
- The most protective factors in terms of maintaining good mental health and resilience have been shown to be use of social support, maintaining a balance between home and work and the degree to which someone is motivated and extended in his/her work
- The most effective ways of supporting staff include the mobilisation of interpersonal support, the provision of greater

control and autonomy, assistance with problem solving, facilitation of interpersonal awareness and provision of feedback and advice

- Managers need to be given sufficient support and training in managing change and the psychological effects of the processes of change and loss. This would allow the expectations of what can be achieved, from both individuals and organisational systems, to be more realistic and is more likely to reduce the levels of cynicism and burn-out amongst staff

- There may be occasions when decisions may have to be imposed on staff but, no matter how seemingly time consuming, *facilitating* decision making such that staff feel more in control and that their expert knowledge and experience is valued will always be of greater benefit in the longer term. The involvement of suggestions, solutions and ideas from practitioners can have a radical effect on how change can be implemented and maintained and is likely to *enhance* morale

- Managers at all levels within an organisation need to be supported actively and taught how to maintain their own personal resources. This will enable them to provide a supportive ethos within the organisation, set a good example of proactive self-care, be more understanding and supportive of the staff whom they manage, be more sensitive to potential burn-out in others, and thus be able to take restorative action sooner

- Support for staff needs to be embedded within an organisational culture, ethos and strategy which is genuinely committed to humane and caring organisational practices

CONCLUDING COMMENTS

The pace of change in the mental health agenda continues unabated and the resulting ongoing demands and responsibilities of all front-line practitioners show no sign of reducing. Those working in mental health services carry increasingly independent clinical responsibility. Roles are often becoming broader and all- encompassing while, at the same time, the expectations from government and the public of what services can provide for those in emotional distress continues to rise. Thus, the provision of appropriate support for staff is even more fundamental and essential than before. No matter how comprehensive policies and strategies are, implementation is totally dependent on the practitioners who care for others and the managers of services. It is essential that all front-line practitioners acknowledge their own humanity and vulnerability and seek out the support required for them to provide for the needs of others; that managers ensure not only that support for staff is provided but also that they themselves receive the support that they need and organisations recognise that a commitment to humane working practices and investing in the well-being of their staff is their best investment for the future.

REFERENCES

Burrow, S. (1995) 'Supervision: Clinical development or managerial control?' *British Journal of Nursing 4*, 879–82.

Butterworth, T., Carson, J. and White, E. (1997) *It's Good to Talk: An Evaluation Study in England and Scotland*. Manchester: University of Manchester, Department of Nursing and Midwifery.

Carson, J., Fagin, L. and Ritters, S. (1995) *Stress and Coping in Mental Health Nursing*. London: Chapman and Hall.

Cottrell, S. and Smith, G. (2000) *The Development of Models of Nursing Supervision in the UK. www.clinical-supervision.com*

Duncan-Grant, A. (2001) *Clinical Supervision among Mental Health Nurses: A Critical Organisational Ethnography*. Portsmouth: Nursing Praxis International.

Fowler, J. (1996) 'The organization of clinical supervision within the nursing profession: A review of the literature.' *Journal of Advanced Nursing 23*, 471–8.

Gilbert, J. (2003) 'Between a rock and a hard place? Training and personal development issues for mental health service managers.' *Mental Health Practice 6*, 10, 31–3.

Grant, A. (2000) 'Clinical supervision and organizational power: A qualitative study.' *Mental Health and Learning Disabilities Care 3*, 12, 398–401.

Hannigan, B., Edwards, D., Coyle, D., Fothergill, A. and Burnard, P. (2000) 'Burnout in community mental health nurses: Findings from the all Wales stress study.' *Journal of Psychiatric and Mental Health Nursing 7*, 2, 127–34.

Marris, P. (1996) *Loss and Change*. London: Routledge.

Moore, K.A. and Cooper, C.L. (1996) 'Stress in mental health professionals: A theoretical overview.' *International Journal of Social Psychiatry 42*, 150–9.

Pocket Oxford Dictionary (1982). Oxford: Clarendon Press.

Todd, G. and Freshwater, D. (1999) 'Reflective practice and guided discovery: Clinical supervision.' *British Journal of Nursing 8*, 20.

Ward, M. (2000) 'Campaign fails to tackle mental health staff crisis.' *Nursing Times 96*, 15.

Williams, S., Michie, S. and Pattani, S. (1998) *Improving the Health of the NHS Workforce*. London: Nuffield Trust.

FURTHER READING

Cutcliffe, J.R., Butterworth, T. and Proctor, B. (eds) (2001) *Fundamental Themes in Clinical Supervision*. London: Routledge. *www.clinical-supervision.com*

CHAPTER 10

FROM GRASSROOTS TO STATUTE

THE MENTAL HEALTH SERVICE
USER MOVEMENT IN ENGLAND

CAREY BAMBER

INTRODUCTION

In this chapter, I describe and explain the large-scale emergence and development of the psychiatric system survivors/mental health service user movement in England. In doing so, I do not intend to contribute to the emerging body of academic literature, which is beginning to chart the detailed history and develop a critical analysis of the user movement. Instead, I hope to provide a basic overview of the development of the movement, its inspirations and aspirations, and some practical examples of user activity in one region – the north-west of England.

'USERS AND MOVEMENTS?'

Throughout this chapter I will refer to people who are involved in this movement as *service users* – a term which is most commonly understood to refer to people who are considered to experience mental ill health and are (generally) in contact with health and social care services who provide some degree of care and/or treatment. In terms of the movement itself:

> The service user/survivor movement is a term used to describe the existence of numerous individuals who speak out for their own rights and those of others, and local groups and national organisations set up to provide mutual support or to promote the rights of current and former mental health service users to have a voice... The term 'movement' implies that these individuals, groups and organisations share some common goals and are moving in a similar direction. (Wallcraft with Read and Sweeney 2003, p.20)

Estimates of the current level of user involvement in England indicate that there are somewhere in the region of 900 active mental health service user groups (Wallcraft *et al.* 2003). With memberships ranging from a handful of people to 1000-plus individuals, user groups clearly have access to large numbers of people. Many others may well be involved on the fringes of user activity (through e-mail groups or on mailing lists of major organisations), but are not outwardly active in the movement. Whilst significant, it is important to note that this only represents a minority of the number of people who are in contact with mental health services in England. That said, the numbers of people involved in voluntary work within the wider community is probably of similar proportions.

The terminology around psychiatric services is the subject of much debate, perhaps reflecting the tension that exists around this peculiar branch of medicine, and its tempestuous socio-political history. Users themselves regularly debate the terminology employed to describe their position in relation to service providers, and providers themselves struggle with the language to describe their client groups. Some users do not accept the term 'user', believing it to have connotations of drug or alcohol misuse; others reject the terms 'clients' or 'customers', which are seen to imply choice, and others prefer the term 'survivor' in an acknowledgement of the ordeal that people have experienced with services.

So where has the user movement been located? Much user activism has historically been located around community and inpatient, adult acute and community mental health services. Secure/forensic, child and adolescent and older people's mental health services have all, to some degree, absorbed some of the rhetoric of involvement and participation; but its impact is yet to be measured and activists from these sectors have tended to be few and far between. Another area, which has yet to be developed, is the primary care arena, although some primary care trusts (PCTs) and some user groups are beginning to work together to try and develop opportunities for involvement and participation.

WORKING WITH PRIMARY CARE

Box 10.1 Liverpool Joint Forum

In Liverpool, a full-time post has been established with the Liverpool Joint Forum, where a worker has begun to develop feedback mechanisms on primary care mental health service users' experiences. The worker has produced a number of reports on primary care interventions, and has identified opportunities for users to be further involved.

Liverpool Joint Forum, CHC Offices, 17 Lime Street, Liverpool L1 1JG

The user movement itself has yet to become fully inclusive, as the Sainsbury Report *On Our Own Terms* highlights:

> There is no such thing as the 'ordinary' service user. There are a wide range of personal experiences of mental distress and use of services, compounded by different racial and cultural backgrounds, gender, age, sexuality, disability and social class. At present the movement is limited in its ability to respond well to this diversity, though some individuals and groups are making efforts to reach out to minority groups. (Wallcraft *et al.* 2003, p.38)

In addition, some of the user movement's struggles have, paradoxically, been predominantly located in a fight for increased and improved care and treatment services, focused around the individual needs of service users. This paradox, whereby many service user groups thus implicitly acknowledge and accede to the dominance of psychiatric expertise, has led to the continued partial fragmentation of the aspirations of a user movement and, in my view, limited its impact and ability to recognise its own power.

To people in the wider community beyond mental health services and psychiatry, the concept of a 'mental health service user movement' must conjure images of the 'lunatics taking over the asylum'. Despite a common understanding of the poor reputation and history of psychiatry, media-fuelled moral panics around people with mental health problems maintain a public perception of danger, and thus the need to remove the source of the problem – the mentally ill. Challenging this perception still eludes the movement in terms of impact and remains an outstanding issue on the 'to do' list of most user groups.

THE EMERGENCE OF A SURVIVOR VOICE

Popular belief in the mental health user movement often charts the development of patients' struggles against psychiatric practices back to the time of the establishment of the first recorded asylum. In the early fourteenth century, the Bethlem and Maudsley hospital in London began to accept vagrants and lunatics. Better known as 'Bedlam', the hospital, established by monks, saw some of the earliest recorded activism by people labelled as mentally disordered, with petitions from the inmates of Bedlam (around the conditions, in particular the food) published in the early seventeenth century.

Although the origins of the branch of medicine we now refer to as 'psychiatry' only truly emerged in the nineteenth century, earlier practices are reflective of the schools of thought governing the 'cure' of madness and mental disorder. It is these cruel and bizarre practices – blood letting, physical and mechanical restraint, immersion and isolation – which still colour the reputation of psychiatric interventions as ill-informed, experimental practices. These practices, alongside the legal authority invested in sequential mental health laws that have authorised the deprivation of liberty and enforced medication on those considered to be a danger to themselves or the public, have combined to create a sense of injustice in those who have been on the receiving end of them. This sense of injustice has acted as a catalyst of protest and shared anger that has motivated thousands of previously apolitical individuals to get involved actively in the user movement. However, one crucial element in the relative success of the mental health service user and survivor movement has been the alliances that have developed between some mental health service personnel and mental health service users.

The active development of a large scale and influential anti-psychiatry movement during the 1960s (see Goffman 1961; Szasz 1961,1971) may well have provided ripe ground for the emergence of this alliance between psychiatric system survivors and health and social care professionals sympathetic to criticism of traditional psychiatric practices. Also influential on these English groups and their allies was the work of the so-called 'anti-psychiatry' psychiatrist and writer R.D. Laing.

Significant in raising public awareness of the experience of inpatient psychiatric care was the publication in 1962 of Ken Kesey's novel *One Flew Over the Cuckoo's Nest*. Influential and ground- breaking in its subject matter, Kesey exposed the worst excesses of institutionalisation and the degrading treatment meted out in some long-stay psychiatric facilities in America, and the 1975 Hollywood film starring Jack Nicholson went on to influence popular thought about psychiatry. Alongside this came the development of new, anti-psychotic medication (chlorpromazine or largactil – which, for the first time, offered the opportunity to dull the more bizarre and seemingly unpleasant symptomology of mental illnesses) and a drive towards a new approach in the provision of psychiatric care. So began the unprecedented and large-scale shift of 'mental patients' from the traditional asylums established during the eighteenth and nineteenth centuries. The closures of the county asylums were an enormous and ambitious attempt to reprovide psychiatric services in a community setting, and the first patients began to be placed in the (unprepared and unaccepting) outside world during the 1970s.

During the 1960s, the Western world was challenged by the rise in new social movements championing the rights of oppressed and minority groups – women, people with physical disabilities, black people and, later, lesbians and gay men. It is within this emerging and shifting new social order that the service user movement as we now understand it had its birth. In England, the Mental Patients Union, developed in the 1970s, grew from a struggle to save the Paddington Day Hospital in London. Paddington offered a unique approach to the provision of psychotherapy (a 'talking treatment'), with its therapeutic community style approach, and its threatened closure created a groundswell of resistance from its user community. One can trace the threads of continuity (Spandler 2002) between the activists around the Paddington, the emergence of the Mental Patients Union and Survivors Speak Out – perhaps one of the better-known service user campaign groups of the 1980s and 1990s.

DEVELOPING LOCAL USER ACTIVISM

Box 10.2 Nottingham Advocacy Group

During the 1980s, local user activists in Nottingham established the Nottingham Advocacy Group (NAG), which drew some of its inspiration from the large-scale developments of the Patients Councils in the Netherlands and other European nations. NAG was one of the first and most successful user-led groups, and is still active today. From its inception in 1986, NAG focused on developing advocacy systems – self-advocacy (users speaking up for themselves) and peer advocacy (service users supporting each other to ensure that their voices are heard) – and its methods were widely replicated across England and Wales over the following ten years.

Nottingham Advocacy Group, The Croft, Albert Road, Nottingham NG3 4JD. Telephone: 0115 910 7300

Although still in existence, Survivors Speak Out has now been eclipsed in prominence in the user movement by other national groups affiliated to or part of the mental health voluntary sector, such as Mindlink (National Mind) or Voices (Rethink, formerly National Schizophrenia Fellowship), and a number of other user-led organisations that have developed outside the voluntary and statutory sector, such as Mad Pride. The groups established within the national independent mental health care organisations have provided a valuable 'reference group' of users across England and Wales for these national bodies to consult, and have also acted as an opportunity for users nationally to influence the work of two of the main players in the national mental health voluntary sector.

MADNESS AND CIVIL RIGHTS

Box 10.3 Mad Pride

Groups such as Mad Pride have functioned outside the more traditional field of influence of the voluntary sector agencies. They have won significant media interest for their direct action (protests outside the Royal College of Psychiatrists annual general meeting in 2001, and the 'Hugs not Drugs' campaigns) and courted publicity in their uncompromising approach in celebrating the experience of madness. Mad Pride describes itself as 'the first great civil liberties movement of the 21st century. Sick of discrimination, marginalisation, medication and being treated like shit, psychiatric patients are preparing to rise from the ghettos and make the world a fit place to live in' (Mad Pride publicity leaflet).

In addition, Mad Pride published its first book in 2000, which featured '24 authors boasting about wild things they've done when they've been losing it and sharing accounts of their liberation through madness' (Curtis *et al.* 2000).

Much of the early work of local user groups concentrated on trying to develop self-advocacy and peer advocacy, and in 1992 the United Kingdom Advocacy Network was founded. Its aims were supporting the further development of local user capacity in self-advocacy and peer advocacy, as well as group advocacy in Patients Councils and community meetings in hospitals and other settings. In addition to self-advocacy and peer advocacy, groups began to emerge focused on self-help and shared experiences – the most notable and perhaps influential of which has been the Manchester-based Hearing Voices Network.

THE SELF-HELP MOVEMENT

Box 10.4 The Hearing Voices Network

The Hearing Voices Network, a user-led national organisation founded in 1988 on the work of Dutch mental health professionals Professor Marius Romme and Sondra Escher, provides support to 147 local self-help groups across the UK (as at July 2003), produces a quarterly newsletter, offers training to users and professionals and operates a telephone helpline for voice hearers.

The Hearing Voices Network,
91 Oldham Street, Manchester M4. Telephone: 0161 834 5768

After 1991 and the NHS and Community Care Act, which enshrined the notion of user involvement in service design, delivery and development, user involvement processes began to become established in the majority of community mental health settings.

In many localities, service users have been involved in small-scale consultations around local service issues and running user groups that began to establish an idea for, or actually began to deliver, user-run or user-led services.

LOCAL ACTIO...

statutory services at all, believing that it may impede their ability to act freely without ties to any organisation. Furthermore, the nature of funding for non-governmental organisations is notoriously fickle, and many groups have almost gone to the wall through underfunding or delays in notification of extended funding. A number of groups owe their continued active existence to the annual 'slippage' round, whereby non-recurring monies may become available as a result in cost savings in statutory services.

SO WHAT DO USER GROUPS DO?

As we have seen, in the early days, user groups frequently located their work and identities within the self- and peer advocacy movements. However, over recent years this focus has begun to shift, and groups have tended to become increasingly responsive to the consultation agenda o health and social care commissioning and provider organisations seekin users' views. The common experience in most areas of adult men health service provision is an expectation that users will be involved in design, planning, delivery, monitoring and evaluation of mental he services.

USER-LED MONITORING

Box 10.7 People's Voice

Members of the People's Voice group in Wigan and Leigh de a set of standards that they felt should be in place on th wards of the local service. The model developed has unde number of refinements to ensure that the quality agenda c to improve and the audit tool that was designed and dev users has now been adopted as the model for user-led across the inpatient areas of the Five Boroughs Partne Trust.

People's Voice, Hyndelle Lodge, King Street, Hindley, W

Research amongst user groups undertaken by the (Wallcraft et al. 2003) indicates that user groups ten following activities:

s
r
th
pa.
are
(12
pay,
appr
proble
with lo
rates w.
turnove
Part of th
tations pl.

- self-help and support   79 per cent
- user involvement   72 per cent
- education and training   69 per cent
- creative activities   41 per cent
- campaigning   38 per cent
- advocacy   38 per cent

Clearly the user movement has played a crucial part in developing informal self-help networks and support, and this has become the core trade of many user groups. Over the years, user groups have begun to offer alternative services, sometimes in partnership with either the voluntary or statutory sector providers. Frustrated by the fixed 'working week' limitations of statutory mental health service providers, and the dominance of a medical approach to service delivery in mental health settings, user groups began to operate informal out-of-hours services – crisis services, drop-in facilities, evening socials, coffee mornings and telephone helplines.

USER-LED SERVICES

Box 10.8 New Way Forward

New Way Forward, a user-run organisation in Trafford, runs a range of drop-in sessions that move across various locations in the borough. The organisation provides a user group with women's space, involvement in local policy development, a community café, a video project, poetry sessions, a gardening project and days out and is also involved in a football tournament that regularly brings 700 service users together for competitions. The football project is about to go international, having participated in a European tournament in 2003.

New Way Forward, Broome House, Seymour Grove, Old Trafford, Manchester M16. Telephone: 0161 912 4389

SOCIAL INCLUSION

Box 10.9 Advocacy West Lancashire

In West Lancashire, Advocacy West Lancashire, in conjunction with local service users, developed a group offering a weekly drop-in session in the café of a local supermarket on a Saturday morning, which aims to break some of the social isolation that affects many service users over the weekends. With £2,000 funding from the local health service, 'Let's Have Coffee' has been a huge success, with large numbers of people dropping in, making new friends and being located in a place that is a mainstream community location rather than a health- or social-care-led drop-in.

Advocacy West Lancs, 4 Church House, Park Road, Ormskirk L39 3AJ. Telephone: 01695 579666

Such informal, socially inclusive services recognise the social impact of mental ill health, and seek to provide a network of informal support to people which goes beyond the narrow statutory provision offered by health and social care services. This tradition of users recognising and creating the types of holistic services that people want is at the very heart of patient and public consultation. This is why service commissioners and providers are now keen to engage users and carers in service design, planning, delivery and evaluation to capture what it is that people actually want.

In terms of involvement, this would appear to have become the second most widespread outcome of the development of local user groups. Whether or not this involvement has emerged as a genuine response to users' campaigns for inclusion and involvement, or whether it has emerged as a result of the creeping legislative and policy frameworks imposed on health and social care providers, is not clear. However, the strength of policy initiatives in the current health and social care climate cannot be underestimated, and the danger is that this fundamentally diverts the purpose and function of user groups and the wider user movement from its original aspirations. This could lead to a situation where the work of user groups is dictated not by the members but by the consultation requirements of the service providers with whom they engage.

REGIONAL NETWORKING

Box 10.10 Local implementation teams

Service user members of more than 20 of the 26 local implementation teams or LITs (local multi-agency task groups focused on the implementation of the standards of the *National Service Framework for Mental Health*) across the north-west of England report mainly positive experiences of involvement. However, many also report that their comments in meetings go unrecorded, they have few opportunities to shift the agenda onto users' issues and they struggle to see clear, identifiable outcomes from their suggestions and comments.

NW LIT Users Network, c/o NIMHE NW, Hyde Hospital, Grange Road South, Hyde, Cheshire SK14 5NY

This policy drive around inclusion and involvement may well originate from what Rogers and Pilgrim (1997) describe as a growing 'consumerism' within health and social care, and may not, therefore, be motivated solely by a sense of justice and fair play.

Education and training has long been a focus of local and national user groups, with training being offered to support users themselves in making choices and speaking up, or in users training staff in provider agencies. In addition, many user groups have encouraged members to participate in work-related training opportunities, such as learning IT skills, first aid and other practical and personal development skills. Many of these skills have added value both to the work of the groups and to the personal development of members; and such training has often been located within user-friendly settings and developed at a pace to suit the needs of people with mental health problems. In addition, many service users have enthusiastically engaged in training around self-management techniques – learning how to cope with and manage some of the distressing symptoms they may experience. This approach is now being celebrated on a national level with the emergence of the notion of 'expert patients'. The expert patients programme covers all aspects of chronic and acute health care, and teaches participants new skills in coping. Drawing on the user-led expertise in organisations such as the Hearing Voices Network, the National Phobics Society and the Mood Swings

Network, people are taught through a range of methods, including diary-keeping, practical skills and assertiveness.

In terms of users' participation in the training of staff, developments have been patchy, with many groups struggling to access 'air time' on accredited training events, or get on the agenda in anything more than a tokenistic way. In some areas, user groups have chosen to focus on training issues as a way forward in challenging and changing some of the institutional discrimination that mental health service users experience from mental health workers, and have established training agencies who focus on the user experience.

TRAINING THE PROFESSIONALS

> ### Box 10.11 Giving Experience Meaning
>
> In Preston, the Giving Experience Meaning (GEM) group has trained service users as trainers, and then developed training programmes that have been rolled out for staff in the local mental health service. In doing so, they have been able to ensure that there is a user perspective in training provided to staff. They have also, of course, contributed to the personal skills of group members, some of who have gone on to gain employment as a result of new skills and new confidence.
>
> GEM, Galloways, Howick House, Howick Park Avenue, Penwortham, Preston PR1 0LS

In other areas, service users have engaged with colleges, universities and deaneries that manage the professional qualification programmes for mental health service personnel and have gained a foothold not only in course presentation, but also in the design and development of course outlines, teaching methods and materials and evaluation. It is hoped these developments will impact on future mental health service personnel in their approach and attitudes to mental health service users, and they are held in high value by the service users as having a significant impact in the early stages of professional training.

Creative opportunities are popular elements of the core work of many user groups, and are often offered in partnership with other providers.

Although the Sainsbury research (Wallcraft *et al.* 2003) illustrates that 41 per cent of groups are involved in the provision of 'creative opportunities', this may well be a growth area as user groups become increasingly skilled and confident in developing alternatives. These alternatives include a wide range of activities such as arts projects, leisure activities, theatre groups, creative writing workshops, poetry groups and others.

RUNNING THINGS FOR OURSELVES

Box 10.12 Tameside and Glossop Mind/Mental Health Forum

A small group of service users from Tameside and Glossop Mind/Mental Health Forum got together to set up a writing group. The group facilitators (two service users) enrolled in a creative writing course at a local university, and run a weekly group for other users. The group has been on a number of trips to see theatre productions, and some of the group members have had the fruits of their labour published in local reports.

Tameside and Glossop Mind,
18–20 Chester Square, Ashton under Lyne, Tameside OL6 7NS

WHERE ARE WE GOING?

The mental health service user movement in England has now reached a point whereby some of its original aspirations around service delivery are being partially delivered – 24-hour services, alternatives to hospital admission/crisis services, user-led alternatives and users involved in service design, development, monitoring and evaluation. In terms of general consultation, service users are pushing against an open door. In some respects, the door is so far open that user groups are being significantly diverted in their task by the agendas of service providers, possibly to the detriment of their groups and their own purposes. In many places service user groups are struggling with the demands on their capacity, with the push to 'field' users and involve them in a range of consultation opportunities across the specialist mental health trusts and other agencies.

KEEPING TRUE TO OURSELVES

Box 10.13 Mad Women

One victim of its own success has been the acclaimed Mad Women group in Liverpool, which has recently decided to end Mad Women in its current form, as it had been diverted in its original aim of being a radical campaigning group and become bogged down with responding to the agenda of other organisations. The women involved voted overwhelmingly to close down the group, citing their disillusionment with the direction of travel the group was having to take. Thankfully, however, women within the group, which has been the source of one of the best newsletters in the user movement, have pledged to return: 'Mad Women is going underground – we'll exist in a changed form and when you least expect it – we'll be back!' (Mad Women, notes from meeting held on 20 June 2003).

In trying to meet these demands, user groups are at risk of losing sight of their own issues and agendas. This is impacting on their ability to plough their own course and develop a strategic, user-led way forward for local user activity.

FACING THE FUTURE

Over the past twenty years, service user involvement has become a commonplace element of general mental health care in England. User groups have made a major contribution to the redesign of mental health care through policy development, yet much remains to be done. Still eluding the movement is the development of real change in the attitudes of mental health service staff, which have been of long concern to service users, and also the creation and take-up of real employment opportunities within the sector for users themselves.

At the end of 2003, the user movement has been faced with a number of new challenges, with the launch in December 2003 of Patients Forums (statutory bodies overseen by the Commission for Patient and Public Involvement) and the publication of the widely criticised Mental Health Bill. Whilst cautiously welcoming the forthcoming statutory Patients Forums established in each of the 571 primary care and NHS provider trusts in England in December 2003, user groups express concerns that such bodies will effectively 'kill off' groundswell voices such as those of local mental health service user groups, and be replaced by a small, undemocratic Patients Forum of publicly appointed individuals. It will be crucial for the ongoing impact of local user groups that the interface with such statutory bodies is established clearly and rapidly to ensure that the forums are closely in contact with the views of local people using services. As for the proposed Mental Health Bill, user activism may well take on a new strength should the forthcoming legislation contain the expected focus on Community Treatment Orders, which are feared by many service users and mental health professionals. United in their opposition, users and professionals have already begun to form new alliances, which may well go on to alter the direction of the mental health service user movement.

In terms of ongoing challenges for the user movement, the biggest challenge still to crack is the discrimination that people with mental health problems face in wider society – in employment, insurance, banking, the media and other sectors. Until mental health service users are truly able to gain meaningful and valued employment within mental health service provision (and elsewhere), until the attitudes of mental health service personnel change towards a recognition of the positive rather than negative aspects of their client group, the mental health service user movement will continue to have a huge agenda for change. In order to meet these challenges, user groups need to become more inclusive in their own right, encouraging and valuing the diversity of people who use mental health services, and become more strategic in their approach. In addition, solutions need to be found for some of the ongoing barriers to involvement and participation – staff attitudes, issues of payment for consultation and other work, and organisational barriers.

We are no longer grateful for being invited to the table – we now want to run the show!

> **Reflective Practice Questions**
>
> - How might I best support the work of mental health service users or those who want to get involved?
> - How would I want to be treated?
> - Is our service structured around the needs of individual service users?

REFERENCES

Curtis, T., Dellar, R., Leslie, E. and Watson, B. (2000) *Mad Pride: A Celebration of Mad Culture*. London: Spare Change Books.

Goffman, E. (1961) *Asylums: Essays on the Social Situation of Mental Patients and Other Inmates*. Harmondsworth: Penguin.

Rogers, A. and Pilgrim, D. (1996) *Mental Health Policy in Britain: A Critical Introduction*. Basingstoke: Macmillan.

Spandler, H. (2002) *From Asylum to Action: Paddington Day Hospital, Therapeutic Communities and Beyond*. Unpublished PhD thesis, Manchester Metropolitan University.

Szasz, T. (1961) *The Myth of Mental Illness*. New York: Harper Row.

Szasz, T. (1971) *The Manufacture of Madness*. London: Routledge and Kegan Paul.

Wallcraft, J. with Read, J. and Sweeney, A. (2003) *On Our Own Terms: Users and Survivors of Mental Health Services Working Together for Support and Change*. London: Sainsbury Centre for Mental Health.

STATUTES

NHS and Community Care Act (1991)

FURTHER READING

Barnes, M. and Bowl, R. (2001) *Taking Over the Asylum: Empowerment and Mental Health*. New York: Palgrave.

Chamberlain, J. (1977) *On Our Own: Patient Controlled Alternatives to the Mental Health System*. London: Mind Publications.

Newnes, C., Holmes, G. and Dunn, C. (1999) *This is Madness: A Critical Look at Psychiatry and the Future of Mental Health Services*. Llangarron: PCCS Books.

North West Mental Health Development Centre (2001) *Good Practice Guidelines for Involving Service Users and Carers in Local Implementation Teams*. Manchester: NWMHDC. *www.nimhenorthwest.org.uk*

Ryan, T. and Bamber, C. (2002) 'A survey of policy and practice on expenses and other payments to mental health service users and carers participating in service development.' *Journal of Mental Health 11*, 6, 635–44.

Shorter, E. (1997) *A History of Psychiatry*. Chichester: John Wiley and Sons.

Snow, R. (2002) *Stronger than Ever: The Report of the Survivor Workers Conference*. Manchester: Asylum Publishing.

USEFUL CONTACTS

Hearing Voices Network
91 Oldham Street
Manchester M4
Tel: 0161 834 5768
Web: www.hearing-voices.org.uk

Mood Swings Network
23 New Mount Street
Manchester M4 4DE
Tel: 0161 953 4105
Web: www.moodswings.org.uk

National Phobics Society
Zion Centre
Stretford Road
Hulme
Manchester M15
Tel: 0870 7700 456
Web: www.phobics-society.org.uk

CHAPTER 11

MENTAL HEALTH ADVOCACY AND EMPOWERMENT IN FOCUS

RICK HENDERSON

INTRODUCTION

This chapter sets out to define and describe advocacy in the context of mental health services. It focuses on 'independent' advocacy – that is, advocacy which is provided independently of health and social care services. Although it can be said that advocacy is part of the training and practice of all mental health professionals, there can be conflicts of interest which mean that an independent advocate is often the preferred option. The issues around conflicts of interest will be explored as the chapter progresses.

The chapter also includes information on why mental health advocacy is needed, how it is currently provided and some of the dilemmas associated with its provision. The current debate surrounding proposals to implement a legal right to 'specialist mental health advocacy' is also examined. Throughout the chapter, case studies are used to illustrate the points raised. Although these are based on real experiences, the names have been changed to protect the individuals concerned.

BACKGROUND

Any description of advocacy in mental health will necessarily begin with a *definition* of what is meant by advocacy. This is not as straightforward as it may seem – there appear to be as many definitions of advocacy as there are advocacy schemes. Advocacy can be crudely defined as giving a voice to the voiceless, yet this definition appears at once patronising and patriarchal. A voice cannot be 'given' by one person to another – it must be 'taken' by the person him- or herself. In this sense, the description of the recipient of advocacy (or, indeed, of mental health services) as 'voiceless' renders them in a position of powerlessness. In fact, the vast majority of people are able to express an opinion or at least an emotional response to a given situation, which can be interpreted as their 'voice' in a broad sense. The issue here is whether the individual's chosen method of communication is acceptable or, indeed, understandable to the listener. For example, a person who refuses to get out of bed and get dressed, or becomes excited or agitated when waiting for a visitor to arrive, may be communicating some extremely important feelings or thoughts. Advocacy is often about ensuring these views are acknowledged and taken seriously, when others may be unable or unwilling to give weight to them.

A more sophisticated, early definition of advocacy is given by John O'Brien:

> [The advocate]...creates a relationship with a person who is at risk of social exclusion and chooses one or several of many ways to understand, respond to and represent that person's interests as if they were the advocate's own... (O'Brien 1987, p.3)

This definition tells us two important things about the advocacy process. First, that the advocate uses 'one or several of many ways' – in other words, a range of advocacy approaches – and second, that the advocate represents his/her partner's views 'as if they were the advocate's own'. This implies a real sense of empathy with the service user's perspective, an understanding of what it must be like to be that person. In this sense, advocacy is neither dispassionate nor impartial – in fact, the advocate is 'partial' to the views and concerns of their partner.

A more pragmatic definition can be found in the publicity leaflet of a local mental health advocacy scheme: 'Advocacy means supporting service users to speak and persuading service providers to shut up and listen' (Independent Advocacy Service 2000). In this definition, the advocate has a dual responsibility. She or he enables, supports and, where necessary, represents the service user's views but, equally important, has a crucial role in ensuring these views get *heard* by powerful people. If the act of speaking up is empowering, then the act of being listened to is doubly so. Many service users describe experiences of not being listened to within the mental health system or worse, are told their views are merely symptoms of ongoing mental distress. A lack of an ongoing, constructive dialogue between users and professionals is a major source of dissatisfaction within mental health services.

CASE STUDY 11.1 JENNY (AGED 33)

'I tried and tried to get him [the social worker] to understand that I really didn't want to stay in the group home any more, I wanted a flat of my own, as I was sick and tired of being told what to do, what to eat, what time to go to bed. But it felt like I was banging my head against a brick wall. He'd made his mind up that it was the best place for me, and nothing I said or did made any difference. I wanted to scream at him, but I knew it wouldn't make any difference. That's why I contacted the advocacy scheme'

Here, Jenny describes a breakdown in communication that could prove damaging to her mental health. She feels angry and frustrated that her attempts to assert her independence are ignored by her social worker. An independent advocate would ensure that Jenny is given the opportunity to put her wishes and concerns to the social worker in a constructive and meaningful way.

The recently produced *Advocacy Charter* offers the following, comprehensive definition:

> Advocacy is taking action to help people say what they want, secure their rights, represent their interests and obtain services they need. Advocates and advocacy schemes work in partnership with the people they support and take their side. Advocacy promotes social inclusion, equality and social justice. (Advocacy Across London 2002, p.2)

This definition contains all of the key elements of the advocacy form. It defines what advocacy is, how it is done and what it aims to achieve. In this way, it reflects the interrelationship between advocacy *processes* and advocacy *outcomes*. In addition to achieving positive outcomes for service users (aftercare, re-housing, changes to medication and so on), advocates aim to develop positive, empowering relationships with people who may previously have had bad experiences of services and service providers. As an independent person, the advocate is able to align him- or herself with the service user and is governed less by a duty of care or a 'best interests' approach, and more by a sense of loyalty to the person and his/her perspectives.

WHAT ADVOCACY ISN'T

In order to understand fully what advocacy is, we must first clarify the distinction between it and other forms of 'informal' support services. Table 11.1 illustrates the point.

Table 11.1 Distinctions between advocacy and other informal support	
Advocacy is	*Advocacy isn't*
Choice	Advice
Equality	Befriending
Justice	Mediation
Support	Counselling
Empowerment	Social work
Protection	
Information	

There is often some confusion about the difference between advocacy and other services, especially advice services. The fundamental difference is that advocates do not express an opinion or give advice about what a person should or should not do. The advocate's role is to provide information to help people make an informed choice, and then to represent that view or support the service user to do so for him- or herself. In an ideal world, the full range of support services described in Table 11.1 would be available free of charge to all users of mental health services. In reality, advocacy can be seen as a means of ensuring these services pay attention to the needs of vulnerable and socially excluded individuals. There is no guarantee that a generic advice agency will have the skills, experience or even willingness to engage with a person with severe mental health problems. In this way, advocates often act as a gateway to other support services whilst at the same time being careful not to duplicate or replace them.

In the United Kingdom advocacy has a history spanning at least two decades. In that time, a number of advocacy models have emerged. The main ones are outlined in Box 11.1.

Box 11.1 Models of advocacy

Casework/formal advocacy

Advocacy provided by paid advocacy 'caseworkers' under the auspices of a formal advocacy scheme. Advocates work with a number of service users on a short- to medium-term basis and adopt a problem-solving approach

Citizen advocacy

One-to-one, volunteer-based advocacy. Usually long term, with the benefit that the citizen advocate is completely independent of health and social care systems

Peer advocacy

Service users or ex-service users supporting each other to speak up

Collective advocacy

Groups of service users coming together to speak out on collective issues, for example via Patients Councils

Self-advocacy

Service users being supported and feeling empowered to speak for themselves

(Henderson and Pochin 2001)

There are now many hundreds of small, local mental health advocacy schemes around the country. Many are entirely independent and often user-led, whilst others are run and managed by larger charities such as Mind, Rethink and the Richmond Fellowship. Funding for independent advocacy comes primarily from statutory services, notably primary care trusts and local authority social services departments. This is supplemented by charitable funding from grantmaking trusts such as the Community Fund and Comic Relief. There are also a number of regional and national advocacy networks, notably the United Kingdom Advocacy

Network (UKAN) and the Greater London Mental Health Advocacy Network (GLMHAN). Despite the large number of schemes, advocacy provision remains patchy, with some areas well-served and others lacking. There is also a distinction to be made between hospital-based and community-based provision – many areas have one but not the other, which can cause problems for service users who make use of both hospital- and community-based mental health services.

In the context of mental health, there is also a clear role for the full range of legal advocacy in relation to the 1983 Mental Health Act (DH 1983). It is this additional legal dimension which sets mental health advocacy apart from other advocacy forms. The powers of the Act go far beyond any other legislation of its kind. For hospital-based mental health advocates, the Mental Health Act looms large as one of the major sources of concern amongst service users. The role of the mental health advocate in the context of detained patients is often to help people to access proper legal advice and representation as well as offering moral and practical support. Mental health advocacy is, to some extent, a *political* activity in that it is often in a position of challenging widely held assumptions and stereotypes about mental illness which exist not just within services, but throughout society. To the extent that the Mental Health Act is in part about social control, then mental health advocacy is, also in part, about social justice.

WHY IS ADVOCACY NEEDED?

There is no denying the grim reality of modern mental health care for many service users. Although we have witnessed an unprecedented shift away from antiquated, Victorian asylums towards 'care in the community', in many areas services are still lacking. The combination of an oppressive Mental Health Act, life-changing medication regimes, the spectre of electro-convulsive therapy (ECT) and a general underfunding of psychiatric services means that, for some service users, mental health services are experienced not as 'healing' but as 'harming'. Research tells us that this is especially the case with people from black and minority ethnic communities, who are significantly over-represented within psychiatric services. A recent survey conducted by the Sainsbury Centre for Mental Health (Keating *et al.* 2002) of over 200 black service users, carers and professionals found that stereotypical views of black people, racism, cultural ignorance and the stigma and anxiety associated with mental illness often combine to undermine the way in which mental health services assess and respond to the needs of African and Caribbean communities.

CASE STUDY 11.2 DERIK (AGED 25)

'They kept talking about something called "cannabis psychosis" and I was thinking, "What does this mean?" It was like a convenient way of them explaining why I was so distressed, but they never looked into my housing, my family problems, my lack of self-worth, to them it was just another black man with a drugs problem.'

CASE STUDY 11.3 SIAN (AGED 42)

'When I was first admitted to [psychiatric] hospital, they showed me to my bed and left me there. The first thing I did was change into my pyjamas – that's what you do in hospital – and went out into the sitting area. Everyone else was in their normal clothes! Instead of helping me, the nurses just laughed. I felt so stupid. Why hadn't they told me? The next few days were just a blur of medication, sleep, a constantly blaring TV and the smell of boiled cabbage. Then one day the doctor came and told me he was recommending ECT. I told him that I didn't want it but he was very persuasive. I had no idea that it would make me lose my memory. The important thing to understand is, at no point did anyone help me to think through the issues. It really felt like there was nobody on my side. It's the loneliest I've ever been.'

Case study 11.3 raises a number of issues which might be taken up by an independent advocate:

1. Why was the patient not given sufficient information at the point of admission?

2. What can be done to address the negative attitude of the nursing staff?

3.   What exactly is the treatment programme for this person and is it appropriate?

4.   Why is ECT being recommended and what information has the patient been given about the treatment and possible side-effects?

5.   What can be done to ensure the patient feels in control of her own care and treatment?

Clearly, there would be a role for an independent advocate in this scenario. By getting to know the patient and looking at things from her perspective, the advocate is able to support her to ask the right questions and make demands of the service providers. The *independence* of the advocate is crucial. Advocates are not a part of the mental health system, nor are they accountable to it. Their independence (both structural and psychological) enables them to be truly 'loyal' to the service user and to represent viewpoints which may make them unpopular with mental health professionals. For these reasons, advocates maintain a reasonable distance between themselves and mental health services:

> Relationships with staff should not necessarily be unfriendly, but advocates must be seen as being independent from staff. All of my advocates are encouraged to avoid conversations with staff in the nursing offices and having familiar sorts of conversations with staff during work hours. (Advocate, quoted in Barnes, Brandon and Webb 2002, p.64)

WHAT DO ADVOCATES DO?

How might an advocate proceed with a service user? First, s/he needs to receive *instruction* from the service user. This can be done formally, via a letter of authorisation, or informally, in conversation. The important thing is that the service user who requests advocacy support is aware of what this entails and knows how to terminate the arrangement if s/he so wishes. The advocate will then begin the process of getting to know the service user, meeting with him or her and building up a picture of what support the person needs. This involves listening, asking questions and obtaining information. The length of time required will vary from individual to individual, but should not be rushed. The advocate's willingness to visit service users in their own homes, or in places where they feel safe and secure, is a key element of the relationship-building process. People may be wary of saying too much on the first visit, but will open up as trust is established. It is not the advocate's role to give advice, express a strong opinion about what is in a person's 'best interests' or, indeed, to persuade a person to do something s/he does not want to. It is useful to draw a distinction here between the advocacy role of *accepting* the service user's viewpoint and the more traditional *assessing* role adopted by service providers. The advocate will neither judge nor dismiss the service user's view, instead working towards a greater acceptance of the person's particular perspective. This is part of what has become known as 'person-centred' planning; that is, putting the service user at the centre of any decisions made about him/her.

There is often an implicit criticism of this advocacy role of 'accepting' what service users say, which is, put crudely, how do we know if people are telling the truth? For an advocate to pursue a non-judgemental approach with their service user, they must accept the service user's view of events. This is not simply naivety, it is a carefully thought-through posture which communicates value and empathy with the service user. In an environment in which users' views are often ignored or dismissed, the act of accepting service users' accounts of what is happening to them is empowering in itself, even if the advocacy process achieves no tangible outcomes. This is especially true, for example, when working in locked wards or forensic settings (Carver *et al.* 2003).

Box 11.2 *The advocate's role*

'I visited this guy in a residential home. He believed the staff were poisoning the food, so was refusing to eat. The staff said he was delusional, they wanted him sectioned and someone even spoke about force-feeding! When I spoke to him on a few occasions, he was adamant that he was not going to eat the pre-cooked food. It was like all trust between him and the staff had broken down.

'He told me he'd been in prison, and worked in the kitchens. He said they used to do all kinds of terrible things to the food as a revenge on the other prisoners. I think this was at the root of his anxiety. In the end, we persuaded the staff to let him prepare his own food in the staff kitchen, but even then they made it really hard for him.'

Here, the advocate demonstrates empathy with the service user whilst being careful not to reinforce his (possibly delusional) views. In doing so, the advocate is setting up the opportunity for trust to be rebuilt between staff and the service user, and adopts a constructive, rights-based approach to resolving the problem.

THE MENTAL HEALTH BILL (2002) AND ADVOCACY

Other chapters in this book examine in some detail the workings of the Mental Health Act and make reference to the many modifications proposed in the draft Mental Health Bill (DH 2002). In relation to advocacy, the White Paper *Reforming the Mental Health Act* (DH 2000) proposed that patients subject to the formal powers of the Act should be given a right of access to independent advocacy. This has huge implications for the mental health advocacy sector. At present in the UK, no adult has the legal right to be represented by a 'lay' (i.e. non-legal) advocate. Although the proposals are limited only to those patients subject to compulsory powers, the question must be asked: 'Where will all these advocates come from?' And, perhaps equally important, 'How will they be trained, supported and monitored?' In answer to these and other questions, the Department of Health commissioned a team from Durham University to undertake a study which sought to make recommendations for good practice in what has become known as 'specialist mental health advocacy' (Barnes *et al.* 2002). The study made a number of recommendations in relation to the funding, management and evaluation of the proposed new advocacy model. The key recommendations of the study are outlined in Box 11.3.

Box 11.3 Durham Report (2002) – Key findings

- Advocates should be paid workers, not volunteers
- Specialist advocacy should be supported by statutory funding
- Advocates should be trained, supervised and accountable
- Specialist mental health advocacy should operate alongside more generic advocacy forms
- There should be national standards for specialist mental health advocacy

(Barnes *et al.* 2002)

Not only is this proposed new right to advocacy radical in a mental health context, it also represents a significant precedent for the advocacy sector more broadly. If one group of vulnerable and socially excluded people have a right to advocacy, then why not others? For obvious reasons, the debate around this proposed legal right is currently a preoccupation for many within the mental health advocacy community. On the one hand, a legal right would provide a safeguard for detained patients and secure vital core funding for advocacy schemes. On the other, increased State involvement in advocacy may bring with it greater regulation, tighter controls and a potential threat to independence.

STANDARDS AND BENCHMARKS

Given that the majority of advocacy services are publicly funded, some form of accountability is essential to ensure that service users have access to effective, appropriate support. At present there are no nationally recognised, advocacy-specific standards for schemes to aspire to. In the absence of such standards, many advocacy schemes have adopted either the PQASSO (Practical Quality Assurance System for Small Organisations) system or the Community Legal Service (CLS) Quality Mark. Both of these are generic quality assurance systems which apply to a broad range of community organisations, including advice services. Specific to advocacy, there is the *Advocacy Charter* (Advocacy Across London 2002) which outlines ten key advocacy principles and has been widely adopted throughout the United Kingdom. The complete text of the charter is reproduced in Box 11.4.

The Durham Report also proposes a number of standards for specialist mental health advocacy which may have wider relevance. In addition, both the UKAN code of practice for advocacy (UKAN 1994) and the *Power Tools* resource pack (Leader and Crosby 1998) offer practical suggestions for providing a good quality mental health advocacy service.

Box 11.4 The Advocacy Charter principles

Clarity of purpose

The advocacy scheme will have clearly stated aims and objectives and be able to demonstrate how it meets the principles contained in this charter. Advocacy schemes will ensure that people they advocate for, service providers and funding agencies have information on the scope and limitations of the scheme's role.

Independence

The advocacy scheme will be structurally independent from statutory organisations and preferably from all service provider agencies. The advocacy scheme will be as free from conflict of interest as possible both in design and operation, and actively seek to reduce conflicting interests.

Putting people first

The advocacy scheme will ensure that the wishes and interests of the people they advocate for direct advocates' work. Advocates should be non-judgemental and respectful of people's needs, views and experiences. Advocates will ensure that information concerning the people they advocate for is shared with these individuals.

Empowerment

The advocacy scheme will support self-advocacy and empowerment through its work. People who use the scheme should have a say in the level of involvement and style of advocacy support they want. Schemes will ensure that willing people can influence and be involved in the running and management of the scheme.

Equal opportunity

The advocacy scheme will have a written equal opportunities policy that recognises the need to be proactive in tackling all forms of inequality, discrimination and social exclusion. The scheme will have in place systems for the fair and equitable allocation of advocates' time.

Accountability

The advocacy scheme will have in place systems for the effective monitoring and evaluation of its work. All those who use the scheme will have a named advocate and a means of contacting them.

Accessibility

Advocacy will be provided free of charge to eligible people. The advocacy scheme will aim to ensure that its premises, policies, procedures and publicity materials promote access for the whole community.

Supporting advocates

The advocacy scheme will ensure advocates are prepared, trained and supported in their role and provided with opportunities to develop their skills and experience.

Confidentiality

The advocacy scheme will have a written policy on confidentiality, stating that information known about a person using the scheme is confidential to the scheme and any circumstances under which confidentiality might be breached.

Complaints

The advocacy scheme will have a written policy describing how to make complaints or give feedback about the scheme or about individual advocates. Where necessary, the scheme will enable people who use its services to access external independent support to make or pursue a complaint.

(Advocacy Across London 2002, pp.2–3,
reproduced with permission)

DILEMMAS IN MENTAL HEALTH ADVOCACY

Below are some of the key dilemmas facing mental health advocacy groups at present. They are included to illustrate the evolving nature of mental health advocacy, and the fact that groups are collaborating to find answers to these and other dilemmas. It is strongly felt that solutions should come from within the advocacy movement itself rather than being imposed by an external agency.

Should mental health advocacy schemes be user-controlled?

There is a long and proud history of collaboration between advocacy schemes and the mental health service user movement. This is illustrated by the fact that UKAN (the United Kingdom Advocacy Network) is, in fact, a network of both advocacy schemes and user groups. UKAN has lobbied heavily over the years for advocacy to be user-led and user-controlled, arguing that this is the only way in which advocacy can retain its focus on empowerment. However, at present many advocacy schemes would struggle to meet the criterion of being 'user-controlled' even though service users are involved in project management and decision making. It is felt by many that complete user control should be an aspiration rather than a requirement at this time.

What is the relationship between advocacy and campaigning?

There is a clear distinction to be made between one-to-one advocacy and campaigning. It is inappropriate for advocates to use individual service users' complaints and concerns as a platform for issue-based campaigning. However, in the context of collective advocacy, a more political approach may be necessary; for example, when challenging new legislation or opposing changes to local service provision. In this way, the collective voices of service users can be a powerful way of raising the profile of particular issues. For this reason, many advocacy schemes work closely with campaigning and survivor-led organisations to give voice to such issues.

Is there a role for volunteers in mental health advocacy?

The authors of the Durham Report on specialist mental health advocacy caused controversy by claiming that advocacy of this nature (supporting detained patients) should be undertaken by trained, paid staff rather than volunteers. Many mental health advocacy schemes have utilised volunteers for several years, and feel that unpaid volunteers bring a wide range of skills and experience to the advocacy role. However, given the complex, often quasi-legal nature of advocacy with people subject to compulsory powers under the Mental Health Act, it may be that volunteers will be unwilling to undertake such work.

How should mental health advocacy be funded?

The present funding arrangements for mental health advocacy are clearly inadequate. At best, current provision is patchy and, at worst, a 'postcode lottery' is in operation which means that some service users have good access to advocacy support whilst others struggle alone. This is due to the differing funding criteria of local health and social care commissioning agencies and the inconsistent nature of charitable funding. There is no strategic approach to advocacy funding at a local, regional or national level. In some European countries a 'per capita' approach to funding is used, based on the number of people admitted to psychiatric hospital. In others, the health and social care budget is 'top-sliced' to fund essential advocacy services. In Scotland, health boards, in partnership with local authorities, are required to produce and publish advocacy strategy documents which outline how the advocacy needs of local communities are to be addressed. Ideally, a mechanism would be sought which enables core statutory funding to be made available without compromising advocacy's independence.

How can mental health advocacy be truly independent?

Independence can be thought of as having three distinct levels – structural, operational and psychological. There is little doubt that mental health advocates are operationally and psychologically independent – this is demonstrated through their face-to-face work with service users – but, for many, structural independence is harder to achieve. For example in London, the Advocacy Across London database shows that over half of all mental health advocacy projects are incorporated into a larger organisation (such as local Mind associations) that also provides other services. These 'other services' may include day care, residential care, befriending or advice services. Such an arrangement may present issues of conflicts of interest if, say, a service user of a care home (run by the same organisation as the advocacy scheme) requests advocacy support to make a complaint about the home. The only way to truly avoid such issues arising is for the advocacy scheme to be established as an independent, advocacyspecific agency.

CONCLUSION

The provision of independent advocacy for people with mental health problems has increased significantly over the past fifteen years. Advocacy is no longer perceived as a marginal activity, but as a central means of ensuring the voices of mental health service users are heard. This is beginning to be recognised in legislation, although we are still a long way from individual service users being given an automatic right to independent support and representation. Advocates make a difference by being independent from statutory mental health provision, and following a set of principles which encourage empowerment, choice and user involvement. The challenge for advocacy schemes in the future is to retain that independence whilst at the same time securing long-term, secure funding for their activities. This will require a commitment from government, from local commissioning agencies and from the advocacy agencies themselves. Ensuring that advocacy is accessible to all sections of the community will also be a priority. Herein lies a challenge for all mental health advocates – to increase both the quality and quantity of advocacy provision without becoming just another 'brick in the wall' of mental health services.

REFERENCES

Advocacy Across London (2002) *The Advocacy Charter*. London: Advocacy Across London.

Barnes, D., Brandon, D. and Webb, T. (2002) *Independent Specialist Advocacy in England and Wales: Recommendations for Good Practice*. Durham: University of Durham.

Carver, N., Morrison, J., Skelton, L. and Wood, P. (2003) 'Independent advocates' perceptions of their work on inpatient wards.' *The Advocate*, June, 14–16.

DH (Department of Health) (1983) *The Mental Health Act*. London: HMSO.

DH (Department of Health) (2000) *Reforming the Mental Health Act*. Cm 50161. London: HMSO.

DH (Department of Health) (2002) *Mental Health Bill Consultation Document*. Cm 5538–111. London: HMSO.

Henderson, R. and Pochin, M. (2001) *A Right Result? Advocacy, Justice and Empowerment*. Bristol: The Policy Press.

Independent Advocacy Service (2000) *Introduction to IAS*. Project leaflet. London: IAS.

Keating, F., Robertson, D., McCulloch, A. and Francis, E. (2002) *Breaking the Circles of Fear*. London: Sainsbury Centre for Mental Health.

Leader, A. and Crosby, K. (1998) *Power Tools: A Resource Pack for Those Committed to the Development of Mental Health Advocacy into the Millennium*. Brighton: Pavilion.

O'Brien, J. (1987) *Learning from Citizen Advocacy Programs*. Atlanta, GA: Georgia Advocacy Office.

UKAN (United Kingdom Advocacy Network) (1994) *Advocacy – A Code of Practice*. London: NHS Executive.

STATUTES

Mental Health Act (1983)

USEFUL CONTACTS

UK Advocacy Network
Volserve House
14–18 West Bar Green
Sheffield S1 2DA
Tel/Fax: 0114 272 8171

Greater London Mental Health Advocacy Network
c/o PO Box 31856
Lorrimore Square
London SE17 3XR
Tel: 020 7820 7868
Web: www.glmhan.org.uk

Prevention of Professional Abuse Network (POPAN)
1 Wyvil Court
Wyvil Road
Vauxhall
London SW8 2JT
Tel: 020 7622 6334
Fax: 020 7622 9788
E-mail: info@popan.org.uk
Web: www.popan.org.uk

Advocacy Across London
PO Box 31856
Lorrimore Square
London SE17 3XR
Tel: 020 7820 7868
E-mail: info@advocacyacrosslondon.org.uk
Web: www.advocacyacrosslondon.org.uk

National Advocacy Network
c/o GAIN
John Haswell House
8–9 Gladstone Terrace
Gateshead
Tyne and Wear NE8 4DY
Tel: 0191 478 3130
E-mail: gain@dial.pipex.com

CHAPTER 12

PERSONAL EXPERIENCES OF MENTAL HEALTH AND ILLNESS

JULIAN AND ERIC (SON AND FATHER)

INTRODUCTION

This chapter draws together the personal experiences of Julian, who has been diagnosed and treated within mental health services over almost two decades, with those of his father, Eric. It is a very personal account of something that is very difficult to describe succinctly or in a manner that can truly communicate the experiences in such a short space. However, it is hoped that these accounts, although not generalisable, provoke thought in readers in a manner that is beneficial to their practice and subsequently to the service users, families and friends with whom they work in the future. The first half of the chapter has been written by Julian and is followed by the experiences and thoughts of his father. The chapter concludes with a number of questions to assist the reader in considering the issues raised in the accounts.

THE SON'S PERSPECTIVE

In November 1986, shortly after returning to the city of my upbringing, after a disastrous relationship, I had what a psychiatric nurse on a ward where I was an inpatient described as 'a severe psychotic breakdown'. The week before, the distillation of the theory of transactional analysis, the book called *I'm OK, You're OK* by T.A. Harris, fell into my lap and gave me tools to navigate a course of some form of self-awareness through the ensuing absurdities of the psychiatric system. I spent six months languishing on an acute ward rather than being chivvied into, counselled about or helped back into the outside world. During this time I was, for the first three months, pumped full of chlorpromazine (and other drugs with names I can no longer remember) by a woman psychiatrist, who clearly stated that she did not practise talking to people but simply listened for five minutes once a week to me talking and then prescribed, or adjusted, existing prescriptions of medication. For the rest of my time on the ward, up until May 1987, the regime of five minutes a week was continued under the auspices of a ward nurse who was my 'key worker'. This nurse did occasionally practise a two-way dialogue as if we were fellow human beings, rather than me being a clinical specimen, and I welcomed this. However, she only ever took me at face value as someone mentally well developed, rather than attempting to read between the lines to the emotional 15-year-old lying behind the sophisticated veneer of an ex-Londoner hospital secretary, which was my persona until September 1986.

In May 1987, I was rescued from my inpatient experience by Mary, an intelligent woman who was a Christian worker with a community-based housing project for people recovering from mental illness. I lived in a house with five other blokes near the local football ground and it was a rough-and-tumble learning experience. My housemates, and a Citizens Advice Bureau where I began working as a voluntary typist, put up with me wearing women's clothes rather well. Everyone just wanted to understand. Sadly I had a bust up with the simultaneously most thuggish and most intelligent of my housemates and left in August of the same year. I camped with friends and with my parents for four months before settling into another shared house with the same project in January 1988 in a more salubrious part of the city and in the more convivial immediate surroundings of men and women living together. Not since May 1986 had I had any statutory community mental health back-up, but I continued to take medication, which made me feel sleepy until 11 o'clock in the morning, until I re-entered the housing project. I also enjoyed the support of the spirited Mary throughout this period. Once back in the housing project I enjoyed good caring support from both paid and volunteer workers with the project. They believed in talking problems through and getting people involved back in mainstream community life. Certainly by June 1988, if not before, every resident was in paid employment; I think there were five, possibly six of us. I came right off medication and felt none the worse for it and worked as a commischef. I felt like an ordinary man again and stopped cross-dressing.

We all benefited from the supported housing policy of talking things through, and I took my belief in what works one step further – 'unless a caring doctor or psychiatrist can clearly demonstrate that you need medication, don't bother with it'. I continue with this belief today, late April 2004. The housing project additionally organised trips and, much more fruitfully, sometimes arranged places on courses; albeit not directly vocational. I was put on a canoeing course free of charge that took me through a couple of fear barriers and gave me one lasting friend. More important, it set a precedent in my eyes of what statutory psychiatric services should, in part, be about.

My time at the housing project ended ignominiously through an unplanned pregnancy within an unhappy relationship and a fight with a fellow resident in early 1989. I was evicted but continued in employment, left behind the statutory and non-statutory mental health services and found housing in the private sector. No follow-up from either was volunteered. Frankly, it seems to me that there should have been some attempt at statutory follow-up. One phone call a month should have been the standard policy just to say 'Hi, are you OK? Fine, just wanted to make sure.' Sadly, statutory services only seem to 'kick in' when a person reaches the crisis stage. Certainly, this was my experience. I sailed along comparatively well, dating women occasionally until November 1989 when I started to walk the streets uneasy with my own company and then desired to self-harm. I put myself in an ambulance and insisted on being admitted to the local psychiatric unit once again. I began to realise I was struggling with guilt over my child and her mother. I had abandoned both soon after my daughter was born and had put them temporarily out of mind as well as out of sight. I did not like the new-found responsibility and felt trapped by it. I began living out a weird form of behaviour as if someone had written a script for my life that I had to act out. I began to compulsively smash windows, behaviour which, not surprisingly, sent me behind bars, until a magistrate decided to give me a lengthy Probation Order commencing in 1990 on condition that I underwent a course of psychiatry. This felt like going back to square one...but not quite.

A now-retired psychiatrist working at the psychiatric unit was authorised to sort me out and put me in the way of an experienced psychologist. She adopted in a more professional, astute and structured way the format which the housing project had successfully employed, that of talking things through as if you were a human being and on equal terms with the welfare practitioner trying to help you. To have professional help from a highly intelligent and skilled practitioner who saw me as her equal, and insisted on meeting me in her cheerfully-homely-cosy-book-covered-plus-nice-picture-or-two office instead of a clinical hospital setting where I was 'an ill service user', was ground-breaking in its impact on me. That woman convinced me I did not need to follow the tedious smashing-windows 'script'. She introduced me to task orientation as a way of dealing with the crippling guilt I felt. I had to learn to live with guilt long term because there was no point in returning to the destructive relationship I had left behind to try to assuage that guilt.

Since seeing the psychologist I have stopped smashing windows. I have achieved a lot in terms of community work and church work. In particular, I have been visiting people and keeping friendships going using task orientation in the face of often anarchic and painful feelings inside. I have recovered some self-esteem and a sense of inner well-being. I have given up smoking and decided to leave off medication, preferring 'white-knuckle raw reality'. I have worked steadily for seven and a half years. In all this I have been helped by a Christian faith and the much stronger presence of Christ Himself in my life. I remain schizophrenic but I lead a responsible independent life, holding down adult – more or less! – relationships in the process and not leaning on, burdening, manipulating or ripping off any person or institution.

On a gentler note, I talked earlier about the pioneering work of the housing project – that had many notable individuals working hard for those residing in the scheme – in finding courses for people to attend. I believe this set, and continues to set, a template for what psychiatry and mental health services could achieve.

I have talked about what has worked for me on several levels already:

1.   Practitioners talking things through with service users.

2.   Practitioners seeing service users as equal to them in merit and worth, even though, at that moment of time at any rate, their service users are 'scoring' far lower in terms of social competence than they are.

3.   Practitioners accepting the wisdom of their service users – (when forthcoming!) as well as giving it. The psychologist who worked with me is a nationally respected figure in her

field, yet she was truly humble and if I said something that challenged her she said 'Wow, I hadn't thought of that before!' in a disarming, humble and friendly way. This in turn brought out the best in me and made me work hard to follow her advice.

4.   Practitioners offering advice/counselling/whatever-you-want-to-call-it in as informal, non-clinical setting as possible.

5.   Practitioners taking the trouble to listen carefully enough to read between the lines of what a service user is saying in order to offer intelligent advice, e.g. task orientation to someone struggling with continuing guilt.

Now I want to go one step further and contend that mental health services should be outward looking and community orientated. They should see themselves as the gateway into mainstream society and I believe psychiatrists, nurses and other professionals should have as part of their role the need to create links with local employers and training providers. The psychologist that I worked with seemed to be as good as it gets right now, but neither she nor anyone else I ever met helped me get out of the world of benefits-dependency and into the world of financial self-sufficiency and earning ability.

When I consider the friends I made in the late 1980s and early 1990s when I was caught up in the statutory mental health services 'system', something like a quarter have progressed into steady employment. Of those who have made it into paid employment, only one that I can think of was helped into it by a health or welfare professional and that professional worked in the voluntary and not the statutory sector. Most of the rest have got stuck in the dead-end world of day centres. This is simply not good enough. There is a clear need for more staff in the statutory mental health services. Personally, I have had to wait six months for an assessment to be considered for a new form of help known as cognitive analytic therapy. It will be four or five more months before I actually get to begin a course of treatment. However, if I was the Whitehall civil servant in the Department of Health responsible for considering applications for more money by the chairman of an NHS trust to pay for more psychiatrists, I would be looking at the percentages of service users who move on into new self-supporting lives in mainstream society and would be saying to the chairman 'No way!'

Often, in the name of offering their service users choice as to what they do with their lives, psychiatrists and mental health nurses unwittingly condemn service users to a lifestyle rut of drop-ins and day centres, be they statutory or non-statutory, which is in practice the negation of choice. It is human nature to want to follow the path of least resistance, and health and welfare professionals should actively help service users who are depressed and feeling worthless into constructive activities. 'Constructive activities' means a paid job or education that is likely to lead onto paid work. Mental health services should be linking up with employers, training providers or nationally recognised charities where people can work voluntarily in order to start on the road back into mainstream society or, indeed, into mainstream society for the first time.

THE FATHER'S PERSPECTIVE

A psychotic illness may have many starting points, and be manifested in many kinds of behaviour. What follows is one experience only; furthermore, it is one person's perspective on that experience. Others in this situation (or observing it) may see things differently.

The trigger for our son's illness was a close relationship (which looked permanent from the outside) going dramatically wrong. This was then followed by a flight to and from India, from which he returned gaunt, disoriented, and almost unreachable. He admitted himself to a psychiatric ward, speaking 'from the edge of a black hole', and accepted the first of several courses of ECT. There was more than one admission, and his behaviour was increasingly florid and unpredictable.

Feelings do not come in separate strands, but on interwoven skeins that are hard to separate out. Uppermost, in our experience, were bewilderment, anxiety and guilt: one cannot account for what is happening. One is anxious about what may happen next, not least what treatments will be imposed; and as a parent one feels guilt. Guilt itself is complex, for it is linked to feelings of ignorance and impotence, to half-memories, and to the free-floating residues of earlier regrets, regrets which have been resolved in the past, but which now still re-emerge. Guilt is not simply in the present. It is expressed in self-questioning: 'Should we have detected earlier signs?', 'Were there any signs?', 'What could we have done about them if they existed?' and 'Have we unwittingly caused all this?' There are no answers, and even when a psychiatrist offers reassurance, one continues to wonder. And, of course, there is the guilt of knowing that one has brought into the world someone who is suffering so greatly.

As the years go by, challenges and the sense of incompetence increase as the illness becomes more extreme and the treatments more experimental. One would not wish to rehearse these matters in detail, but a list of 'challenges' gives a sense of the changing course of the illness: regression and, at an appropriate period in the regression, a degree of sexual ambiguity; unexpected episodes of criminal damage and physical threats; the loss of a basis for rational discussion and for sharing affection; a further intense relationship (with a patient); occasional false memories and accusations; loss of control over money; telephone calls from the police in the small hours over dumped clothes; court appearances. I have inevitably suffered with each event; but how much greater must have been our son's suffering if these were the only responses available to him.

The failure of ECT was followed by the experimental use of medicines: medicines which changed his body shape and turned him into a zombie; psychiatric comments that he would never get better; the feeling that we had lost the son we had loved, and that he had become an unpredictable stranger. Happy shared memories became irrelevant to him and, for us, they became a mockery of current hopelessness.

In addition, there were, of course, uncertainties in our dealings with neighbours, friends and colleagues. What did they make of the situation, and how much of it could properly be shared with them? The demands and routines of work, rather than family and social life, became the primary source of safe feelings and reassurance.

What were the sources of help?

Friends and colleagues were major sources of support; we encountered many positive responses, some of which were unexpected. But not all responses were positive. Thus, while some treated us as they always had done and looked for no explanations, offered no unrealistic hopes, accepted our sadness and, so far as they could, shared it with us, some others became distant, possibly unable to cope with our distress. Others looked for rational explanations, and these were the most difficult to deal with. In our Western culture, families (and particularly parents) can be simplistically blamed for virtually every personal and social problem; so we became sensitive to covert attitudes that something must have gone seriously wrong in our earlier parenting.

Professional help

In some respects, the behaviour of the professionals mirrored the responses of friends. Clearly there is a problem, when the patient is an adult, of how far professionals consider it appropriate to involve parents or other adults. For example, the choice of treatments (and their possible outcomes) was never discussed with us. We were invited to attend a hospital case-conference, but only to be asked questions about our son's earlier behaviour. In seeking patterns and explanations of this development of the illness, some professionals seemed to imply the primacy of parental responsibility; perhaps we were over-sensitive to this, but that was how it felt. The atmosphere at the case-conference was cold; no reference was made to how we might be feeling; and we left the hospital with less hope and more guilt than when we arrived.

I have regularly visited our son during his times in hospital admissions. The nurses were unfailingly smiling and benign, but offered no guidance about what was happening or whether our visits were appropriate or detrimental. We were not given advice on how we should respond to our uncommunicative son or how we might best deal with his visits home at weekends, with his discharges to hostels, or with his final discharge to an (unfurnished) council flat. We accept that there probably were discharge plans and plans for community care, but we were not informed. Two local authority social workers did, in contrast, visit us at home for a short period and showed concern for our anxieties. This was a welcome relief, but short-lived as we had no priority in the work of the local authority services. We sought the support of a counselling service within the general practice. This helped a great deal, but was inevitably removed from our underlying concern to discover how we could be more effective helpers in the care of our son.

The symptoms of illness gradually lifted. He courageously refused further medication – courageously in that he suffered waking nightmares from time to time – as he recognised that it was doing him more harm than good. We have now reached a plateau of mutual affection and goodwill, even though we are occasionally subject to misunderstandings. Anxiety about the future remains with us all, however, particularly in regard to suitable employment.

How could the services have been improved?

I can offer the following only from my personal experiences as a parent of someone who has suffered a debilitating illness and from our contacts with the system that is there to help respond to this. Others with similar experiences may see things differently; however, I feel that services can be improved:

1. Parental anxieties should be recognised from the outset of the illness. If community care is to make sense, it needs to be planned well in advance of discharges from hospital, and the family given some guidance and support as potential contributors to effective planning.

2. There should be greater openness about diagnostic and prognostic considerations. Even if the outlook is bleak and the diagnosis is uncertain, it is better to know than to remain adrift on a sea of speculation.

3. The tentative explanations of theories that underpin the actions of professionals should be shared. Visits to hospital wards and aftercare hostels, whether by parents or friends, should be given coherence rather than regarded as random and virtually meaningless events.

4. It needs to be remembered that the family, as well as the patient, has to live with the long-term effects of what the professionals have defined as treatment or help.

5. Meaningful occupation is an important component of mental health. Our son has a degree and other qualifications, but these have not formed a focus of aftercare discussions with him. Neither has he had direct and personal support in seeking employment, or in negotiating with potential employers. A link between psychiatric and mental health interventions and subsequent employment-related independence would be a real help.

6. Similarly, someone needs to accompany a discharged patient in his/her enrolment for social benefits, bearing in mind that the patient may unwittingly provide false information about his/her financial means. Our son fell into this trap, to an amount of several hundred pounds of alleged overpayment. It needs to be remembered that, even when an illness shows sufficient abatement for discharge from hospital, cognitive

and affective distortions may remain, and may seriously affect the understanding and response of civil servants.

There is a more general issue affecting the well-being of adult patients. Sometimes, the concept of self-determination (the adult's right to freedom of choice) gets in the way of purposeful welfare planning, and the longer-term safety and well-being of patients. This is especially so in respect of their relationships with each other, and the consequences of these. Sometimes, self-determination can be used as an excuse for professional idleness, indecision and irresponsibility. Perhaps self-determination, as a phrase, should be forbidden to any mental health staff member who cannot explicate its precise relevance to the current achievement of a professional task.

CONCLUSIONS

The views presented here are those of two people and may not be generalisable; however, they are deeply personal and relevant to both parties and probably have a resonance with many other service users and parents. These experiences have been provided not to damn the system that has tried to support the family but to offer an insight to professionals of what might be an 'alien' viewpoint in the hope that it can encourage empathy and thought in professionals reading this work.

Reflective Practice Questions

- How common do you feel these experiences are in general among people who use mental health services and their families?
- Do you feel that people who use the service you work in would identify with these experiences?
- What might you do to improve your empathy towards people who use mental health services and their families through hearing their narratives?
- What mechanisms exist within your service to learn from the experiences of users and families and how do you know if these mechanisms are effective?
- How do you and the service you work in involve users and families in service development and delivery?

CHAPTER 13

CARER PERSPECTIVES

ALISON PEARSALL AND LILLIAN YATES

INTRODUCTION

There has been a considerable amount written about the journey (or care pathway) of mental health service users through systems of health and social care. This chapter seeks to describe the parallel experience of the carer of someone with a mental illness and his/her journey through services. The needs of carers, also formally recognised in mental health policy (DH 1999), are explored before examining some of the issues that this raises for mental health service development. Practical examples and vignettes of how services can meet the needs of and support and involve carers are provided to illustrate good practice in this important area.

In the context of this chapter a carer is defined as someone who provides unsalaried and regular care for a person with mental health problems; such individuals include partners, siblings, parents, friends and other relatives. There are many terms used to depict the role of a carer; for example, a salaried professional, a voluntary worker or a family member. For the purpose of this chapter we will be focusing on 'primary' carers, those people who provide the main support to people, often to the point where their own quality of life may at times be compromised.

We aim to highlight areas where the role of carer can support the interventions of services and vice versa. We aim to do this by initially outlining the recent policy context that recognises the valuable role of carers within the modernisation of mental health services, the rationale for this and how issues of carer involvement can be tackled at each stage of the user's journey through services. Professionals can demonstrate regard for carers as co-clients or co-workers, each producing distinct and separate approaches. Each can benefit the cared-for and carer but, importantly, must be recognised, negotiated and agreed by all stakeholders for relationships to work positively.

The user movement was established over twenty years ago to ensure the voice of users is heard throughout the mental health system (see Chapter 10 in this volume). However, the carer's voice has been slower to be heard. The Carers National Association (CNA) has advanced understanding on the politics of caring, although the CNA is not specific to mental health, as are many user organisations.

Service users and carers may share similar issues of stigma, oppression and discrimination; however, each has very distinct, separate and sometimes conflicting needs. Therefore, a separate voice is required for carers as their needs can often be hidden and at times misunderstood. It is vital that both the service user and carer feel central to services which are geared to meet both sets of need. Similarly, both service users and carers must be enabled to have a sense of control to be the participants, rather than recipients of care (National Institute for Mental Health in England 2001).

It has been estimated that 15 per cent of the adults in England have a caring responsibility and make a contribution to the health care and social industry (Office of Population and Censuses and Surveys 1992) and has remained almost constant over the past ten years (National Statistics 2002). However, we may never know the full extent to which carers provide support to people with mental health problems, particularly if they are not actively engaged within the care processes of professionals. It could be argued that mental health services would struggle to deliver much of the basic support provided by carers and their care is vital to the functioning of the mental health system. Whilst caring is unequivocally rewarding, it potentially places immense pressures on individual carers and on family units. If unsupported this can lead to fragmentation and breakdown of the family and, ultimately, to the service user's relapse.

POLICY CONTEXT

Mental health carers occupy an ambiguous position in relation to service delivery and development and often sit on the perimeter of the health and social care system. They are part of its required responses and concerns, whilst often being beyond its remit. Therefore, in reality, carers form part of the taken-for-granted and hidden service provision on which we all so vitally depend (Twigg and Atkin 1994). Recent policy documents, including the Carers Strategy (DH 2002a), have, however, acknowledged the vital role of carers and the fact that there has previously been a lack of strategic direction in supporting this in the past (DH 1999).

Caring for Carers, Standard 6 of the National Service Framework for Mental Health (NSFMH) (DH 1999), places responsibility on health and social care agencies to identify carers of people with mental illness who receive care from secondary mental health services. There is a requirement under the Carers (Recognition and Services) Act 1995 to provide an annual assessment of the main carer's needs that is reinforced specifically in mental health through the NSF. The carer can expect a Carers Support Plan that should ensure the carer understands where and how to access services, including at a time of crisis and outside office hours. It is the responsibility of local services to ensure that an assessment of the carer's needs is undertaken, to develop support plans and to provide sensitive, practical and emotional support.

INVOLVING CARERS
Why involve carers?
Involving carers as soon as possible in supporting their relatives or friends with mental health needs provides many positive effects – for the service user, carer and mental health staff. Carers can experience varied emotions, particularly at the outset of their experience of caring, including bewilderment, anxiety, guilt and denial. Providing information can minimise frustration, anxiety and anger that may be vented on the service user. Involving carers from an early stage encourages them to understand challenging behaviours in terms of an illness model that can help them to separate the person from the symptoms. Improving carers' understanding through support and education can also reduce relapse rates in users (Kuipers 2000; Vaughn and Leff 1981).

CASE STUDY 13.1

Simon is 31 years old and diagnosed with bipolar disorder. Simon's mother and sister are his main carers. It was only after years of care provision that Simon's mother and sister came to understand his illness. In the formative years of caring the women would whisper together, presuming that their quietness would relieve Simon's agitation. Instead, their private conversations aggravated him and put a further strain on their vital caring relationship. Simon would become acutely paranoid towards them during psychotic relapse.

This tension arising within family units is not an isolated incident. Furthermore, it can be avoided by the provision of information about the particular illness, symptoms, treatment and management techniques. Early intervention teams, primary care workers and mental health liaison services often see people in the first acute illness stage, when the provision of information is crucial. It is also important to give contact and helpline numbers to ensure that the family unit has a lifeline to future support.

Questions for discussion

1.   Are potential tensions between service users and carers routinely identified and by whom?

2.   How can these be relieved in order to optimise the service user's continued recovery?

Carers are vital in supporting the development of service user's self-determination and self-control, without which the user may become consumed by the negative symptoms of their illness. However, although useful in helping separating the user from the condition, the illness model has dangers. Carers may become over-involved emotionally and take over key parts of the service user's life, such as areas of responsibility and decision making, because s/he is viewed as being 'ill'. This can lead to the user's perception of him- or herself as 'ill', in need of care, and can hinder or prevent recovery. It can also have a major impact on the user's development of insight and concordance with treatment, particularly medication, and reinforce dependency.

How carers can be involved

Involving carers brings many benefits, but ignoring carers can result in many drawbacks. Carers who feel ignored and undervalued in their caring role may lose their ability to cope and can become ill themselves. Carers need to be identified in their own right, not merely as a by-product of the structures created for the service user. Traditionally, carers who are fortunate enough to be supported are helped by services designed primarily for the service user. Most carers are grateful for the benefits gained through the service user's care; however, this may not be the best way of enabling and supporting carers.

The recognition of carers, with their own distinct identity, is essential to the operation of a modern mental health system. The assumptions that professionals make about the carer role, its responsibilities and the impact of caring can produce either dividends or further difficulties for carers and, in turn, service users. Presumptions about carers' availability, knowledge of mental ill health, the level of care they are able to provide and their ability to cope with the demands of caring can have profound implications. Hence, actively engaging and involving carers in the care and treatment of their friend or relative is vital for all concerned.

Listening to carers

Carers need time to talk to someone who will actively listen. This is often best done by those who are providing services to the person they are supporting, although there are occasions where others may be better placed due to conflicts of interests in carer and user needs (e.g. Patients Advice and Liaison Services or carers support workers). It is also vital that the carer feels safe and comfortable with the professional with whom s/he is speaking and that, when appropriate, the professional will sensitively and proactively act on the information provided by the carer. General practitioners (GPs) are obviously key personnel in the identification and support of carers and, therefore, require the support of mental health services to undertake this task.

Good Practice Points

Developing a checklist for GPs and primary care staff in the identification and support for carers would be a useful initiative. Practices should consider the following questions when developing such a checklist:

- Are you able to identify carers of people with mental health problems within your registered patient population?
- Can you identify people experiencing mental health problems among your registered patient population?

- Do you check carers' physiological, psychological and emotional health when an appropriate opportunity arises? For example, on an annual basis?
- Do you routinely inform carers that they are entitled to receive a carer's assessment from social services, which should be reviewed on an annual basis?
- Do you check with service users whether they agree to their health details being disclosed to their carer?
- Are you aware of the existence of a carers' support group or carers' centre in your area? Do you tell carers about such provision and related services?

(Adapted from DH 1999, p.72)

Informing carers

Carers often thirst for information about the illnesses with which their family or friends have been diagnosed initially and over time. They also may have a need for more information about the organisation of health and social care in order that they can be involved in helping to improve these systems. Carers have frequently been heard to say 'I didn't know what I didn't know, until I found it out'. There is no single process for providing carers with information systematically and often they feel as though they stumble across useful information by chance. Having briefing packs on each of the main forms of mental illness and the local services that are available to support the service user and carers should be commonly available within all mental health services.

While there may be many aspirations within current mental health policy and a vision that describes a comprehensive and high quality service system, the truth is that there may be differences between what service providers would like to see available and what might exist. Carers, as much as anyone else, recognise that the health and social care purse is not bottomless and it is therefore essential that they are made aware of the resource limitations placed on services to avoid the creation of false expectations. Across different parts of the country there are often financial disparities that can result in significant variations in the support services provided to carers and service users. Clearly, it is also essential for carers to be appraised honestly of service pressures, priorities and proposals. This is particularly helpful where carers want to put something back into their mental health system by becoming involved in service development work, for example in the local implementation teams (LITs).

CARERS AND SERVICE USERS
Supporting carer needs

As highlighted earlier, carers' physical and mental health can suffer if left unsupported or left with inadequate back-up. In addition, however, numerous studies have found that there are frequently high levels of expressed emotion (EE) within families where a service user with a severe and enduring illness frequently relapses (for a summary see Barrowclough and Tarrier 1992). Typically, high EE is synonymous with hostility towards the service user and over-involvement in the everyday activities. This frequently results from a lack of information about the service user's condition and how to support it and the lack of external support for those undertaking the role of primary carer(s).

People who are the main carer(s) of service users who are eligible for the Care Programme Approach (CPA) have the right to an annual assessment of their needs and support plan (DH 1999). Support plans should be developed that provide carers with contact numbers which are available 24 hours a day and information about how to respond to a crisis with clear contingency plans; ideally, they should be linked to the CPA plan for the service user the carer is supporting. This recognises that supporting the carer is also key to supporting the service user.

Balancing the needs of carers and service users

Carers want to see their service user recover and live independently. However, the experience for many people with serious mental illness is that they move in and out of services, particularly where their insight is impaired. Carers can sometimes feel they are the sole person responsible for identifying relapse and referring service users back into services, often when they are seriously ill. This can place the carer in a dilemma, in that s/he can be the person who instigates admission, perhaps against the user's wishes, thereby impacting on the relationship with his or her relative or friend. Pathways into the mental health system need to be clear to the carer to ensure that access to assessment and treatment is swift and there are limited opportunities for mixed messages between users, carers and professionals.

Situations can arise when carers alert services of the need for increased support or interventions and the views of professionals and carers may differ in respect of user needs. While this is inevitable from time to time carers should not be left in situations where their safety is compromised as it has been shown that extreme acts of violence, including manslaughter and murder, are more likely to be committed against family members or carers than against a stranger (Estroff and Zimmer 1994). Carers' ability to assess and manage risk can be extremely useful to professionals and should be valued as a part of the information gathering that directs carer and treatment decisions (Ryan 2002). There can be conflicts of interest that professionals need to balance, especially in relation to safety issues, particularly where carers are living in the same household as users.

Practitioners can be unclear about what to do when a different viewpoint or conflict between the service user and carer arises. A general principle is that the obligation for care lies with the service user and therefore the expressed needs or wishes of the carer can be negated. People who experience non-psychotic illness are deemed to exercise appropriate insight, understanding and to function adequately enough to make their own decisions without impaired cognitive functioning. Essentially, carers of people with psychosis (i.e. severe, enduring mental illness) may be in a stronger position to request information due to the perceived risks to the service user, the public and, indeed, the carer themselves.

Practitioners may say that they are bound by confidentiality; that is, if the service user decides not to involve the carer then that is what has to happen. However, it is important that these decisions are recorded and often reviewed as the position may change over time. This can be particularly significant where the service user lives with the carer and aspects of the illness or behaviour could place the carer at potential risk. In contrast, carers may feel that professionals expect them to provide private and sensitive information about service users and their relationship with them, particularly at times where service users' communication is unclear. Practitioners need to be aware of the possible effect that this could have on the relationship between the service user and carer.

CARE PATHWAYS AND THE INVOLVEMENT OF CARERS

Accessing services

It is important that the carer is involved from the very beginning in the service user's journey within mental health services and that this is a positive experience for both service user and carer. Carers can help to corroborate issues of fact when professionals are undertaking assessments of the service user's mental health and also provide support and reassurance during stressful times such as when a user is being admitted to hospital.

Often service users and carers are tired and frustrated by the time they use mental health services. It is therefore essential that front-line practitioners take sufficient time to ensure that they are made to feel comfortable, safe and supported. The entry points to mental health care are crucial as they pave the way for the service user's and carer's journey through services.

Good Practice Point

Repeating the mental health state examination (i.e. a comprehensive assessment of the individual's personal/social/psychiatric/family history, current functioning, symptoms and willingness to engage with treatment/management options) that has been carried out with a service user, is a useful way of obtaining further information and corroborating that which the service user has provided. It also informs the carer about the assessment, provides a structure for carer participation and can improve the risk assessment process, as information can be cross-referenced.

Confidentiality and information sharing

Upholding a service user's confidentiality is important in establishing and maintaining a positive and therapeutic relationship, based on mutual respect and trust. It is therefore essential that the service user and carer are informed of how confidentiality operates in practice within the service.

Some teams may operate a team confidentiality protocol whereby information about service users is shared among the team. Records are open to all team members to ensure that they are able to provide swift intervention to all individuals known to the team as necessary. This approach is best exemplified in assertive outreach teams where team-working is central to how support is provided.

Service users and carers should be made aware on entering services that it may be necessary at certain times to share or act on particular information in order to manage and minimise the risks that individuals can pose to themselves, their family or the general public. Decisions to break the expected confidence should ideally be taken by the multi-disciplinary team and should always, unless there are exceptional circumstances, involve the care coordinator, the service user and carer.

Admission to inpatient units

It can be a terrifying ordeal for a person with an acute mental illness to be admitted to a psychiatric ward and considerable effort is often put into reassuring the person. However, it is also stressful to leave your loved one in a mental health unit, particularly on their first admission. Good practice dictates that practitioners proactively take the time to meet or contact carers, to explain the care and treatment programme and to answer any questions they may have. Carers find it useful to be provided with written information and contact numbers for the ward, as they may find it difficult to retain this if only given verbally due to the stress of the events at hand.

Good Practice Point

Information packs should be available on the ward to ensure that the provision of information is standard custom and practice. Information should include:

- Ward contact details
- Visiting times
- Names of the consultant psychiatrist, ward manager and the service user's key nurse (the main nursing contact)
- Details of family support groups or specialist workers (based in the hospital and outside)
- Details of carer organisations
- Details of medications
- An overview of the illness with which the service user has been diagnosed (if a diagnosis has been made)

- Information about recovery, including service user and carer perspectives
- Information about the Care Programme Approach (CPA) and the Mental Health Act 1983
- A map detailing the ward and the hospital/unit (carers may find it useful to pass on to relatives or friends who have not been to the hospital previously)
- Details of bus routes and timetables

The key nurse should arrange to meet with the carer(s) during the inpatient admission, along with the service user, if appropriate. The main aim should be to keep them informed of the care programme, to allay any potential anxieties and answer any questions they may have. Any periods of home leave, particularly where the service user lives with the carer, should be discussed and planned with both the service user and carer. Often such leave is decided at 'ward rounds' and consideration will need to be given to whether the dates for leave are convenient. In cases where the carer's safety has been compromised in the past by the user, his or her views will be very important and contingency and crisis arrangements will need to be put in place before any leave periods are finalised. It is important that leave is reviewed after the service user returns to the ward and that the staff know what happened during the time at home. The service user's account of leave alongside the carer's views will be essential to the whole programme of care and help in assessing progress.

Planning for Discharge

Discharge planning and preparation should commence soon after admission, with discharge criteria being set as part of the care programme. This should be shared routinely with the service user and carer. Carers need to be customarily invited to attend all reviews, ward rounds and multidisciplinary team meetings. The care team should consider the needs of carers who are employed and offer times that encourage their attendance.

> **Good Practice Point**
>
> Carers in employment should not be placed under additional pressure by having to take more time off work to attend reviews. Ward review times should be flexible and include early evenings, when required.

Carers should be empowered to take a full and active part in the review and therefore should be appropriately supported. It is important for the key nurse to explain the review process and check out any support needs the carer may have.

Carers should routinely be involved in pre-discharge meetings to ensure that appropriate arrangements are in place prior to the user leaving hospital. There should be a care plan activated before a person leaves the ward, and a written copy should be provided to both service user and carer. This should provide clear information on aftercare and who will be providing support.

For service users who are identified as being at increased risk, such as those who have a high risk of suicide (for example, those who have a psychotic illness and have self-harmed prior to admission), policy guidance suggests that a home visit should be made within seven days of discharge from inpatient care (DH 1999, 2002b). It is important as part of this follow-up plan that contact with the carer is featured, particularly if s/he lives with the service user, to clarify the service user's progress and well-being.

Outpatient reviews and the Care Programme Approach

Another major area of mental health activity is the outpatients department or community clinics. Unfortunately, it can be difficult to get an appointment with a consultant psychiatrist outside of office hours unless through an emergency domiciliary visit. Carers who are in employment or who have other commitments can often feel under extreme pressure to attend for outpatient appointments.

As with the inpatient stay, written information in the form of a leaflet should be provided to the service user and carer that they can take away and digest. Leaflets will need to be specifically tailored to meet the needs of minority groups or people with additional difficulties such as sub-

CASE STUDY 13.2 A CARER'S STORY

I am what the NSF Standard 6 refers to as a 'carer'; I didn't think of myself as a carer for a long time, I was John's mum. John had been a good student; it was a pleasure to go to parents' evening at school and be told he was bright and well mannered and in the top set for all his subjects. The change came in his final year at high school. Parents' evening was very different – he was no longer the blue-eyed boy and his behaviour at home was awful.

The weeks before his admission to hospital were terrible; he didn't sleep, didn't eat and was uncontrollable. Finally, he lost touch with reality. It was so frightening, he couldn't stop talking and he went on and on for hours. He was completely irrational but I still tried to reason with him. I sent for the emergency doctor who was as out of his depth as we were. He left telling us John would be better when he had slept.

John woke and of course he wasn't fine so I sent for our own doctor. He told me to take him up to the hospital. I was distraught; taking John onto a squalid, dormitory ward full of mentally ill adult men was the second worst moment in my life. The worst was leaving him there.

John was given anti-psychotic drugs; these didn't help, they just gave him side effects. He was no longer manic, just a stiff, lost, frightened boy; still hallucinating, still delusional, and very ill. John was on the ward for five months under section 2 and then section 3. I didn't know that these were sections of the Mental Health Act. It was horrendous; he attempted suicide twice. Finally, his doctor told me 'He is not getting any better, I don't know why'. Soon after he was discharged and I found him sitting on the doorstep when I got home from work. My GP referred John for a second opinion.

This time both John and I were involved, listened to and cared about. The doctor spoke to John on his own, then to me and then to both of us together at every meeting. Slowly he came back to us, he became the young man I knew he should always have been; thoughtful, kind and caring. The journey to recovery had started.

Questions for discussion

1. How can services positively and routinely involve carers in the assessment process?

2. How can services listen and respond to carers' concerns about service users?

3. How can services support carers who have experienced substantial difficulties in accessing services?

stance dependency or learning disabilities. Having information available also assists staff in explaining processes to service users, carers and other allied professionals. Explanation of the aims and objectives of aftercare, the process and outcome of all outpatient reviews, medications and the rationale for their use, anticipated benefits, efficacy and any potential side-effects are all useful to both users and carers. Having these things in written form puts less pressure on users and carers at reviews and they do not have to worry about retaining information given to them verbally.

The CPA was designed to underpin the delivery of quality mental health care and to target appropriate levels of support to those who most require it (DH 1990). Therefore, it is important that users and carers are provided with appropriate and accessible information in order that they can take full advantage of what the CPA process has to offer. The CPA is the cornerstone of aftercare and the active involvement of carers in the assessment, intervention and evaluation will be vital to successfully supporting the user and also the carer in the community (Chapter 3 in this volume).

CONCLUSION

Caring for an adult with mental health problems has received less attention in accounts of care giving, perhaps because it is viewed as entirely different to caring for people with physical disabilities. There are stark contrasts; for example, carers of people with mental health problems may feel implicated in the mental health condition, at least as a causal agent in its manifestation. It is also more difficult to recognise many forms of mental illness, objectify conditions and symptoms, access treatment services and, importantly for carers, to separate the 'illness' from the relationship. Therefore, it is important to engage carers along with service users in a programme of education about illness and symptomatology. However, more important than understanding 'illness', it is vital that users and carers acknowledge recovery (see Chapter 1 in this volume). Without an appreciation of 'wellness', conditions such as schizophrenia can seem like a terminal illness. Once a diagnosis has been made, the way that this is communicated, the supporting information that is provided and how questions are answered will be crucial to how services work with the user and any carers from this point.

There are many opportunities for practitioners, users and carers to work together within common objectives. However, the mechanisms for effective channels of communication must be developed and reinforced throughout services. With genuine commitment to joint working and information sharing the service user's journey through mental health services may be very successful, which, in turn, can have significant benefits for the carer.

REFERENCES

Barrowclough, C. and Tarrier, N. (1992) *Families of Schizophrenic Patients: Cognitive Behavioural Interventions*. London: Chapman and Hall.

DH (Department of Health) (1990) *Joint Health and Social Services Circular: The Care Programme Approach for People with a Mental Illness Referred to the Specialist Psychiatric Services*. HC (90) 23/LASSL(90/11). London: DH.

DH (Department of Health) (1999) *National Service Framework for Mental Health: Modern Standards and Service Models*. London: Department of Health.

DH (Department of Health) (2002a) *Developing Services for Carers and Families of People with Mental Illness*. London: DH. (Also available at: *www.DH.gov.uk/mentalhealth/devservcarers*)

DH (Department of Health) (2002b) *National Suicide Prevention Strategy for England*. London: DH.

Estroff, S.E. and Zimmer, C. (1994) 'Social networks, social support, and violence among persons with severe persistent mental illness.' In J. Monahan and H. Steadman (eds) *Violence and Mental Disorder: Developments in Risk Assessments*. Chicago, IL: University of Chicago Press.

Kuipers, E. (2000) 'Working with carers: Interventions for relative and staff carers of those who have psychosis.' In T. Wykes, N. Tarrier and S. Lewis (eds) *Outcome and Innovation in Psychological Treatment of Schizophrenia*. Chichester: John Wiley and Sons.

National Institute for Mental Health in England (2001) *National Institute for Mental Health in England: Role and Function*. London: DH.

National Statistics (2002) *Carers 2000*. London: The Stationery Office.

Office of Population and Censuses and Surveys (1992) *General Household Survey: Carers*. London: HMSO.

Ryan, T. (2002) 'Exploring the risk management strategies of informal carers of mental health service users.' *Journal of Mental Health 11*, 1, 17–25.

Twigg, J. and Atkin, K. (1994) *Carers Perceived: Policy and Practice in Informal Care*. Buckingham: Open University Press.

Vaughn, C. and Leff, J. (1981) 'Patterns of emotional response in the relatives of schizophrenic patients.' *Schizophrenia Bulletin 7*, 43–44.

STATUTES

The Carers (Recognition and Services) Act (1995)

Mental Health Act (1983)

USEFUL CONTACTS

Carers National Association
20/25 Glasshouse Yard
London EC1A 4JT
Tel: 020 7490 8818
Fax: 020 7490 8824

Contact a Family
209–211 City Road
London EC1V 1JN
Tel: 020 7608 8700 (office)
Tel: 0808 808 3555 (helpline)
Fax: 020 7608 8701
E-mail: info@cafamily.org.uk
Web: www.cafamily.org.uk

Crossroads Caring for Carers
Crossroads Association
10 Regent Place
Rugby
Warwickshire CV21 2PN
Tel: 0845 450 0350
Fax: 01788 573653
E-mail: communications@crossroads.org.uk
Web: www.crossroads.org.uk

Department of Health
Web: www.carers.gov.uk/index.htm

Making Space
46 Allen Street
Warrington WA2 7JB
Tel: 01925 571680
Fax: 01925 231402
Web: www.makingspace.co.uk

Princess Royal Trust for Carers
142 Minories
London EC3N 1LB
Tel: 020 7480 7788
Fax: 020 7481 4729
E-mail: info@carers.org
Web: www.carers.org

CHAPTER 14

BLACK AND MINORITY ETHNIC MENTAL HEALTH

MELBA WILSON, LINDA WILLIAMSON, RHIAN WILLIAMS AND SANDRA GRIFFITHS

INTRODUCTION

This chapter assesses progress regarding developments in black and minority ethnic (BME) mental health. It discusses the political, legislative and policy context in which BME mental health has developed and continues to develop, primarily from the perspectives and experiences of African Caribbean and Asian communities.

It aims to:

- identify and set in context the policy framework which relates to BME mental health
- reflect on the impact
- discuss solutions and approaches for good practice
- present good practice examples of work in relation to BME communities.

The chapter also focuses on the mental health needs and issues arising for refugees and asylum seekers. This is because it is becoming increasingly clear that there is a need for concentrated care and attention in this area.

CONTEXT

The National Institute for Mental Health's new strategic framework on BME mental health (NIMHE 2003) acknowledges the problems which exist for BME people who need to access mental health services. These include:

- an overemphasis on institutional and coercive models of care
- professional and organisational requirements that are given priority over individual needs and rights
- institutional racism within mental health care.

The strategy emphasises that change will occur only when 'those who use mental health services are identified, first and foremost, as citizens with mental health needs, which are understood and located in a social and cultural context' (NIMHE 2003, p.7).

There is well-documented evidence about the nature of BME people's engagement with mental health services – much of it negative. The Department of Health and Home Office (1992) have long acknowledged that black people who come to the attention of psychiatric services are more likely to be:

- removed by the police to a place of safety under Section 136 of the Mental Health Act 1983
- detained in hospital under Sections 2, 3 and 4 of the Act
- diagnosed as suffering from schizophrenia or other forms of psychotic illness
- detained in locked wards of psychiatric hospitals
- given higher dosages of medication.

They are also less likely than white people to:

- receive appropriate and acceptable diagnosis or treatment at an early stage
- receive treatments such as psychotherapy or counselling.

During the past decade numerous reports and initiatives have chronicled the mental health needs of BME communities in Britain. One of the most recent of these (Keating *et al.* 2002) makes a qualitative case for change. It incorporates the voices of people from BME communities in an effort to create greater awareness and spell out the inconsistencies and inadequacies of mental health service delivery as experienced by users and carers.

In particular, the report highlights gaps in information provision, notes a perceived lack of accountability to families and carers, and underscores the widely held view within black communities that there is an unwillingness on the part of service providers to translate the wealth of evidence and feedback into systematic change in care and treatment.

AFRICAN CARIBBEAN COMMUNITIES

McKenzie (2002, p.14) has argued that the lack of a definition of mental health from a British African Caribbean perspective and the 'use of diagnostic criteria based on white European norms rather than on the values and experience of the African-Caribbean population' is problematic.

Further evidence (Hunt *et al.* 2003; Keating, Robertson and Kotecha 2003; McKenzie 2002) suggests that people from BME communities experience a number of social and environmental risk factors which adversely affect their mental health. These include high unemployment rates; poor housing; racism; low educational expectations, particularly for African and Caribbean boys (Greater London Authority/London Health Observatory 2002); isolation; and a lack of access to opportunities for personal development.

CASE STUDY 14.1

Lisa is of African Caribbean origin and is living in B&B accommodation with her four-year-old daughter. She has been homeless for the past two years. Prior to that she lived at various temporary addresses.

She is very depressed and has twice attempted suicide and self-harm. Her GP sent her for an assessment by the community mental health team. They said she was isolated and depressed and advised counselling at the GP surgery. She will not be moved by the Housing Department as she has passport irregularities. She is very angry and upset, as she was sent to Britain by her family when she was aged 13 years to stay with a relative. She thought this was for a holiday and feels she had no part in this decision.

The rest of her family is in the Caribbean and she is not now close to them. She will have to wait in B&B accommodation until her immigration hearing. She is currently pregnant again and cannot take anti-depressants. The waiting list for counselling is at least three months long. She expresses negative thoughts and feels powerless about directing her own future. There seems little joined-up thinking about her problems.

(Wandsworth Primary Care Trust Team for Homeless
Refugees and Asyum Seekers)

Questions for discussion

1.   What would you regard as Lisa's primary need?

2.   How would you reconcile Lisa's immigration and health care needs?

3.   Where are the opportunities for multi-agency working?

4.   What are the barriers to developing a joined-up solution for Lisa? How could they be overcome?

A report by the black mental health charity Footprints (UK) (2003), which works primarily with African Caribbean service users, has identified continuing issues of concern about care and treatment as:

- the need for better assessment to promote more culturally acceptable interventions
- concerns about medication, including high dosages and polypharmacy, resulting in numerous adverse side-effects
- negative staff attitudes.

Keating *et al.* (2002) have highlighted the point that black people see using mental health services as a degrading and alienating experience and that their perception is that services respond to them in ways that mirror some of the controlling and oppressive dimensions of other institutions in their lives, e.g. exclusion from schools and contact with police and the criminal justice system.

For a good practice example, see Box 14.1.

Box 14.1 Mellow Camaipgn

The Mellow Campaign is a pioneering project that is addressing a complex range of factors that influence the mental health of young African and Caribbean men and their experience of mental health services. One of its initiatives has been a 12-week programme that was developed as a joint venture between the Harmony Project (a community project aimed at promoting good mental health for BME communities in Newham) and the Mellow Campaign. The programme was delivered in Hackney and Newham from May to October 2001.

The aim was to run a series of personal development programmes for young African and Caribbean men/boys with mental health difficulties, aged 16 to 30 years. These programmes would utilise creative expression and sporting activities to:

- increase their awareness of issues that affect their mental/emotional well-being
- increase their willingness to seek help earlier
- develop more effective coping mechanisms.

The programme was developed and coordinated by a development worker, a young African Caribbean mental health practitioner, with experience of engaging hard-to-reach black youth. His role was to support the session leaders, as well as carry out a wide range of duties in relation to preparing for and running the course and supporting the participants. He reported on a day-to-day basis to the Harmony Project, with Mellow taking a strategic role in over-seeing the project.

Outcomes

Outcomes included some participants setting goals. One participant wanted to challenge his employer about his rate of pay; he was able to develop the assertiveness skills to be able to do so. Another participant took up employment; while another felt empowered within his family to ask for his own time and space 'to do his own thing...'. Other outcomes included one participant staying out of hospital for a sustained period and another ending his persistent suicide attempts, although he is still a heroin user.

Key lessons

- Shared ownership of programmes needs to be established between service providers and referral agencies
- There is a need for continuous engagement with hard-to-reach young men leading up to and during the programme (e.g. drop-in sessions and Community Engagement Posts – there is now a joint community engagement officer post in Newham)
- In developing programmes for young men who have a high risk of hospitalisation and contact with the police and who have chaotic and isolated lifestyles, the programme needs to flexible enough to respond to the needs and mood of the clients and the staff must be prepared to be proactive and possess strong motivational skills

- Future programmes for young men who have difficulty recognising and discussing their emotional difficulties need to be designed in consultation with the young men concerned, and to be free of the language and features of institutional mental health services
- Practitioners should not forget that young people with mental health difficulties share the same interests as those young people without known mental health difficulties

Key questions

1. Do you know the ethnic and cultural composition of your client communities?

2. Is there an understanding of the key mental health needs of your client communities?

3. How will/do you consult with specific client groups to ensure service provision is relevant to their needs?

4. What is your knowledge of youth culture and youth services in your locality?

5. How can local youth services assist you in developing services/programmes that appeal to young people?

ASIAN COMMUNITIES

The provision of mental health services to people from Asian communities has been of growing concern within Asian communities, as well as amongst some mental health professionals.

As with the indigenous population, a wide range of mental health problems exist. These include depression, anxiety, eating disorders and various psychotic disorders (Chakraborty and McKenzie 2002; Reid-Galloway 2003). Within Asian communities, distress is particularly high amongst women and often linked to social isolation, domestic violence and abuse, immigration issues and racism (Chantler *et al.* 2001). Evidence from Mind (Reid-Galloway 2003) also points to underpinning issues that have a bearing on how Asian mental health service users experience services. These include a lack of access to interpreters, misdiagnosis of presenting complaints and a lack of knowledge and therefore little awareness about how to effectively incorporate aspects of culture into service provision.

However, Chantler *et al.* (2001) have cautioned against service providers viewing mental health problems of people in Asian communities solely in terms of a failing of the community. They argue instead for solutions to be sought 'in the contexts and services whose responsibility it is to support them' (p.32). For good practice example, see Box 14.2.

Box 14.2 *Vishvas Counselling and Resource Centre*

This newly launched resource, under the auspices of the Confederation of Indian Organisations (UK), focuses on the mental health needs of the South Asian community. The South Asian Counselling and Resource Centre is a nationwide initiative focusing on two main areas – counselling and the development of a mental health resource centre.

The project offers culturally sensitive counselling in different Asian languages to men and women across the five London boroughs of Southwark, Lambeth, Hillingdon, Wandsworth and Barnet. The objective is to encourage clients to reach the best solution to their problems by adopting a sympathetic and non-judgemental approach.

The South Asian Counsellors' Database is being developed to facilitate networking and sharing of information. The project holds regular meetings of the Asian Mental Health Forum, which serves as a platform to discuss theoretical, ethical and practical issues experienced by those working in the field of cross-cultural mental health.

The Confederation of Indian Organisations is a national body which works to ensure the development and recognition of the South Asian voluntary and community sectors.

REFUGEE AND ASYLUM-SEEKER COMMUNITIES

Currently there are some 20 million people who are classed as refugees under the 1951 Convention (UNHCR 2003). Asylum seekers can obtain status as refugees in Britain if they meet the 1951 UN Convention's definition of a refugee. Article 1 of the convention states that they must have a 'well-founded fear of persecution on the grounds of race, religion, nationality, membership of a particular social group or political opinion' (UNHCR 2003).

In 2000, applications for asylum to the UK, excluding dependants, amounted to 80,315 (UNHCR 2003).

According to the British Medical Association, the health status of asylum seekers on arrival suggests that one in six refugees (17%) has a physical health problem severe enough to affect their life, and two thirds have experienced significant anxiety or depression (BMA 2002). Refugees and asylum seekers in London are estimated to number between 350,000 and 420,000, or about one in 20 of the city's resident population (GLA 2001).

The GLA outlines the health problems which may affect refugees and asylum seekers as involving a range of physical problems associated with torture and abuse. In addition, the GLA report also identifies that people in this client group can also suffer a range of mental and emotional problems.

CASE STUDY 14.2

Martha, a service user from the Democratic Republic of Congo, has been registered with a GP for some weeks. The health worker for asylum seekers had notification that she had moved into the area and arranged to visit with an interpreter to assess the situation. Martha had been sleeping badly, had nightmares, poor concentration and memory, suffered flashbacks (vivid intrusive memories of traumatic events) and felt permanently anxious.

She disclosed that she had witnessed violence and seen atrocities involving family members. This resulted in the enforced chronic separation of her family and the death of her child.

Although Martha had been registered with her GP for some weeks, no one had picked up on her physical and mental problems or known anything of her history. The health worker had the time and interpreter to explain how the NHS works with regard to appointments for GPs and mental health appointments and who and what the relevant disciplines actually address. The Liaison Psychiatry Service was explained, as was a referral to the Medical Foundation for the Care of Victims of Torture.

(Wandsworth Primary Care Trust Team for Homeless
Refugees and Asylum Seekers)

Questions for discussion

1. Are patients given the chance to explain their current medical problems with the aid of a professional interpreter?

2. Is sufficient time allowed for appointments?

3. Have refugee and asylum-seeking patients got access to mental health and appropriate counselling services?

4. Does the organisation have a dedicated worker for refugees and asylum seekers, and have the professionals looked at the information advocating personal health records to ensure 'joined-up' care for these patients?

Thompson (2001) notes that refugees suffer an incidence of mental illness several times greater than that of the general population. Atakan (2002) outlined the most frequently seen mental health problems amongst refugees as depression, anxiety, phobias and post-traumatic stress syndrome. Related issues of language difficulties, social and economic isolation, loneliness and lack of awareness about health systems in the UK can exacerbate their difficulties. Asylum seekers are often cut off by language and culture and, since the government's dispersal programme to spread refugees throughout the country, they may also be cut off from the more established refugee communities (Thompson 2001).

For a good practice example, see Box 14.3.

Box 14.3 Department of Health Asylum Team

At a national level the Department of Health has set up an Asylum Team to explore areas of good practice and to coordinate asylum-seeker health issues. For example, hand-held records for refugees and asylum seekers are being piloted and it is hoped that, with training, staff will be able to use them appropriately to improve the care pathway, and facilitate better communication between medical services, other disciplines and the client. Other areas have also been using their own locally devised hand-held records and are linking into this group.

These records, when used properly, have proven effective, e.g. one Somali-speaking service user with a child with diabetes and epilepsy was able to access appropriate services almost immediately following dispersal from London as she carried all the relevant information and contact details with her in her hand-held records.

(Wandsworth Primary Care Trust Team for Homeless Refugees and Asylum Seekers)

STRATEGIES FOR CHANGE

A number of initiatives have been proffered in recent years to address these issues by developing a cohesive framework for mental health. They include the following.

The National Service Framework for Mental Health (NSFMH)

The NSFMH (DH 1999) is an important driver and was a key step in actively signalling that health services must ensure that the needs of people from BME communities are incorporated in the planning processes for mental health care. The framework emphasised the need for diverse communities to be consulted about the ongoing effectiveness and suitability of services.

The National Health Service Plan

The NHS Plan (DH 2000) is underpinned by ten core principles that are aimed at ensuring that people who use mental health services are at the centre of determining how services are delivered. *The NHS Plan* contains an explicit recognition of the diversity that exists within Britain.

Black mental health strategy

The recently published strategy on black mental health (NIMHE 2003) again underscores the government's commitment to race equality and outlines the underpinning roles of the NSFMH and *The NHS Plan* in ensuring that its modernisation programme within mental health is delivered.

Social exclusion and mental health

The government has also recently committed itself to tackling mental health inequities through the work of the Social Exclusion Unit (SEU). The Office of the Deputy Prime Minister announced major areas of work to address mental health and social exclusion. A key strand of this work will be to explore the risk factors that influence the development of mental health problems; these include 'being a member of a minority group' (SEU 2003).

All of these initiatives are expected to be integral to the performance management of the NHS through the priorities and planning framework (DH 2002a). This sets out what is expected of local NHS organisations over the next three years.

Race equality schemes

Another important development in promoting more appropriate service delivery to BME communities is the enactment of the Race Relations (Amendment) Act (RR(A) Act) 2000. It places a general duty on all public authorities to:

- eliminate unlawful discrimination
- promote equality of opportunity
- promote good relations between people of different groups.

Organisations operating within the spirit and intent of the RR(A) Act can do much to promote a better quality of mental health services for people from BME communities. This offers scope for involving, acknowledging and, importantly, resourcing the independent black voluntary sector to develop services as part of mainstream provision; services which meet real need and avoid stigma and stereotyping.

REALITIES VERSUS STRATEGIES

The impetus to generate change is clear. Achieving real progress, however, is slow and intermittent and indications are that finding and funding ways to fundamentally address service changes continue to elude policymakers and service providers.

Keating *et al.* (2002) point to key impediments to change which include fears on the part of service users about the willingness of statutory service providers to deliver services which meet their needs and their views that there is too much reliance on stereotypical assumptions and there are also fears and frustration amongst professionals about feeling unable to speak openly and honestly about issues of race and culture.

Mental health reform

The impending reform of the Mental Health Act 1983 is a major cause of concern amongst a range of mental health service users, but particularly for people from BME communities. The reform, as set out in the *Mental Health Bill: Consultation Document* (DH 2002b), is based on a need to have a new legal framework that covers the compulsory treatment of people who are suffering from mental disorders, including mentally disordered offenders.

There is widespread agreement that such provisions will impact disproportionately negatively on people from BME communities. In its response to the consultation on the draft bill a coalition of black mental health organisations and individuals (Afiya Trust 2002) outlined the concerns of people in BME communities about the proposed legislation. It was noted that the proposals in the draft bill would:

- have little impact on reducing the already high numbers of people from BME backgrounds already in the mental health system
- not change the means by which people from BME backgrounds enter the mental health system or improve the care they receive within it
- do little to lessen the stigma of mental illness
- strengthen the belief that mental illness is synonymous with criminality
- infringe on individual human rights.

(Afiya Trust 2002, p.9)

GOOD PRACTICE AND INNOVATION
Understanding the black voluntary sector

There is concerted and consistent work within BME communities to challenge and change existing policy and practice. Much of it is led and championed in the independent black voluntary sector, which many would argue functions as a lifeline for BME service users. Keating (2002) identifies a number of characteristics of black-led initiatives. These are that they are most often client-centred/led, regarded as providing culturally appropriate services and, crucially, are mainly under-resourced.

It is within the independent black voluntary sector where much occurs that is positive, innovative and culturally relevant to meeting the needs of BME service users. Black-led initiatives make critical observations about psychiatry and offer a perspective that involves an understanding of the political reality of black people's experiences and the hardships they endure (Keating 2002; NHS Executive/ Mental Health Task Force 1994).

Keating (2002) identifies three main models that typify the service provision provided by the black voluntary sector as being:

1.   ethno-specific agencies

2.   multicultural agencies

3.   multi-agency partnerships between black communities and the statutory sector.

THE ETHNO-SPECIFIC AGENCY

These offer services to a specific minority ethnic community and aims to provide a culturally appropriate service through its practice and staffing arrangements (Christie and Smith 1997; Keating 2002). This model of provision is underpinned by a philosophy that argues that mainstream society is racist and therefore black service users need a safe space to reclaim their culture and build a network that reflects their cultural traditions.

MULTICULTURAL AGENCIES

These agencies are run by people from different ethnic and cultural backgrounds for a range of ethnic and cultural traditions (Keating 2002). They are underpinned by notions of pluralism and the premise that Britain is multi-ethnic and services should be configured to reflect this.

Partnership, pluralism and pragmatism

It is possible to argue, however, that most black voluntary sector agencies are increasingly a hybrid which encompass the first two models identified by Keating, and are at the forefront of developing a new strand of multi-agency partnerships. These have as their basis *culturally determined* service provision within a mainstream context.

The organisations at the vanguard of this change have developed a pragmatism, born out of a history of underfunding and short-term funding, which has left a littered playing field with regard to development within the small and independent black voluntary sector. Many recognise that, in order to create real change, it is important to have clarity of focus, a better-than-working knowledge of how the system operates and a determination to succeed. Their defining characteristics are:

- an insistence on developing mental health services which have cultural integrity within the context of specific client groups/communities
- an unwillingness to operate on the fringes
- a healthy scepticism with regard to unsupported statements of good intention
- pragmatism in seeking solutions to develop within a mainstream context.

In addition to those already mentioned there are a number of others that are worth highlighting.

PATTIGIFT

This is a new service being developed in Birmingham which, again, is focused specifically on the mental health needs of people from African Caribbean communities. Pattigift is being set up as an alternative to hospital admission. The aim is to provide an acute psychiatric service, which will include assessment, treatment and care. In addition it aims to provide an extended seven-day-a-week day service of health promotion work with carers and African-centred therapy and care courses (Pattigift 2002).

THE AFIYA TRUST

This is a multifocused organisation that works to promote equity in health. A key focus is on mental health. Currently plans are underway to develop a national BME mental health network and to develop a training model that enables lay people from BME communities to access training for employment in the NHS to work specifically with black and minority ethnic clients.

MAAN, THE SOMALI MENTAL HEALTH PROJECT

This Sheffield-based project was set up in 1992 on a voluntary basis to facilitate access to mental health services. It has established community-based facilities in a linguistically and culturally sensitive environment and is now supported by statutory health services (Seebohm, Secker and Grove 2003).

SOCIAL ACTION FOR HEALTH

This London-based organisation utilises community development and regeneration approaches to encourage community participation and involvement. A specific area of focus is refugee and asylum-seeker communities in East London. Work has included training for service users to become more confident in communicating in formal environments and information projects to enable better and accessible information in hospital wards (Social Action for Health 2002).

CONCLUSION

The impetus for change and improvement for mental health service delivery to BME communities can be seen. Many people who use mental health services, however, would argue that what is less tangible is change in hospital wards, day centres, residential homes and engagement with community mental health teams; in essence, at the coal face.

There is scope for substantial and sustainable change. It will require a recognition by mental health professionals of the strengths that service users and their families can bring in reshaping service delivery, partnership working involving agencies, community groups and mental health professionals and, most importantly, agreement by service providers and service users on clear and mutually agreed goals and outcomes about what constitutes improved care and treatment.

REFERENCES

Afiya Trust (2002) *A Collective BME Response to the Draft Mental Health Bill*. London: The Afiya Trust.

Atakan, Z. (2002) *The Most Commonly Experienced Psychological, Physical and Social Problems of Refugees*. Presentation to Borderline Conference, June.

BMA (British Medical Association) (2002) *Asylum Seekers: Meeting their Healthcare Needs*. www.bma.org.uk

Chakraborty, A. and McKenzie, K. (2002) 'Does racial discrimination cause mental illness?' *British Journal of Psychiatry 180*, 475–7.

Chantler, K., Burman, E., Batsleer, J. and Bashir, C. (2001) *Attempted Suicide and Self-Harm: South Asian Women Project Report*. Manchester: Manchester Metropolitan University.

Christie, Y. and Smith, H. (1997) 'Mental health and its impact on Britain's black communities.' *The Mental Health Review 2*, 1, 5–14.

Confederation of Indian Organisations (November 2002) South Asian Counselling and Resource Centre. Newsletter of the Confederation of Indian Organisations. Issue 1, September 2003.

DH (Department of Health) (1999) *National Service Framework for Mental Health: Modern Standards and Service Models*. London: DH.

DH (Department of Health) (2000) *The NHS Plan: A Plan for Investment, a Plan for Reform*. London: The Stationery Office.

DH (Department of Health) (2002a) *The NHS Plan: Improvement, Expansion and Reform: The Next Three Years. Priorities and Planning Framework 2003–2006*. London: DH.

DH (Department of Health) (2002b) *Mental Health Bill: Consultation Document*. London: The Stationery Office.

Department of Health and Home Office (1992) *Review of Health and Social Services for Mentally Disordered Offenders and Others Requiring Similar Services*. London: HMSO.

Footprints (UK) (2003) *Tell it Like it Is: Giving Voice to African and Caribbean Mental Health Service Users*. London: Footprints (UK).

GLA (Greater London Authority) (2001) *Refugees and Asylum Seekers in London: A GLA Perspective*. London: GLA Policy Support Unit.

Greater London Authority/London Health Observatory (2002) *Health in London: 2002 Review of the London Health Strategy High Level Indicators*. London: London Health Commission.

Hunt, I., Robinson, J., Bickley, H., Meehan, J., Parsons, R., McCann, K., Flynn, S., Burns, J., Shaw, J., Kapur, N. and Appleby, L. (2003) 'Suicides in ethnic minorities within 12 months of contact with mental health services.' *British Journal of Psychiatry 183*, 155–60.

Keating, F. (2002) 'Black-led initiatives in mental health: An overview.' *Research Policy and Planning 20*, 2, 9–19.

Keating, F., Robertson, D. and Kotecha, N. (2003) *Ethnic Diversity and Mental Health in London: Recent Developments*. London: King's Fund.

Keating, F., Robertson, D., McCullough, A. and Francis, E. (2002) *Breaking the Circles of Fear: A Review of the Relationship between Mental Health Services and African and Caribbean Communities*. London: Sainsbury Centre for Mental Health.

McKenzie, K. (2002) 'A community-embedded psychiatry.' *OpenMind 114*, March/April, 14–15.

Mind (2002) *Mind Briefing on Proposed Mental Health Act Reforms*. London: MIND.

NHS Executive/Mental Health Task Force (1994) *Black Mental Health: A Dialogue for Change*. London: DH.

NIMHE (National Institute for Mental Health England) (2003) *Inside/Outside: Improving Mental Health Services for Black and Minority Ethnic Communities in England*. London: DH.

Office of the Deputy Prime Minister (2003) Press Release 032. March.

Pattigift (2002) *Pilot of the Pattigift Mental Health Centre for African Caribbean People: Operational Policy*. Birmingham: Pattigift.

Reid-Galloway, C. (2003) *The Mental Health of the South Asian Community in Britain: Mind Factsheet*. London: MIND.

Seebohm, P., Secker, J. and Grove, B. (2003) *Hidden Skills, Hidden Talents*. London: Institute for Applied Health and Social Policy, King's College London.

Social Action for Health (2002) *Community Development and Regeneration: Reflection, Theory and Practical Action.* London: SAH. *www.safh.org.uk*

SEU (Social Exclusion Unit) (2003) *Mental Health and Social Exclusion: Consultation Document.* London: Office of the Deputy Prime Minister.

Thompson, A. (2001) 'Refugees and mental health.' *Diverse Minds Magazine 9*, 6–8.

UNHCR (United Nations High Commission for Refugees) (2003) *Basic Facts. www.unhcr.ch/cgi-bin/texis/vtx/basics,* visited 15 May 2003.

STATUTES

Mental Health Act (1983)

Race Relations (Amendment) Act (2000). Chapter 34

CHAPTER 15

GENDER AND MENTAL HEALTH

BARBARA HATFIELD

INTRODUCTION

The differences between women and men in terms of the occurrence of mental health problems are well documented in a literature that spans some three decades. More research attention has been devoted to mental health problems amongst women than men, with some exceptions. The evidence points to key issues in the social context of women's lives and their experiences of broader inequalities that contribute to increased mental health vulnerability, particularly in relation to the common mental health problems of anxiety and depression. However, it is also important to acknowledge that specific areas of mental health vulnerability are more common in men. Men are, for example, more likely than women to experience drug or alcohol dependence and more likely to commit suicide (Mental Health Foundation 2003a and 2003b). The relationship between mental health vulnerability and social disadvantage appears to be mediated by gender.

The more severe mental disorders (psychoses) occur in smaller proportions of the population, and there is less difference between women and men in the estimated rate at which they occur (Office for National Statistics 2001). However, the experience of living with serious mental health problems over the long term can pose different issues for women and men.

A further dimension affecting the impact of the social context and social expectations upon women and men is that of age, or life stage. For example, in young adulthood, issues of independence from family of origin, the formation of new intimate pair-bonds, reproduction and entry to the labour market might be salient in different ways for women and men. At later life stages, issues of becoming a long-term provider or carer, developing longer-term 'social capital' or becoming economically secure might predominate. Mental ill health can critically affect the individual's performance in any of these domains, and the implications may be very different for women and men. For women, the parenting role is viewed as central, and psychosocial issues to do with relationships and parenting can reverberate throughout the life span and have implications for the mental health of both mothers and children.

This chapter will examine some key issues in mental health, for which considerations of gender and life stage are an important part of the context of intervention.

Good Practice Point

Mental health workers need to appreciate the significance of the social context for mental health, including both the socio-economic context and how this affects women and men at different life stages

---

THE ISSUE OF PAID WORK

The present government's social inclusion agenda has a strong focus upon employment and leisure participation (Department of Health 1998; Social Exclusion Unit 2003). People with mental health problems have low rates of employment, but there is evidence that even those with severe and long-term conditions can benefit from participation in the workforce (Evans and Repper 2000). Paid work can have both economic and social benefits for the individual, as well as providing a structure of daily activity. However, it is important to acknowledge that work can also be a significant source of stress.

The landmark study of depression in poorer women (Brown and Harris 1978) identified a causal model within which paid employment emerged as one 'protective factor' in the development of depression. In terms of family composition, there have been significant social changes since the 1970s with a substantial increase in the number of poor female-headed households. When parents break up, it is overwhelmingly mothers who retain care of their children. In terms of their ability to enter the employment market, women with young children are placed at a disadvantage. The availability, cost and quality of child care are key considerations. The physical and emotional stress of managing the work and parenting roles potentially affect all working mothers, but particularly those who are lone parents.

More recent studies have raised important questions about the mental health impact of work for mothers of young children. In one study, employment was found to be beneficial for mothers of older children but not mothers of pre-school children (Haw 1995). Elliott and Huppert (1991) examined the relationship between employment and psychological well-being of British married women, and found that those with a youngest child aged less than five years had the poorest mental health. Employment for lone mothers is associated with poorer mental health, particularly for those who work full time (Baker and North 1999; Brown and Moran 1997;). It is not difficult to imagine the restricted lives of lone mothers, working and also responsible for housework and child care, particularly for mothers who work in low-paid roles. Whilst men may also experience unemployment or low pay, the sole responsibility for the care of children is less likely to fall upon their shoulders.

Although women now have far greater access to the workplace than in previous generations, traditional divisions of work in the home have been shown to persist. In couple households where both partners work, the burden of domestic tasks tends to fall unequally on women; this inequality in itself has been shown to have an impact upon women's mental health (Bird 1999).

Good Practice Point

Mental health practitioners need to be aware that employment can have a negative impact on mental health, particularly for lone mothers

---

POVERTY

Closely linked to the issue of paid work is the experience of living in poverty. Studies over the last 50 years have consistently shown the close association of mental ill health and poverty (Sheppard 2002). In some cases this will be due to illness that prevents individuals from entering or retaining employment; in other cases, poverty is part of the matrix of disadvantage that may contribute to the development of mental health problems. For women, particular vulnerability to poverty is associated with lone parent status, and with later life.

Female-headed households with young children have become a significant area of policy concern in the UK and the USA. In the USA, the syndrome of mothers being abandoned with the sole care of children and living on welfare benefits has been dubbed 'the feminisation of poverty'. Increasing rates of divorce, separation and single parenthood have been shown to contribute to the growth in female-headed households in the USA, whilst inadequate levels of benefits and child support cement these households in poverty (Rodgers 1990). Similar trends are evident in the UK. Poverty can result in women and children obtaining less than optimal basic resources such as food and housing; social networks may also consist of stressed households of others living in poverty; at times families may have to share accommodation; and poverty also leads to a high level of interaction with and dependency upon bureaucratic systems to obtain resources from the State (Belle 1990; Buck 1997).

In the USA, there has been a political backlash against the phenomenon of female-headed households who are dependent on state welfare benefits for longer-term survival, and the long-term right to benefits has been ended (Orloff 2001). Similar trends are discernible in Australian policy towards single mothers (Hancock 2001), with lone parenthood being re-cast as a lifestyle choice for which the individual must pay. Whilst social policy in the UK is at present less punitive towards lone parents, attempts have been made through the Child Support Agency and the Working Parents' Tax Credit to discourage dependency on benefits where possible. Both of these developments have led to unprecedented administrative problems, leaving lone parents unable to exercise their entitlement for protracted periods of time. This in itself testifies to the difficulty of attempting to legislate for family complexity.

The mental health consequences of poverty and lone parenthood have been well documented and forcing lone mothers back to work is likely to compound their mental health vulnerability (Baker and North 1999; Brown and Moran 1997;). The quality of their parenting is likely to be impaired at crucial periods of their children's development, leading to further mental health consequences for future generations.

Good Practice Points

- Mental health workers need to be aware of the impact of poverty, and to be prepared to work in ways that maximise practical and economic resources of women
- Mental health practitioners need to have knowledge about the benefits system, and about resources in kind that may be available for mothers with young children

---

Leanne's situation in Case Study 15.1 is in many ways typical of that facing young mothers living in poverty.

CHILDHOOD ADVERSITY AND ADULT MENTAL HEALTH

There is a wide literature on the impact of child abuse on adult mental health, and a somewhat more limited literature on the impact of more general social disadvantage in childhood. The Newcastle '1000 families' study (Sadowski *et al.* 1999) identified that multiple family disadvantages in childhood substantially increased the risk of depression in adulthood.

CASE STUDY 15.1 LEANNE

Leanne is 28 years old and lives in a council house in a large northern city. Leanne left school without formal qualifications and subsequently worked in a series of jobs in fast-food outlets. She enjoyed work, and hopes to return to work in the future. Leanne has two sisters older than herself and a younger brother who is serving a term of imprisonment for serious drugs offences. Her father died some years ago, but had deserted the family when Leanne was 13 years old. Her mother drinks heavily and is hostile to Leanne's four children, but visits and attempts to borrow money from Leanne and her sisters. Leanne has some contact with her sisters, both of whom are lone parents and live locally. She also visits her brother in prison.

Leanne has four children aged 11, 9, 4 and 2 years, and is a lone parent. She is dependent upon benefits for income. She was briefly married to the father of her third child, and currently the father of her youngest child visits occasionally to see his son. Two of her children suffer from chronic asthma, and the nine-year-old has epilepsy with frequent seizures.

Leanne has many casual friendships as she has lived in the area all of her life. However, she has no close friends, and admits that she finds it difficult to make friends, saying that she 'never knows what to say'. Leanne has been diagnosed with depression by her GP who prescribes anti-depressants, and referred Leanne for a course of cognitive therapy, but she only attended once. A social worker from the local authority children's services is involved with the family following concerns raised by the local primary school that Leanne seemed uninterested in the children, and the children seemed apathetic and neglected. A nursery place has been provided for the two younger children on a full-time basis, and a school holiday play-scheme has been financed for the older children. However, Leanne dropped out of a mother's group after one attendance.

Leanne is experiencing

- Poverty
- Poor family support
- Childhood adversity
- High level of demand to care for others
- Poor educational achievements
- Minimum standard housing and neighbourhood
- Poor social networks and support
- High level of agency intervention
- Chronic stress of sickness in children

Questions for discussion

1. What sort of individual help might benefit Leanne?
2. How could her community support her?
3. What specific help might benefit the children?
4. What resources are available for women like Leanne in your area?

For women, depression was particularly linked to the quality of parenting in early life. A further study suggests that loss of a parent in childhood, either by divorce or death, has a stronger impact on the development of depression in women than in men (McLeod 1991).

Women are more likely than men to report a history of sexual abuse in childhood. One review of existing literature on childhood sexual abuse identified that likely effects in adulthood include anxiety, fear and suicidal ideas, as well as a greater likelihood of re-victimisation (Beitchman *et al.* 1992). A further study (of women) confirms an increased likelihood of social, interpersonal and sexual difficulties in adult life (Mullen *et al.* 1994) and increased mental health vulnerability following childhood sexual abuse (Mullen *et al.* 1993).

Good Practice Point

Mental health practitioners need to be aware of the emotional needs of women who have been victims of childhood abuse.

PARENTING

The birth of a child confers some additional mental health vulnerability on women, with a proportion becoming acutely depressed, and a few developing psychotic symptoms. Some women will need brief intensive psychiatric help in this period. In the longer term it is difficult to disentangle the independent effects of parenting on mental health, taking account of other disadvantages such as poverty and lone parenthood. In general the evidence points in the direction of a greater vulnerability to depression in women with children under the age of five (Brown and Harris 1978; Elliott and Huppert 1991).

Mental health practitioners seeking to help women with young children need to be aware of both the mother's mental health needs and the needs of the children at their particular stage of development. In general, poorer mental health will affect the parenting capacity of mothers (Gopfert, Webster and Seeman 1996). A depressed mother may find it hard to respond warmly to her children, and to give young children age-appropriate attention. Studies of neglected children have identified that, commonly, mothers who neglect are depressed (Bifulco *et al.* 2002). Within the broad framework of the Children Act 1989, children's needs are deemed to be 'paramount', and the support of parents is crucial to this. The guidance for assessing children in need points out that attachment problems in children can follow from parental deprivation, personality difficulties or mental illness (Department of Health, Department of Education and Employment and the Home Office 2000). Community initiatives to help young children and their families can bring benefits to both stressed mothers and young children. The current 'Sure Start' projects have been set up in socially deprived areas to offer this type of support to both mothers and their children (Department for Education and Skills and Department for Work and Pensions 1995–2003).

Women with severe mental illnesses are more likely than men with similar illnesses to marry and have children, possibly because schizophrenia in particular has an earlier onset in men, and women have children before the onset of the illness. One study identified that 63 per cent of severely mentally ill women in contact with community mental health services were mothers, with a majority having had more than one child (Howard, Kumar and Thornicroft 2001). A woman with persistent severe mental illness is likely to experience serious difficulties in parenting young children (Gopfert *et al.* 1996) without substantial support, and there may be a risk of losing her children to alternative carers. Practitioners will be aware of severely mentally ill women who have lost all contact with their children over years of separation. In one UK study, African women and women who were recent immigrants had a higher likelihood of their children entering State care (Howard *et al.* 2001), highlighting the support needs of these groups.

Good Practice Points

- Mental health practitioners need to be aware of the Children Act principles and guidance, and should recognise the importance of community initiatives as well as mental health interventions in supporting mothers with young children
- Where children are involved, mental health practitioners may need to work closely with child care professionals in supporting the family as a unit
- Mental health practitioners need to recognise the impact of separation from children upon severely mentally ill women. Women may need support in maintaining appropriate contact with their children, or in keeping significant reminders of them

GENDER AND ETHNICITY

The over-representation of African and Caribbean people in coerced mental health services has been well documented, and is particularly evident for young males (Wall *et al.* 1999). Involvement of the police and courts in hospital admissions, and admission to medium and high secure facilities, is more common (Sainsbury Centre for Mental Health 2002). Mental health practitioners need to be aware of the need to engage young men with mental health problems from minority communities before a crisis begins to arise, and to offer services that are attractive and culturally appropriate. At present, the evidence is that black people do not believe that the mental health system can offer positive help and so delay seeking help (Sainsbury Centre for Mental Health 2002).

A further issue that has been identified concerns the over-representation of younger Asian women in rates of suicide (DH 1994; Wilson 2001). Women within Asian communities may have needs for services that take account of their cultural and religious beliefs (Hatfield *et al.* 1996; Wilson 2001) and that are offered by women practitioners. Specific projects to address psychological distress and its causes amongst Asian women may be vital as an addition to mainstream mental health services (for example, Bhardwaj 2001).

Women in black and ethnic minority families, like their white counterparts, are predominantly responsible for caring for children or vulnerable family members. One aspect of race and gender stereotyping is for professionals to perceive black and ethnic minority women as more likely to choose to care for others in the family and to be seen as 'natural carers'. The reality is that the stress and burden of care may be experienced within a social context that includes racism and the social isolation of minority groups (Atkin and Rollings 1996). Exploring and using wider community facilities may be problematic if women are not confident of transport or of appropriate support for their specific needs within mainstream facilities and services.

YOUNG MEN AND MENTAL HEALTH

The life stage of young adulthood (broadly speaking under forty years of age) is one that holds specific mental health vulnerabilities for men. The evidence is that a first diagnosis of schizophrenia in men is generally made at a significantly younger age than for women, and is often characterised by more severe and disabling symptoms and poorer outcomes than women experience (Lewis 1992). This can seriously impair young men in terms of their progression to the fulfilment of important social roles in adult life, particularly those of work and close pair-relationships. Mental health practitioners will be familiar with young men on their caseloads who are debilitated by mental illness, to the extent that they are restricted in both of these important social domains. Whilst appropriate medication and early psychological interventions can both be crucial in treating the symptoms of schizophrenia, mental health practitioners should also be active in identifying any employment opportunities and day activities that reduce social isolation, and in providing family support. This 'broad spectrum' approach to intervention is endorsed within the *National Service Framework for Mental Health* (DH 1999).

Recent concerns have also surrounded the increasing rate of suicide in younger men (DH 2001). The trend is mirrored throughout the developed world (Hawton 1998). It has been suggested that social factors contribute to this trend, specifically unemployment and the increasing casualisation of the workforce leading to longer-term occupational uncertainty, the widespread increase in the illicit use of drugs, and family and relationship breakdown that leaves young males isolated (Hawton 1998). Women may seek help more readily, be more willing to reveal feelings of hopelessness and despair, and be more socially embedded in relationships than men (Murphy 1998).

Studies of individuals assessed and detained under the Mental Health Act 1983 indicate an over-representation of young men with psychosis (Hatfield and Antcliff 2001; Hatfield, Huxley and Mohamad 1997). More of the young men live alone or with parents than do women in a similar situation (Hatfield and Mohamad 1995). Since 1991 there have been more men than women in residential mental health facilities in Britain for the first time this century (Prior and Hayes 2001).

The picture is one of a sub-group of young men with mental health problems who have limited support from the wider social structure. A group of studies of patients presenting as psychiatric emergencies identifies a particular group of young men, referred directly from the community, likely to be unemployed, self-harming and possibly using drugs. Most were not in contact with mental health services and were not psychotically ill. Many failed to attend follow-up appointments. There is a suggestion that mental health services as currently offered are failing to reach a group of young men with serious psychosocial difficulties (Hatfield, Spurrell and Perry 2000; Perry, Hatfield and Spurrell 2002; Spurrell, Hatfield and Perry 2003).

Good Practice Point

Mental health practitioners need to recognise the scale of exclusion of many young men with mental health problems from mainstream social support and opportunities

---

Jude's difficulties, described in Case Study 15.2, mirror those of many young men referred to mental health services.

CASE STUDY 15.2 JUDE

Jude is 24 years of age and lives temporarily in a supported hostel provided by a mental health charity, in a small market town in a predominantly rural region of the East Midlands. Jude's parents and sister (who is 19 years old) live in a town about 25 miles away. They own a small catering business and own their own home.

Jude went to university when he was 18 to follow a computing course, but dropped out after one year, saying he had lost interest. He had a few temporary jobs, but longer and longer periods without employment. This led to serious conflict with his father, who saw Jude as 'lazy'. Jude remembers his father attacking him once with a piece of piping during an argument. Eventually Jude left home, and went to live in a 'squat' with a number of young homeless young people who used cannabis on a regular basis. He broke off all contact with his family; even when his mother traced and contacted him, he refused further contact.

Jude was detained by the police following an incident where he attacked another man in a pub. A psychiatric assessment was arranged, and Jude was admitted to hospital under the Mental Health Act 1983 (Section 2), with florid symptoms of schizophrenia. His father refused to visit, and Jude continued to refuse all contact with his family. On discharge Jude was still deluded, although his acute symptoms responded to some extent to medication which he takes regularly. He was placed in a hostel,

---

where staff have found he needs help with basic self-care and managing his benefits. Jude is on the periphery of social relationships in the hostel and spends a lot of time in his room alone listening to rock music. He takes few initiatives and seems uninterested in planning for the future. His mother and sister both telephone, and occasionally staff can persuade Jude to exchange a few words with them.

Jude is experiencing

- a severe mental illness, possibly associated with heavy cannabis use
- potential loss of all support from family
- separation from community of origin and no current community links
- lack of long-term residential stability
- lack of employment or day activity
- limited social networks or leisure activities
- survival dependent on high level of service involvement.

Questions for discussion

1. What should Jude's care plan contain?
2. How can hostel staff work in ways that address issues of gender and life stage in Jude's case?
3. What strategies would you use to engage Jude's family?

MENTAL HEALTH POLICY AND GENDER

The landscape of mental health policy has undergone important changes in the last two decades, as the longer-term impact of substantial psychiatric hospital bed reductions has become apparent. Within the stream of policy directives that have driven the development of community-based services, issues of race and culture have been prominent in terms of the development of appropriate services for diverse ethnic groups. In comparison, there have been relatively few references to issues of gender sensitivity, although longstanding concerns about the safety of hospital wards have been taken up (DH 2000b).

The NHS Plan (Department of Health 2000a) states that women-only day service places will be provided in every health authority from 2004. In 2002, the Women's Mental Health Strategy was published (DH 2002) providing a broad review of issues likely to face women with mental health problems. The document provides detailed guidance on the development of gender-sensitive mental health services and on organisational and workforce development. Specifically, it states that assessment and care planning for women should address:

- experience of violence or abuse
- parenting and caring responsibilities
- social and economic support
- physical health
- ethnicity and culture
- dual diagnosis with substance misuse
- risk assessment and management.

(DH 2002, p.40)

There are clear workforce implications of providing a gender-sensitive mental health service. The vulnerability in many women's lives arises from gendered experiences of stress and distress. Women need to be confident that mental health services reflect an awareness of women's specific issues and needs. Service features discussed in the document are:

- access to women-only services and facilities
- access to female professional help if that is the choice of the individual woman
- the importance of training in gender-sensitivity for all mental health practitioners.

It is also acknowledged that many of the issues affecting the lives of women mental health service users will also affect the lives of women staff; for example, domestic violence or the responsibility of caring for young children or other dependent relatives.

If women are to be able to choose a woman worker, the issue of the differential recruitment of women to some mental health posts is important, particularly in primary care, where many of the mental health needs of women are addressed.

Whilst the focus of the strategy document is women's mental health, the content of gender-awareness training for mental health workers needs to be 'broad spectrum', encompassing both the psychological and socio-economic domains of women's and men's lives. The training of front-line mental health practitioners should equip them for active intervention across the range of problems, including negotiating with statutory and voluntary welfare agencies and groups, understanding systems of resource allocation and recognising the needs of young children. Training should be provided by agencies and trainers with a clear social perspective, as well as those whose skills are based on psychological or therapeutic models.

CONCLUSION

Gender and life stage are important aspects of the wider context of social inequalities through which mental health problems are mediated. The examples in this chapter illustrate the ways in which particular issues impact differentially according to gender and life stage, and the challenges that are posed to mental health practitioners as a result.

REFERENCES

Atkin, K. and Rollings, J. (1996) 'Looking after their own? Family care-giving among Asian and Afro-Caribbean communities.' In W.I. Ahmad and K. Atkin (eds) *Race and Community Care*. Buckingham: Open University Press.

Baker, D. and North, K. (1999) 'Does employment improve the health of lone mothers?' *Social Science and Medicine 49*, 121–31.

Beitchman, J.H., Zucker, K.J., Hood, J.E., DaCosta, G.A., Akman, D. and Cassavia, E. (1992) 'A review of the long term effects of child sexual abuse.' *Child Abuse and Neglect 16*, 101–18.

Belle, D. (1990) 'Poverty and women's mental health.' *American Psychologist 45*, 3, 385–9.

Bhardwaj, A. (2001) 'Growing up young, Asian and female in Britain.' *Feminist Review 68*, 52–67.

Bifulco, A., Moran, P., Baines, R., Bunn, A. and Stanford, K. (2002) 'Exploring psychological abuse in childhood: Association with other abuse and adult clinical depression.' *Bulletin of the Menninger Clinic 66*, 3, 241–58.

Bird, C. (1999) 'Gender, household labour and psychological distress: The impact of the amount and division of housework.' *Journal of Health and Social Behaviour 40*, March, 32–45.

Brown, G. and Harris, T. (1978) *Social Origins of Depression: A Study of Psychiatric Disorder in Women*. London: Tavistock.

Brown, G. and Moran, P. (1997) 'Lone mothers, poverty and depression.' *Psychological Medicine 27*, 21–33.

Buck, M. (1997) 'The price of poverty: Mental health and gender'. *Critical Social Policy 17*, 79–97.

Department for Education and Skills and Department for Work and Pensions (1995–2003) *Sure Start*. Reports and Guidance. London: The Stationery Office.

DH (Department of Health) (1994) *Health of the Nation. Key Area Handbook: Mental Illness*. Second edition. London: HMSO.

DH (Department of Health) (1998) *Modernising Mental Health Services: Safe, Sound and Supportive*. London: The Stationery Office.

DH (Department of Health) (1999) *National Service Framework for Mental Health: Modern Standards and Service Models*. London: DH.

DH (Department of Health) (2000a) *The NHS Plan: A Plan for Investment, a Plan for Reform*. London: The Stationery Office.

DH (Department of Health) (2000b) *Safety, Privacy and Dignity in Mental Health Units.* London: DH.

DH (Department of Health) (2001) *Safety First: Five-Year Report of the National Confidential Inquiry into Suicide and Homicide by People with Mental Illness.* London: DH.

DH (Department of Health) (2002) *Women's Mental Health: Into the Mainstream. Strategic Development of Mental Health Care for Women.* London: DH Publications.

Department of Health, Department of Education and Employment and the Home Office (2000) *Framework for the Assessment of Children in Need and Their Families.* London: The Stationery Office.

Elliott, B. and Huppert, F. (1991) 'In sickness and in health: Associations between physical and mental well-being, employment and parental status in a British nationwide sample of married women.' *Psychological Medicine 21,* 515–24.

Evans, J. and Repper, J. (2000) 'Employment, social inclusion and mental health.' *Journal of Psychiatric and Mental Health Nursing 7,* 15–24.

Gopfert, M., Webster, J. and Seeman, M. (1996) *Parental Psychiatric Disorder: Distressed Parents and Their Families.* Cambridge: Cambridge University Press.

Hancock, L. (2001) 'The care crunch: Changing work, families and welfare in Australia.' *Critical Social Policy 21,* 1, 119–40.

Hatfield, B. and Antcliff, V. (2001) 'Detention under the Mental Health Act: Balancing rights risks, and needs for services.' *Journal of Social Welfare and Family Law 23,* 2, 135–53.

Hatfield, B. and Mohamad, H. (1995) 'Women, men and the Mental Health Act 1983.' *Research, Policy and Practice 12,* 3, 14–22.

Hatfield, B., Huxley, P. and Mohamad, H. (1997) 'Social factors and the compulsory detention of psychiatric patients in the UK: The role of the Approved Social Worker in the 1983 Mental Health Act.' *International Journal of Law and Psychiatry 20,* 3, 389–97.

Hatfield, B., Mohamad, H., Rahim, Z. and Tanweer, H. (1996) 'Mental health and the Asian communities: A local survey.' *British Journal of Social Work 26,* 315–36.

Hatfield, B., Spurrell, M. and Perry, A. (2000) 'Emergency referrals to an acute psychiatric service: Demographic, clinical and social characteristics and comparisons with those receiving continuing services.' *Journal of Mental Health 9,* 3, 305–17.

Haw, C. (1995) 'The family life cycle: A forgotten variable in the study of women's employment and well-being.' *Psychological Medicine 25,* 727–38.

Hawton, K. (1998) 'Why has suicide increased in young males?' *Crisis: Journal of Crisis Intervention and Suicide 19,* 3, 119–24.

Howard, L., Kumar, R. and Thornicroft, G. (2001) 'Psychosocial characteristics and needs of mothers with psychotic disorders.' *British Journal of Psychiatry 178,* 427–32.

Lewis, S. (1992) 'Sex and schizophrenia: Vive la difference.' *British Journal of Psychiatry 161,* 445–50.

McLeod, J. (1991) 'Childhood parental loss and adult depression.' *Journal of Health and Social Behaviour 32,* September, 205–20.

Mental Health Foundation (2003a) *Factsheet: Mental Health Problems.* London: Mental Health Foundation.

Mental Health Foundation (2003b) *Factsheet: Statistics on Mental Health.* London: Mental Health Foundation.

Mullen, P.E., Martin, J.L., Anderson, J.C., Romans, S.E. and Herbison, G.P. (1993) 'Childhood sexual abuse and mental health in adult life.' *British Journal of Psychiatry 163,* 721–32.

Mullen, P.E., Martin, J.L., Anderson, J.C., Romans, S.E. and Herbison, G.P. (1994) 'The effect of childhood sexual abuse on social, interpersonal and sexual function in adult life.' *British Journal of Psychiatry 165,* 35–47.

Murphy, G. (1998) 'Why women are less likely than men to commit suicide.' *Comprehensive Psychiatry 39,* 4, 165–75.

Office for National Statistics (2001) *Psychiatric Morbidity Among Adults Living in Private Households.* London: The Stationery Office.

Orloff, A. (2001) 'Explaining US welfare reform: Power, gender, race and the US policy legacy.' *Critical Social Policy 21,* 1, 96–118.

Perry, A., Hatfield, B. and Spurrell, M. (2002) 'Specialist service use following psychiatric emergency presentation: An 18 month follow-up study.' *Health and Social Care in the Community 10*, 6, 457–63.

Prior, P. and Hayes, B. (2001) 'Changing places: Men replace women in mental health beds in Britain.' *Social Policy and Administration 35*, 4, 397–410.

Rodgers, H. (1990) *Poor Women, Poor Families: The Economic Plight of America's Female-Headed Households.* New York: M.E. Sharpe Inc.

Sadowski, H., Ugarte, B., Kolvin, I., Kaplan, C. and Barnes, J. (1999) 'Early life family disadvantages and major depression in adulthood.' *British Journal of Psychiatry 174*, 112–20.

Sainsbury Centre for Mental Health (2002) *Breaking the Circles of Fear: A Review of the Relationship between Mental Health Services and African and Caribbean Communities.* London: Sainsbury Centre.

Sheppard, M. (2002) 'Mental health and social justice: Gender, race and psychological consequences of unfairness.' *British Journal of Social Work 32*, 779–97.

Social Exclusion Unit (2003) *Mental Health and Social Exclusion.* London: Office of the Deputy Prime Minister.

Spurrell, M., Hatfield, B. and Perry, A. (2003) 'Characteristics of patients presenting for emergency psychiatric assessment at an English hospital.' *Psychiatric Services 54*, 2, 240–5.

Wall, S., Churchill, R., Hotopf, M., Buchanan, A. and Wessely, S. (1999) *A Systematic Review of Research Relating to the Mental Health Act 1983.* London: Department of Health.

Wilson, M. (2001) 'Black women and mental health: Working toward inclusive mental health services.' *Feminist Review 68*, 34–51.

STATUTES

Mental Health Act (1983)
The Children Act (1989)

CHAPTER 16

SUBSTANCE MISUSE AND MENTAL HEALTH

MARK HOLLAND AND VALL MIDSON

INTRODUCTION

This chapter explores the familiar issues of problematic substance use within the context of mental illness. It examines the policy background (DH 2002) and recommended approaches, guidance and technologies (Barrowclough *et al.* 2001; Holland, Baguley and Davies 1999) that inform good practice. It provides a practical guide for carers, helpers and practitioners alike in meeting the needs of arguably our most challenging client group.

Case studies are used to explore issues of both practice and service provision. In this respect 'dual diagnosis', the presence of both mental health and substance use conditions, will be defined. Speculative models of cause and course will be examined and the growing interventions evidence base identified in order to illustrate the complexities facing service users and their carers and practitioners, many of whom work across the entire health and social care spectrum, and aid them in their efforts.

WHAT IS DUAL DIAGNOSIS AND WHY DOES IT OCCUR?
Definitions and aetiological models

Dual diagnosis is a broad term that, at best, promotes an understanding of two interwoven complex conditions (in this case mental illness and substance misuse) and, at worst, gives service users a vague yet stigmatising label. The term is expedient in conceptualising the phenomenon of substance misuse and mental health but requires considerable exploration if service users and services are to benefit. In addition, the array of interchangeable terms such as 'complex needs', 'comorbidity', 'concomitant substance misuse and mental illness', 'mentally ill chemical abusers', 'multiple needs' and so on can be misleading.

Many services and user organisations have sanctioned the following definition which whilst, broad and encompassing, essentially conveys the duality of these two conditions:

> A mental health problem and a substance misuse problem, both of which require some form of intervention, and may or may not have been medically diagnosed. (Alcohol Concern 1999, p.1)

A narrower definition applicable to this text might be:

> The combination of severe mental illness (usually psychotic) and problematic substance use.

In practice settings it is common to hear discussions concerning the *primacy* of conditions, i.e. what came first, or cause and effect (Mueser, Bennet and Kushner 1995; Rosenthal 1998). This can subsequently lead care along a one-way route where treatment is determined by what is judged to be the cause. For instance, a person with stimulant addiction and paranoid delusions may have their psychotic symptoms attributed to stimulants and therefore receive a focus upon stimulant use. In reality there are two problems here: first, it can be difficult to distinguish symptoms of stimulant use and psychosis, particularly within care environments, and, second, should a root cause be discovered both conditions are likely to be so well established that simultaneous treatment is in fact necessary.

There are four aetiological models speculating on the occurrence of dual diagnosis (Hambrecht and Hafner 2003):

1. Substance misuse is a precipitating, if not causal, factor for psychosis.

2. Substance misuse is a consequence of pre-existing severe mental illness.

3. A third common factor causes both disorders.

4. Comorbidity is nothing but an incidental association.

A similar group of models are described by one of the authors of this chapter (Holland 2002) which reflects expert opinion in favour of substance misuse as a secondary problem that both exacerbates existing mental illness and acts as a catalyst or trigger for the development of mental illness in people with a high degree of vulnerability. This remains speculation but is an area of considerable investigation and discussion; particularly since substance misuse and mental illness sequence onset studies are inconclusive (Duke, Pantelis and Barnes 1994; Rabinowitz *et al.* 1998).

Why do people misuse substances?

Table 16.1 lists the likely reasons why people with a mental illness *might* use substances and is formatted as an *aide mémoire* for practitioners when undertaking assessment and care planning.

The reports by people with a dual diagnosis as to why they use substances varies little from the general substance (mis)using population who report the need to ameliorate feelings of dysphoria (anxiety and variations in mood) and gain a sense of well-being. Many people with severe forms of mental illness also suffer from clinical levels of depression and anxiety. This, combined with a health policy of deinstitutionalisation, increased availability and lower price of street drugs, poor assertiveness skills and social isolation, probably conspires to produce the increased levels of substance misuse in psychiatric populations (Regier, Farmer and Rae 1990).

WHAT DOES IT MEAN TO EXPERIENCE COEXISTING SERIOUS MENTAL HEALTH PROBLEMS AND SUBSTANCE MISUSE?

For carers and professionals

For health care professionals and carers, the presence of these two conditions, both long-term and relapsing in nature, constitutes a major challenge (DH 2002). Managing or supporting service users in this area is intensified by the very fact that many of the service users are not ready to address their substance misuse problems, whilst their carers and professionals believe they should. This often leads to polarised viewpoints and escalating tension in the caring relationship because of this failure to find shared and acceptable goals.

For service users and services

I was pushed around like a tennis ball. The alcohol people said I had a mental illness and the mental illness group said I had a drink problem. Neither of them did very much for me. (Rorstad and Chesinski 1996, p.9)

Table 16.1 Reasons reported by dual diagnosis service users for their substance misuse

Substance used	'Reported' and 'claimed' effects	Comments and cautionary notes
Cannabis	Alleviates distress from auditory hallucinations Relieves anxiety for short periods Relieves muscle tension and involuntary movements caused by anti-psychotic medication	Associated with increased paranoid thoughts, auditory hallucinations, anxiety and panic Heightened sensory and perceptual experiences Amount and strength of cannabis can increase over time
Alcohol	Relieves tension and promotes relaxation Short-lived euphoric feeling produced Numbs emotional pain Produces a feeling of greater confidence Aids sleep	Combined with other depressant drugs may have stronger sedative effect and affect breathing In high doses can lead to strong dependence syndrome Associated with accidents, greater harm to self and others Service users open to greater level of exploitation Prolonged use leads to signs of depression for many Insomnia
Amphetamine and other stimulants	Involvement and acceptance into social group Counteracts anti-psychotic side effects such as limb stiffness Increases energy levels and motivation by stimulating nervous system Improves sexual satisfaction Delays sleep	Can cause nervousness and paranoid thoughts Associated with increasing conviction of delusional beliefs Strong correlation with violence and aggression Can lead to depression and suicidal thoughts Intravenous complications such as HIV, hepatitis and blood clots Sleep disturbance

continued...

Table 16.1 continued...

Substance used	'Reported' and 'claimed' effects	Comments and cautionary notes
Opiates	Numbs painful thoughts and feelings Helps with relaxation and reduces distress and intensity of auditory hallucinations Generates a feeling of warmth and contentment Acceptance into social group	Purity problems and equipment hygiene can lead to infections, blood clots, HIV and hepatitis when used intravenously Strong dependence syndrome develops quickly Financial hardship and social exclusion Greater likelihood of depression, suicide, neglect and exploitation, including prostitution In overdose or when mixed with alcohol, benzodiazepines and other depressants can cause respiratory arrest May reduce some psychotic symptoms
Benzodiazepines and other minor tranquillisers such as Zopiclone	Relieves 'come down' from stimulants Relieves anxiety and tension Short-lived sense of euphoria and confidence Aids sleep	Higher likelihood of suicide and accidental death by overdose Dose usually escalates over time Alone or in combination with other depressants can lead to respiratory arrest Sudden withdrawal can produce rebound psychotic symptoms

The quote above effectively conveys both the despondency a service user can feel and the justification services can hold when substance misuse and mental health services work separately.

Mental health and substance misuse services are usually funded, housed and managed separately. They even hold different care philosophies at times; such as harm reduction and motivation-sensitive interventions from substance misuse services on the one hand, and abstinence-focused treatment from psychiatry on the other. Substance misuse services usually require intrinsic motivation from their service users, while mental health services ordinarily work with service users regardless of their readiness to change.

Such differences, be they philosophy based or organisational, serve to obstruct care provision for the dual diagnosis service user rather than assist his or her recovery (Alcohol Concern 1999; Rooney and Cyster 1999). Services for the dually diagnosed in the UK today range from the least effective, *sequential* form (Rorstad and Chesinski 1996) to *joint working* (parallel services) models (Holland 1998), to the more sophisticated *integrated* treatment model (Mueser, Drake and Noordsy 1998) where one service delivers all.

Commissioners, managers, practitioners, service users and carers can follow the guidance set out within the *Mental Health Policy Implementation Guide: Dual Diagnosis Good Practice Guide* (DH 2002) for development purposes. It sets out the actions needed to meet two realistic goals:

1. Existing services should address their staff's training needs in detection, assessment and effective treatment for people with dual diagnosis.

2. Substance misuse and mental health services should work collaboratively through the use of local agreements in relation to direct client care *and* the mutual provision of mental health or substance misuse expertise through advice, supervision and coaching.

PRACTICE ISSUES
Detection, assessment and treatment issues

As a guiding principle to detection, assessment and management it should be recognised that comorbid mental illness and substance misuse is common and attempting to establish cause and effect in the short term or even the long term can be difficult, even impossible. Therefore, all service users should have access to mental health and substance misuse treatments on the basis of their health *needs*, not on ill-defined or ill-judged *causes* which may exclude them.

Detection of substance misuse

Studies have shown that at least a third of service users with severe mental illness will also have a habit of significant misuse of drugs or alcohol (Menezes *et al.* 1996). These prevalence rates may be higher in inpatient settings and vary in relation to local demography. Comorbid severe mental illness and substance misuse may be the norm rather than the exception and it is important, therefore, to have a high index of suspicion for substance misuse in mental illness services, and vice versa, to ensure service users receive the appropriate approach and treatment. Cast a wide net: it is preferable to misidentify a service user not experiencing a dual diagnosis than to miss others who do.

Index of Suspicion (Mueser, Bennet and Kusher 1995):

- young males (don't exclude women though)
- family history of substance misuse
- homelessness
- disruptive behaviour (childhood conduct disorder, anti-social personality disorder)
- isolation and poor familial relationships
- history of trauma or post-traumatic stress disorder
- repeated hospitalisation
- legal problems
- physical presentation.

Ask the service user

The best way to detect substance misuse is to ask users in an open and frank way. Service users will usually reveal their misuse of drugs and alcohol if asked sympathetically and if assured that negative consequences will not automatically follow. Some degree of knowledge of common drug-using terminology can be helpful, but is not vital. Ask the service user to explain any terms that are unclear and remember that slang can vary across the country and may be misunderstood or misused by certain service users themselves. It is important to consider asking service users about substance misuse whilst they are on their own – not in the presence of relatives or friends.

Assessment

Assessment is an ongoing process and not only informs future treatment but also constitutes treatment in its own right. Particularly important is the process of engagement, which usually takes place at this information-gathering stage (Carey 1996).

Making a comprehensive mental health and substance misuse assessment, incorporating a risk assessment (see Table 16.2), full histories and engaging with the service user, is best done progressively making use of an assessment framework that reflects both the evidence-based practice in each domain and the longitudinal nature of dual diagnosis intervention. Substance Treatment Options in Psychosis (STOP) (Kavanagh *et al.* 1998) provides such a framework, integrating substance misuse and mental health interventions. It can be tailored to individual needs and recognises harm reduction (Strang 1993) and engagement (Sainsbury Centre for Mental Health 1998) as key principles.

Treatment considerations

By using a psychosocial (PSI) framework practitioners can combine evidence-based assessments and interventions in mental health (Lancashire *et al.* 1996) with effective substance misuse practice (DH 1998; O'Brien and McLellan 1996; Seivewright and McMahon 1996). This approach is often referred to as an 'integrated treatment' model (Mueser *et al.* 1995).

Within this approach goals should be established collaboratively with harm reduction (Strang 1993) and motivational techniques (Rollnick 1995) conceptualised within the transtheoretical model of change (DiClemente and Prochaska 1985) and applied even when abstinence is unrealistic. This merely means matching an intervention to the service user's agreed area of need.

The battery of assessment tools identified in Table 16.2, whilst valuable to structured care planning and evaluation, may not be applicable in all circumstances. Case Studies 16.1 and 16.2 illustrate the complexity of assessment and treatment in dual diagnosis. Practitioners are advised to exercise discretion and maintain practice supervision throughout their interventions with service users and carers, particularly since the evidence base to dual diagnosis work remains limited (Ley *et al.* 1999). The case studies look at issues, consequences and interventions

Table 16.2 Comprehensive assessment and treatment in dual diagnosis

Domain	Assessment
Mental health	KGV Psychotic Symptom Rating Scale (Kraweicka, Goldberg and Vaughan 1977) Hospital Anxiety and Depression Scale (HADS; Zigmond and Snaith 1983)
Social function	Social Functioning Scale (Birchwood *et al.* 1990)
Medication and side-effects	Liverpool University Neuroleptic Side Effect Rating Scale (LUNSERS; Day *et al.* 1995)
Family assessment	Knowledge about mental health problems and substance misuse (Barrowclough *et al.* 2001; Falloon *et al.* 1993)
Risk assessment	Worthing Weighted Risk Indicator (Worthing Priority Care NHS Healthcare Trust 1995)
Substance misuse	Drug Abuse Screening Test (DAST; Skinner 1982) Michigan Alcohol Screening Test (MAST; Selzer 1971) Substance Abuse Treatment Scale (SATS; Mueser, Drake *et al.* 1995) Clinical Drug Use Scale (CDUS; Mueser, Drake *et al.* 1995) General areas: • Substance use risk assessment – injection sites, equipment, quality of drug and injection technique environment, knowledge of drug, alcohol and effects, support/risk from peers • Parallel time line of mental health/life events and substance use • Functional analysis; What, When, Where, How, Who with, Why, feelings before and after, effects
Physical health	Full physical examination and nutritional state
Coping skills	Coping strategies incorporating substance misuse in response to psychiatric symptoms, social situations, anger, paranoid ideation, lethargy, assertiveness. Strategies amenable to enhancement should be elicited (Coping Strategy Enhancement or CSE; Tarrier *et al.* 1990)

for details of working with complex service users, but you are also recommended to refer to the reading list at the end of this chapter.

The average amount of money spent per person, per year on drug misuse is £10,000 (Bramley-Harker 2001). There is growing concern and evidence of exploitation of vulnerable people by substance misusers to obtain money. The authors' own experiences and, anecdotally, those of the police and probation service show an increase in substance misusers 'befriending' and often moving in with vulnerable people to gain access to their benefits, their homes and facilities (Manchester Mental Health Service, Police and Probation Service 2002). Case Study 16.2 especially highlights some of these issues.

CONCLUSION

There is sufficient evidence available for practitioners, carers and service users to effectively address mental health problems and substance misuse when occurring simultaneously. The striking issues that undermine effective approaches such as poor liaison, separately designed and funded services, service users' reluctance to change and how this determines entry into service or affects staff and family attitudes, and other issues of engagement or risk, clearly make effective intervention challenging to apply.

This chapter has set out to exemplify, through research review and experiential practice, how practitioners can influence the outlook for arguably the most complex client group in psychiatry. It has not provided a comprehensive range of interventions and it has not examined in detail numerous specific areas of intervention. However, it illustrates the key obstacles and promotes a realistic perspective on recovery that must be long term in duration, engaging in nature and progressively incremental.

CASE STUDY 16.1
BOB AND HIS SENSITIVITY TO DRINK

Bob is a 45-year-old man who lives with his second wife Jean and adult son Brian (from his previous marriage). They live in a three-bedroom council house. Bob was diagnosed with schizophrenia when he was 27 years old; he has had several admissions to hospital over the years, usually as a result of him stopping his neuroleptic medication (the last admission was eight years ago). Jean works part-time and Brian is in full-time employment. Bob spends most of his day tidying the house, shopping with Jean after work and occasionally accompanying a friend on a delivery round. Bob attends the weekly local drop-in and depot neuroleptic clinic for medication management and peer support. He has always been an active participant in this group.

Over the past year Bob had started to experience an increase in psychotic symptoms. He was hearing voices, especially at night, telling him that everyone else was being taken to another planet. There were messages hidden in TV programmes telling people to 'prepare to leave' and he also believed that the CIA had implanted a 'chip' in certain people's brains (people with a diagnosis of schizophrenia). Jean and Brian reported that he would wake them up during the night demanding that they 'hide from the CIA' and threatening them with violence if they refused to comply. This has led to increased irritability, arguments and, on occasions, violence within the family. Bob was also using Jean's sleeping tablets to help him sleep, often taking three times the recommended amount. Jean was threatening to leave the family home and at times Bob was exhibiting signs of depression and anxiety.

During discussions with Bob and his family the community psychiatric nurse (CPN) found that previously Bob and Jean's social life had consisted of an occasional meal or drink in the pub. In the last year Bob and his son had joined the darts team in their local pub and Jean would often accompany them. This meant that Bob was going to the pub twice a week and on both occasions he reported drinking two or three pints of lager, and two or three brandies. Neither Bob, Jean nor Brian saw the increased alcohol consumption as being a factor in the difficulties they were experiencing; they all felt that it was an acceptable and enjoyable part of their social life.

Key issue

This case study presents a familiar problem in dual diagnosis: the assumption that 'normal levels of substance use', often socially and culturally acceptable, are unlikely to cause ill effects.

As with many service users with a diagnosis of schizophrenia, Bob demonstrated a hypersensitivity to alcohol, probably due to the dopaminergic effect exerted by the majority of psychoactive compounds (McGuire et al. 1995; Mueser et al. 1990). Even though his alcohol consumption fell within recommended weekly units and he was only drinking twice a week the effect on his mental health was catastrophic. He was spending at least half of his time experiencing increased paranoid delusions with subsequential effects on his behaviour and feelings.

Key interventions

A range of interventions was used over a period of time with Bob and his family, including psychosocial interventions (Holland, Baguley and Davies 1999), motivational interviewing (Rollnick 1995), harm reduction (Carey 1996) and family education and support (Barrowclough et al. 2001). Critical to success were health promotion and Bob's attitude to medication including the effects of other substances. The decision to use harm reduction strategies (e.g. reduce alcohol intake) was made because at that time Bob was showing no motivation to abstain and poorly timed strategies might jeopardise further treatment success (Drake et al. 1996).

Questions for discussion

1. How relevant are Bob's alcohol consumption, delusional beliefs and auditory hallucinations in assessing the risk of harm to others?

2. What steps might you take to reduce the risk of harm to others?

3. Although Bob's alcohol intake has increased, it remains below or around the recommended 'safe' drinking level for a man. Is he more vulnerable, as a result of mental illness, to the effects of psychoactive substances such as alcohol than someone without a serious mental illness?

4. What might Bob identify as 'good' about drinking and 'not so good' and would such an exercise be useful in changing his substance misuse?

CASE STUDY 16.2
JOHN AND HIS SOCIAL VULNERABILITY

John is a 26-year-old man who was diagnosed with schizophrenia seven years ago. He has spent periods 'living rough' and in homeless hostels. During these times he has used cannabis, heroin and crack cocaine.

Since discharge from hospital 18 months ago John has been living alone in a one-bedroom flat in a tower block. He receives income support and disability living allowance. His rent and council tax are paid through housing benefit. John has never fully engaged with mental health or drug services, often missing appointments and not responding to home visits. He has been prescribed methadone and neuroleptic medication by his GP.

The GP receptionist reported to the CPN that recently when John was collecting his prescription he looked dishevelled and agitated, he had lost weight and was 'accompanied' by two known drug users.

Key issue

Over several days a number of visits were made to John's flat and eventually the CPN gained access. The flat was neglected; the TV, radio and microwave were missing; and there were needles, syringes and other drug paraphernalia lying around. There were two people asleep in the bedroom and John had apparently been sleeping on the settee. John claimed that the two people were friends and were staying with him; they claimed that they 'were looking after John'.

During the next few days it became apparent that the 'friends' had moved into John's flat two months earlier. They had sold his possessions, accompanied him to collect his benefits and bought drugs, which they 'shared' with him. They accompanied him to collect his methadone prescription, which they either sold or used themselves. They had been sending John to various GPs to get prescriptions for benzodiazepines. John had been arrested three times in the past two months for shoplifting and the council were threatening eviction following complaints from other tenants.

John and his clothes were very dirty. He had lost weight. He was agitated and excitable at times. He had a number of inflamed injection sites on his arms and legs and had apparently been sharing 'works' with his friends. John was also adamant that he wanted to continue the current arrangement with his friends.

At this point there were so many issues that the situation felt overwhelming; however, through practice supervision and team support, the CPN managed to negotiate and prioritise with John a number of short-term interventions.

Key interventions

The CPN accompanied John to the local needle exchange where he was given clean needles, syringes and filters, and education and advice regarding safer injecting. John was started on a course of hepatitis vaccinations and given attention to the inflamed injection sites. No effort was made to stop John's drug use at this time but these harm reduction strategies would diminish the associated risks.

An assertive multi-agency approach was agreed including joint appointments with the drugs worker, the GP and the CPN at the GP surgery (John would often agree to see at least two out of three workers). This avoided confusion with appointments and the care planning therein.

In the medium term a case conference was arranged with all relevant people invited, including John, the GP, the drugs worker, the housing officer, community police and the CPN. John also wanted his friends to be invited. Within hours of them being invited they moved out of the flat.

From the case conference a number of possible interventions were identified, including:

- close monitoring of drug misuse through self-report, urine screening and other collateral sources enabling appropriate prescribing of substitute medication
- continuing joint appointments at the surgery enabling closer liaison and fewer appointments for John to attend
- a review of John's housing and support needs
- ongoing education around mental illness and drugs misuse.

Questions for discussion

1. John is open to exploitation by others; however, he may view such contact as better than none at all. What social, leisure, vocational or employment opportunities might exist in your area for him?

2. Given that John is difficult to engage, how would you address the high risk issues such as infected injection sites, contracting infection through shared paraphernalia, fraudulently obtaining prescription drugs and risk of eviction from tenancy?

3.   The CPN felt overwhelmed, a common feeling for
       practitioners and carers in complex dual diagnosis work.
       What support/supervision would you expect as John's care
       coordinator/key worker and how would you ensure it was
       forthcoming?

REFERENCES

Alcohol Concern (1999) *Dual Diagnosis, Alcohol, Drugs and Mental Health: A Report on Eight Mapping Projects*. London: Alcohol Concern.

Barrowclough, C., Haddock, G., Tarrier, N., Moring, J., Lewis, S., O'Brian, R., Schofield, N. and McGovern, J. (2001) 'Randomized controlled trial of motivational interviewing and cognitive behavioral intervention for schizophrenia patients with associated drug or alcohol misuse.' *American Journal of Psychiatry 158*, 1706–1713.

Birchwood, M., Smith, J., Cochrane, R., Wetton, S. and Copestake, S. (1990) 'The Social Functioning Scale: The development and validation of a new scale adjustment for use in family intervention programmes with schizophrenic patients.' *British Journal of Psychiatry 157*, 853–9.

Bramley-Harker, E. (2001) *Sizing the UK Market for Illicit Drugs*. London: Home Office Research, Development and Statistics Directorate.

Carey, K.B. (1996) 'Substance use reduction in the context of outpatient psychiatric treatment: A collaborative, motivational, harm reduction approach.' *Community Mental Health Journal 32*, 6, 291–306.

Day, J., Wood, G., Dewey, G. and Bentall, R. (1995) 'A self rating scale for measuring neuroleptic side-effects: Validation in a group of schizophrenic patients.' *British Journal of Psychiatry 166*, 650–3.

DiClemente, C.C. and Prochaska, J.O. (1985) 'Processes and stages of change: Coping and competence in smoking behaviour change.' In S. Shiffman and T.A. Wills (eds) *Coping and Substance Abuse*. New York: Academic Press.

DH (Department of Health) (1998) *Stimulant Needs Assessment Project*. London: DH.

DH (Department of Health) (2002) *Mental Health Policy Implementation Guide: Dual Diagnosis Good Practice Guide*. London: DH.

Drake, R.E., Mueser, K.T., Clark, R.E. and Wallach, M.A. (1996) 'The course, treatment and outcome of substance disorder in persons with severe mental illness.' *American Journal of Orthopsychiatry 66*, 1, 42–51.

Duke, P.J., Pantelis, C. and Barnes, T.R.E. (1994) 'South Westminster schizophrenia survey: Alcohol use and its relationship to symptoms, tardive dyskinesia and illness onset.' *British Journal of Psychiatry 164*, 630–6.

Falloon, I.R.H., Laporta, M., Fadden, G. and Graham-Hole, V. (1993) *Managing Stress in Families: Cognitive Behavioral Strategies for Enhancing Coping Skills*. New York: Routledge.

Hambrecht, M. and Hafner, H. (2003) 'Temporal order and aetiology.' In H.L. Graham, A. Copello, M. Birchwood and K. Mueser (eds) *Substance Misuse in Psychosis: Approaches to Treatment and Service Delivery*. Chichester: John Wiley and Sons.

Holland, M.A. (1998) 'Substance use and mental health problems: Meeting the challenge.' *British Journal of Nursing 7*, 15, 896–900.

Holland, M.A. (1999) 'How substance use affects people with mental illness.' *Nursing Times 95*, 24, 46–8.

Holland, M.A. (2002) 'Dual diagnosis: Substance misuse and schizophrenia.' In N. Harris, S. Williams and T. Bradshaw (eds) *Psychosocial Interventions in Serious Mental Illness*. London: Palgrave Macmillan.

Holland, M., Baguley, I. and Davies, T. (1999) 'Hallucinations and delusions 2: A dual diagnosis case study.' *British Journal of Nursing 8*, 16, 1095–102.

Kavanagh, D., Young, R., Boyce, L., Clair, A., Sitharthan, T., Clark, D. and Thompson, K. (1998) 'Substance Treatment Options in Psychosis (STOP): A new intervention for dual diagnosis.' *Journal of Mental Health 7*, 2, 135–43.

Kraweicka, M., Goldberg, D. and Vaughan, M. (1977) 'A standardised psychiatric assessment scale for rating chronic schizophrenic patients.' *Acta Psychiatrica Scandinavica 55*, 299–308.

Lancashire, S., Haddock, G., Butterworth, T., Tarrier, N. and Baguley, I. (1996) 'Training mental health professionals to use psychosocial interventions with people who have severe mental health problems.' *Clinician 14*, 6, 32–9.

Ley, A., Jeffrey, D.P., McLaren, S. and Siegfried, N. (1999) *Treatment Programmes for People with Both Severe Mental Illness and Substance Misuse.* The Cochrane Library, Issue 2. Oxford: Update Software.

Manchester Mental Health Service, Police and Probation Service (2002) Case conference.

McGuire, P., Jones, P., Harvey, I., Williams, M., McGuffin, P. and Murray, R. (1995) 'Morbid risk of schizophrenia for relatives of patients with cannabis associated psychosis.' *Schizophrenia Research 15*, 277–81.

Menezes, P. R., Johnson, S., Thornicroft, G., Marshall, J., Prosser, D., Bebbington, P. and Kuipers, E. (1996) 'Drug and alcohol problems among individuals with severe mental illnesses in South London.' *British Journal of Psychiatry 168*, 612–19.

Mueser, K.T., Bennet, M. and Kushner, M.G. (1995) 'Epidemiology of substance abuse among persons with chronic mental disorders.' In A.F. Lehman and L. Dixon (eds) *Double Jeopardy: Chronic Mental Illness and Substance Abuse.* New York: Harwood Academic Publications.

Mueser, K., Drake, R., Clark, R., McHugo, G., Mercer-McFadden, T. and Ackerson, T. (1995) *Toolkit for Evaluating Substance Abuse in Persons with Severe Mental Illness.* Manchester and Concord, New Hampshire: Human Services Research Institute.

Mueser, K., Drake, R. and Noordsy, D. (1998) 'Integrated mental health and substance abuse treatment for severe psychiatric disorders.' *Journal of Practical Psychiatry and Behavioural Health*, May, 129–39.

Mueser, K., Yarnold, P., Levinson, D. Singh, H., Bellack, A., Kee, K., Morrison, R. and Yadalam, K. (1990) 'Prevalence of substance abuse in schizophrenia: Demographic and clinical correlates.' *Schizophrenia Bulletin 16*, 31–56.

O'Brien, C.P. and McLellan, A.T. (1996) 'Myths about the treatment of addiction.' *The Lancet 247*, 237–40.

Rabinowitz, J., Bromet, E., Lavelle, J., Carlson, G., Kovasznay, B. and Schwartz, J. (1998) 'Prevalence and severity of substance use disorders and onset of psychosis in first time admission psychotic patients.' *Psychological Medicine 28*, 1411–19.

Regier, D., Farmer, N. and Rae, D. (1990) 'Co-morbidity of mental disorders with alcohol and other drugs of abuse: Results from the epidemiological catchment area (ECA).' *Journal of the American Medical Association 264*, 2511–18.

Rollnick, S. (1995) 'What is motivational interviewing?' *Behavioural and Cognitive Psychotherapy 323*, 325–34.

Rooney, P. and Cyster, R. (1999) *Complex Needs/Dual Diagnosis in Manchester, Salford and Trafford.* Salford and Trafford Health Action Zone: Research and Service Development Centre and Manchester.

Rorstad, P. and Chesinski, K. (1996) *Dual Diagnosis: Facing the Challenge.* Kenley: Wynne Howard Publishing.

Rosenthal, R.N. (1998) 'Is schizophrenia addiction prone?' *Current Opinion in Psychiatry 11*, 45–48.

Sainsbury Centre for Mental Health (1998) *Keys to Engagement: Review of Care for People with Severe Mental Illness who are Hard to Engage with Services.* London: The Sainsbury Centre for Mental Health.

Seivewright, N. and McMahon, C. (1996) 'Misuse of amphetamines and related drugs.' *Advances in Psychiatric Treatment 2*, 211–18.

Selzer, M.L. (1971) 'The Michigan Alcoholism Screening Test: The quest for a new diagnostic instrument.' *American Journal of Psychiatry 127*, 1653–8.

Skinner, H.A. (1982) 'The Drug Abuse Screening Test.' *Addictive Behaviours 7*, 363–71.

Strang, J. (1993) 'Drug use and harm reduction: Responding to the challenge.' In N. Heather, A. Wodak, E. Nadelmann and P. O'Hare (eds) *Psychoactive Drugs and Harm Reduction: From Faith to Science*. London: Whurr Publications.

Tarrier, N., Harwood, S., Yusopoff, L., Beckett, R. and Baker, A. (1990) 'Coping strategy enhancement (CSE): A method of treating residual schizophrenic symptoms.' *Behaviour Psychotherapy 18*, 283–93.

Worthing Priority Care NHS Healthcare Trust (1995) *Weighted Risk Indicator: Suicide, Violence and Self Neglect*. Worthing: Worthing Priority Care NHS Healthcare Trust.

Zigmond, A.S. and Snaith, R.P. (1983) 'Hospital Anxiety and Depression Scale.' *Acta Psychiatrica Scandinavica 67*, 361–70.

FURTHER READING

Alcohol Concern (2001) *'Dangerous Cocktails'. Your Mental Health Medication and Alcohol: What are the Facts?* London: Alcohol Concern.

Bazire, S. (2000) *Psychotropic Drug Directory: The Professionals' Pocket Handbook and Aide Memoire*. Salisbury: Mark Allen Publishing.

British Medical Association and Royal Pharmaceutical Society of Great Britain (2003) *British National Formulary*. London: British Medical Association.

Graham, H., Copello, A., Birchwood, M. and Mueser, K. (eds) (2003) *Substance Misuse in Psychosis: Approaches to Treatment and Service Delivery*. Chichester: John Wiley and Sons.

Heather, N., Wodak, A., Nadelmann, E. and O'Hare, P. (eds) (2003) *Psychoactive Drugs and Harm Reduction: From Faith to Science*. London: Whurr Publications.

Keene, J. (1997) *Drug Misuse: Prevention, Harm Minimization and Treatment*. London: Chapman and Hall.

Miller, W.R. and Rollnick, S. (1991) *Motivational Interviewing: Preparing People to Change Addictive Behaviour*. New York: Guilford Press.

Rorstad, P. and Checinski, K. (1996) *Dual Diagnosis: Facing the Challenge*. Kenley: Wynne Howard Publishing.

Seivewright, N. (2000) *Community Treatment of Drug Misuse: More Than Methadone*. Cambridge: Cambridge University Press.

Tyler, A. (1988) *Street Drugs: The Facts Explained, the Myths Exploded*. London: Coronet.

USEFUL CONTACTS

www.alcoholconcern.org.uk
www.ansa.uk.net
www.druginfozone.org
www.drugscope.org.uk
www.dualdiagnosis.co.uk
www.mind.org.uk
www.nta.nhs.uk
www.swsahs.nsw.gov.au/areaser/midas

CHAPTER 17

TOWARDS *NO SECRETS*

THE USE OF MULTI-AGENCY POLICIES AND PROCEDURES TO PROTECT MENTAL HEALTH SERVICE USERS FROM ABUSE

RUTH INGRAM

INTRODUCTION

This chapter explores the use of multi-agency policies and procedures for the benefit of mental health service users. The main text discusses barriers to the use of the *No Secrets* framework (DH and the Home Office 2000) by people experiencing mental health distress and the services working with them. Four case studies illustrate the use of adult protection procedures in a mental health context. All the examples are drawn from the author's experience of real situations but have been rewritten to ensure confidentality. The chapter concludes with actions that can be taken by mental health service providers to implement *No Secrets'* multi-agency adult protection work.

DEFINITIONS

The term *people experiencing mental health distress* is used throughout this chapter to describe those who are currently experiencing unwanted emotions or mental processes that reduce their quality of life. People receiving mental health services are described as *mental health service users*.

The term *impairment* is used to describe a difference in ability which makes a person less able than most others to carry out an activity in the same way that most do it. An impairment may be physical, sensory or mental. It may be temporary or permanent. A person's impairment may be obvious or not.

The term *disabled person* is used to describe someone who is disabled by society, because most activities are organised in such a way as not to be accessible to someone with these impairment/s.

BACKGROUND

No Secrets – Guidance on Developing and Implementing Multi-agency Policy and Procedures to Protect Vulnerable Adults from Abuse (DH and the Home Office 2000) gave social services responsibility to lead a multi-agency process to achieve its aims. It was followed with letters to health service chief executives and to police authority chief constables, stressing the importance of their cooperation.

The aim of *No Secrets* is to protect all adults who 'may be in need of community care services' and 'who are not otherwise able to protect themselves' from abuse (DH and the Home Office 2000, paragraph 2.3). Abuse is defined as 'Any violation of an individual's human or civil rights by any other person or persons' (DH and the Home Office 2000, paragraph 2.5). Physical, sexual, emotional and financial abuse are specified and, significantly, so are institutional abuse, neglect and discrimination.

The guidance coincided with the implementation of the Human Rights Act 1998 and was issued alongside many other changes to the health and social care system. Some of them contain aims for decreasing the risk of abuse of people using services through increasing partnership with service users and improving the quality of care received throughout the system (e.g. Care Standards Act 2000; Department of the Environment 2001; DH 2001, 2002). In addition, relatively new legislation addresses issues of violence and abuse (Family Law Act 1996, Part IV; Protection from Harassment Act 1997) and measures which enable people to give 'best evidence' (Youth Justice and Criminal Evidence Act 1999; Home Office 2000).

The development of adult protection policies and procedures is local. This allows for the active involvement of all partner agencies and for variation in the tone and detail of their implementation. Many local authorities have created a post of adult protection coordinator, with the remit to champion the work. There is a growing body of expertise in the use of the *No Secrets* framework to protect individuals experiencing abuse in their own homes and in care settings.

ABUSE OF PEOPLE EXPERIENCING MENTAL HEALTH DISTRESS

There is evidence that the prevalence of violence and abuse directed at people experiencing mental health distress is higher than for the general population. The evidence is available:

- at an anecdotal level:

  Nearly all my clients are experiencing violence and abuse. (Care manager, community mental health team)

- from service user-led research:

  It was like being between hell and hell – do I stay here and put up with this [hospital] or go back home where I'm not coping at all, back to that hell [domestic violence]? (Re*Sisters* 2002, p.30)

- from the whistle-blowing that has exposed the abuse of women in secure mental health hospitals such as Broadmoor:

  I conducted a survey...interviewing a random selection of 28 of the 67 women residents... The survey results showed a very high level of incidence of verbal abuse, sexual harassment, sexual abuse and five alleged rapes. (Wassell 2003, p.16)

- from research:

  ...it is suggested that abuse/harassment by psychiatric staff involves 5–9% of staff... People may seek out employment where the vulnerable may be exploited...and there needs to be an effective policy of vetting staff and volunteers. (Public Policy Working Committee of the Royal College of Psychiatrists 1996, p.9)

The abuse described includes abuse in people's own homes, in care settings and in the community (harassment/hate crime). A survey of mental health service users carried out by MIND (Reid and Baker 1996) found that:

- almost half the respondents had been harassed or abused in public places
- more than half felt threatened or afraid of attack
- a quarter had moved house due to harassment.

There is evidence, too, that experience of violence and abuse is a key factor in actually *causing* mental health distress. This is a likely explanation for the high proportion of women mental health service users who have experienced childhood abuse and/or domestic violence (DH 2003, pp.15–16).

> My problems were caused by a bad marriage and domestic violence. It wasn't just physical, the emotional side made me ill – being abused, put down. Your self esteem and confidence goes. I just couldn't cope any more, like your brain is overloaded. (Re*Sisters* 2002, p.30)

It is therefore important that people are asked about their experience of violence and abuse when accessing mental health services for the first time. It may be that any further development of their mental health distress will be prevented by access to safety and services that enable recovery from the trauma of abuse. If the abuse is current then the *No Secrets* framework can be used to access safety and support.

CASE STUDY 17.1 MIRIAM

Miriam's husband Rasheed is away working in Saudi Arabia. She lives with her parents-in-law and her husband's younger brother Hanif. Her son Rakesh is two and daughter Tani is six months; Rasheed hasn't been home since before Tani was born, and Miriam hasn't had a letter for three weeks.

Miriam attends a mum's support group at the local nursery where the support workers have been increasingly worried about her. She has changed from a happy, outgoing young mother and is now very quiet, and seems very obsessive about Tani's cleanliness. She was found crying in the toilets. Miriam tells the support worker that she tried to take an overdose, that she is a useless wife and mother and now she hasn't even managed to kill herself. Her mother-in-law blames her for Rasheed being away, criticises her care of Tani and has hit her across the face for not cooking enough food when guests turned up unexpectedly. Later Miriam whispers that Hanif has made her have sex with him; he threatened that otherwise he would tell his mother to throw her out.

The workers persuade Miriam to go to her GP, who prescribes anti-depressants, but also offers to find out what other help might be available. With Miriam's permission, an adult protection referral is made to the multi-agency mental health team. A community psychiatric nurse (CPN) meets Miriam the next day at the nursery and tells her about options such as having her mother-in-law arrested for a section 47 assault. Miriam chooses not to involve the police at that time. She is offered a place in an Asian's women's refuge or in a hostel for parents experiencing mental health distress and their children, but chooses not to leave home unless things got worse. She decides to meet with an outreach worker from the refuge.

Together, the CPN, the support workers from the women's centre and Miriam make a plan. This includes Miriam making a record of what has happened (in case she wants or needs to take legal action in the future), avoiding contact with Hanif and programming the telephone number of the police and of the women's refuge into her mobile in case she decides she needs to leave. She keeps a small bag with things for the children and photocopies of essential documents at the nursery. She is supported to apply for a house through a local housing association and starts to attend a group for Asian women who have experienced postnatal depression. It is arranged that the nursery can be reimbursed when Miriam uses their telephone to tell Rasheed what is happening.

With this support, Miriam manages to keep herself and the children safe within her in-laws' house for another six weeks. Once a house has been allocated, Rasheed comes home and tells his parents that he and Miriam want to live by themselves.

BARRIERS TO THE USE OF *NO SECRETS*

No Secrets is intended to be relevant to people experiencing mental health distress. These people fit the definition of *vulnerable adults*, as they 'may be in need of community care services' and sometimes, like the rest of the population, 'are otherwise unable to protect themselves and the Home Office from abuse' (DH 2000, paragraph 2.3).

However, despite the high levels of abuse, it appears that, in most parts of the country, there is a lack of engagement of mental health services with adult protection work (Adult Protection Coordinators Network 2003). There appear to be some barriers stopping service users gaining protection through this framework, barriers that need to be overcome by those promoting adult protection work and by mental health workers and service users. Four of these are explored below.

One barrier may be the historical roots of *No Secrets*, which drew on campaigns against the abuse of older people and those with a learning disability. At a local and national level, it is important that these campaigns are connected to similar work by mental health organisations such as Mind and Survivors Speak Out, and that all are included in developing local adult protection work.

A second barrier is the label 'vulnerable adult'. One of the reasons put forward for not using the *No Secrets* policy and procedures with people experiencing mental health distress is the assertion that they are not 'as vulnerable' as the people the policy is intended to cover. This thinking may arise partly from 'disablism' within mental health services and by service users themselves not wanting to identify with the image they have of 'the disabled'. The lack of inclusion of mental health service users in the wider disability movement may also be limited by discrimination towards them from other disabled people.

It is also possible that the term 'vulnerable adult' is not appropriate to any disabled people, *including* those experiencing mental health distress. The use of the label has been challenged as offensive and misleading by other groups of service users I have met, including those who claim the identity of 'disabled person'. One reason is the implication in the word 'vulnerable' that the cause of the abuse lies with the person experiencing it.

The social model of disability, developed by people with physical and sensory impairments, has good theoretical links with current campaigns to combat discrimination of people experiencing mental health distress. The model sites the cause of disability (and therefore vulnerability) with society, rather than with people's impairments. Applied to the high prevalence of abuse of disabled people, it locates the cause with societal oppression. Within the model, the 'Three As' (**a**ttitudes, **a**ccess and **a**ssistance) are used to explain how this works.

Some disability arises from the still-prevailing *attitudes* that disabled people are 'not quite so human as the rest of us'. This belief tends to come in different flavours, depending on the impairment involved; for example, people with physical and sensory impairments are brave and pitied, whilst people with mental health distress are dangerous and contaminating. All flavours lend justification to 'care' practices that treat some human beings as 'other'; they justify a culture in which care is left 'to the experts', to 'care' practices which would be challenged if used on any 'normal' human being and to the isolation of people in institutions or in their own homes. Discriminatory attitudes also flavour how the community at large treats disabled people, including those with visible mental health issues. Disabled people may be targeted for harassment and hate crime, such as the vandalism of their property, verbal taunts, theft and assaults.

Lack of *access* and lack of *assistance* can also create isolation from mainstream society and be barriers to achieving safety. Assistance may be a personal assistant, an advocate or technology that can be used to enable a person to do something s/he cannot do without it.

Isolation and lack of access can prevent people comparing their own experiences with that of others, and prevents the naming of abuse or denied human rights. Access to help from other people to stop abuse may be limited by lack of contact with those outside the mental health system, and by lack of assistance to gain information about hospital complaints procedures. It may also be limited by attitudes – 'she has a diagnosis of schizophrenia, we can't believe what she says'.

Care is supposed to be safe. However, institutions are well known for posing a risk of abuse (Kingston, Bond and Palmer 2003). Physical isolation is one component of this situation, another is the cultural/professional isolation that can grow up around the experts who deal with people that 'the rest of us couldn't'. Isolation allows power and control to run unchecked by outsiders, to the detriment of all workers and service users.

Within the social model of disability, people experiencing mental health distress are just as 'vulnerable' as others covered by *No Secrets*. This is not because of their distress, but because of the oppression of, and discrimination towards, those labelled as mad. Within that framework, the label of 'vulnerable' is factual, and useful, to challenge the factors in society which support the abuse of disabled people. Nevertheless, it is fraught with difficulty and locates the cause of abuse with the victim. This compounds the harm already caused by the abuse, as it colludes with the sense of shame and blame that survivors often feel.

> I couldn't believe it so who would believe me? He was a nice amiable nurse that everyone liked – I suppose that wouldn't have happened if I wasn't mentally ill. (Re*Sisters* 2002, p.31)

It is important that adult protection work locates the cause of abuse with the perpetrator. It is by naming the perpetrator (and/or the institution) and his/her abusive behaviour (and/or its dysfunctional systems) that the victim becomes free from any shame attached to the abuse s/he has experienced. If the responsibility for the abuse stopping is placed on those whose behaviours cause/allow the harm to occur, then the changes needed can be named.

My own preference is to replace the label 'vulnerable adult' with the phrase 'all disabled people' to include those experiencing mental health distress.

A third barrier appears to be a combination of two factors: the high prevalence of abuse of people experiencing mental health distress, and a perception by mental health workers that the adult protection procedures are over-bureaucratic. As many work in multidisciplinary and even multi-agency teams, they may believe that there is no added value in using adult protection procedures. However, because many multi-agency mental health teams are now well established, they run the risk of having made cultural norms within which abuse of service users is accepted – not because it is believed to be right, but because exposure to high levels of abuse has led to a coping mechanism of acceptance. One challenge is to model good practice use of the *No Secrets* framework to break through such learned helplessness and to achieve safety for service users. A second challenge is to integrate adult protection procedures with existing practice, such as the Care Planning Approach (CPA), so that there is no duplication of bureaucracy. If such moves are not made, mental health service users will continue to be denied access to safety via agencies that enforce the law and regulate care settings.

CASE STUDY 17.2 COLLIN AND ANGUS

Angus spent many years of his life living in a hospital for people with mental health distress and he now lives in a hostel called 'Number 14'. It used to be a care home but last year all the service users were given papers to sign, and told that now they had rights like other people renting flats. Nothing seems to have changed though. Angus dreams of going on holiday to the Shetland Islands, where, he was told, his mother came from. He likes the music he's heard from the islands and wants to save up and get a mini hi-fi, but he never seems to have enough money just to get through the week. Sometimes he gets really angry, for instance when the deputy made him wait so long to get his bus pass that he punched the cupboard door and was sent to his room instead of going out.

Angus' friend Collin smokes a lot of cigarettes and does not want to cut down even though the doctor says it would help him avoid so many chest infections. The staff say they are helping him by keeping his cigarettes and lighter in the office. They will only let him have a cigarette every hour, even if he's desperate. Once Angus saw Tim (the manager) hold Collin up against the wall and threaten him not to come early again or he would not get any more cigarettes that day.

Friday is Angus' day at the resource centre, where last week someone called Angela (from social services) came to talk about 'direct payments' – giving people themselves the money that goes towards their 'care package', so they can choose what to spend it on. Angus thought he could save up the money from not going to the resource centre, and go to the Shetland Islands instead. Angela wanted to know why he could not afford to go anyway. He told her that he only got £10 per week spending money and it went mostly on lunches. She seemed genuinely concerned and offered to find out if he should be getting more. When Angela asked if he was happy where he lived, he told her about what had happened to Collin and how it made him angry and scared.

Angela's team leader agreed with her that the adult protection procedures should be used to help Collin and Angus. The adult protection unit chaired a meeting including Angela, representatives from Supporting People and the police, and five mental health team workers, all of whom had contact with people who lived at 'Number 14'.

The meeting learned that two other serivice users had made complaints about Tim. One was to the police, who said that they could not investigate because the service user was not a reliable witness; and one was to a community psychiatric nurse (CPN) who was helping the person look for a flat of his own. A number of actions were agreed, including the suspension of Tim, pending a police investigation of alleged assault of Collin and any subsequent disciplinary investigation; a police interview of Angus, Collin and the other two service users who had complained, jointly with their CPNs; a financial audit of the hostel; a review of each service user's money; and the provision of support services for service users from independent advocates.

A fourth barrier, associated with the charge of over-bureaucracy, is the view put forward by Williams and Keating (2000) that adult protection procedures are not appropriate for use in mental health settings. The procedures are thought counteractive to developments that increase people's involvement as partners in planning and managing their care, because they 'take over' the autonomous decision-making powers of people experiencing mental health distress.

It is true that the empowerment of people who have experienced abuse should be central to all adult protection procedures. We know that abuse is about the misuse of power and control over another person, often within a cultural, social and legal context which legitimises that misuse of power ('an Englishman's home is his castle'). The experience of abuse can take away a person's sense of ability to control his or her own life, and s/he may become completely dependent on the perpetrator for any sense of him- or herself as a human being (Herman 1992). Surviving and thriving, after living with abuse of all kinds, depends on regaining a sense of one's self as an autonomous human being; regaining control is key to recovery and to establishing self-sustained, enduring safety. This means that it is 'good practice' for adult protection procedures to include a disabled person as the central partner in assessing any risk of abuse s/he is facing, and in planning and implementing his or her protection plan. This includes the right to choose not to take any action and not to engage with services.

However, there are some situations where organisations have a duty to act to stop abuse happening, with or without the person's consent. *No Secrets* has not changed these imperatives, as they are based in existing legislation and guidance. However, it provides a structure through which the existing powers and duties of organisations can be harnessed together to provide protection from abuse. Even (or especially) in these situations, a paramount concern of any adult protection work must be the empowerment of those who have been victims of the abuse. The availability of independent advocacy is a key component in ensuring that this happens.

Situations where organisations have a duty to act to prevent abuse, whatever the expressed wishes of the person, are threefold:

1. the person is at risk of serious harm

2. the person experiencing abuse does not have the mental capacity to give consent to the use of the *No Secrets* framework

3. the abuse is being caused by a person or people employed to provide care, or taking place in a setting where a statutory organisation has an overriding public duty to ensure it is safe for all service users.

CASE STUDY 17.3 DONNA

Donna had been having lots of anxiety attacks before she went into hospital, despite the GP's medication. In her head she could see shadows moving and hiding and she could not get away from them. She kept coming out in sweats and had not slept more than two hours a night for weeks. Once she took five times the maximum number of pills and when she woke up her heart had been racing really hard. Donna had to stop work. She felt useless, ashamed, helpless and very scared. One night she knew the room was full of insects sent to poison her and when they got into her skin she tried to cut them out with her hairdressing scissors.

For a few days after admission to hospital Donna could not think straight. The injection they had given her had made everything hazy and she kept drifting away. One time she was sure there was a man in her bed. He smelt of tobacco, the same brand her dad used to smoke. She began to get better sleep and started to feel more like herself, although the shadows were still whispering about her.

When she visited the community room, Donna sometimes noticed that a man was watching her. He seemed very familiar, with yellow fingers and tobacco in a familiar blue packet. She found out that the man's name was Ted and then remembered that he lived in the next street to her. Donna told her key nurse that he made her feel uncomfortable. A few days later Ted literally bumped into her as she was coming out of the toilet. He pushed her inside and started pulling her blouse open. Luckily it was the disabled toilet and she could reach the safety cord. The staff came pretty quickly but to Donna it felt like forever at the time.

The incident was reported in the 'untoward incident log' and the risk manager, Alan, was happy that the staff had acted correctly. Ted was moved to the all-male unit and waited to hear whether his rehabilitation programme would include a group designed to prevent sexual offending. Donna had signed her statement and Alan faxed his incident form to the adult protection unit. He was surprised when the coordinator rang back later that morning to set up a strategy meeting.

It transpired that a former patient had complained about being sexually assaulted by Ted to her social worker, who had alerted the adult protection unit and the police. They had recorded similar complaints by two separate women of sexual assault by Ted; both women had withdrawn their statements at the thought of having to describe what had happened to them to a court. The adult protection strategy meeting resulted in police interviews with Donna and the hospital staff. Ted was arrested. Donna is now receiving support from STARS (Surviving Trauma After Rape Services) and being helped to understand the criminal justice processes. She has started to remember some of the sexual abuse she experienced as a child and her panic attacks seem to have stopped, even though she is hardly taking any medication.

The Crown Prosecution Service have the file and will decide whether to proceed with the case. Four more women gave statements about Ted to the police. They were all offered post-trauma therapy and support to give evidence in court. Ted, who had been a voluntary patient, is now held in hospital under the Mental Health Act 1983 and is receiving a forensic psychiatric assessment. Nurses have placed posters about sexual abuse and domestic violence helplines on the notice boards near the public telephones.

Situations covered in the third point are those in which other people may face a risk of abuse, from the same source, in the present or in the future; for example, when a service user is abused by an employee of the organisation, by another service user or by the system and culture of the organisation (institutional abuse). Some may be situations where organisations have not listened to complaints by service users and have not taken seriously their responsibilities to provide a safe service.

For example,

- allegations of sexual assault of mental health service users by professionals:

  Anna was subjected to physical and emotional bullying and degradation by nurses whilst an inpatient in a psychiatric unit. The Trust attempted to dismiss her complaints about her treatment on the basis that she was ill at the time. (POPAN 1999, p.7)

- the institutional abuse of older people with dementia:

  A culture developed within the Trust that allowed unprofessional, countertherapeutic and degrading – even cruel – practices to take place. These practices went unchecked and were even condoned when brought to the attention of the Trust. (CHI 2000, p.2)

- and the sexual abuse of women service users at Broadmoor by other service users (see earlier quote from above by Wassell 2003).

The persistence and courage that has been needed by many of those who expose such situations underlines the dangers of cultural isolation in mental health services. It is of note that four of the twelve current (at time of writing, August 2003) and completed investigations by the Commission for Health Improvement (CHI) concern abuse occurring in NHS settings, two of them providing mental health services to older people. CHI's recommendations to make these services safe include an 'effective implementation of the protection or vulnerable adults policies' (CHI 2003, p.66). This engagement would break cultural isolation and enable mental health service users to access their rights to safety through contact with outside agencies, including the police and regulatory bodies.

CASE STUDY 17.4 ROWAN HOUSE

Consuela was called 'Suela' at home in Nicaragua where she had been a nurse in the accident and emergency unit at Managua's central hospital. She had a degree from the university there and had received up-to-date training. Her husband Ernesto is a very talented engineer, brought to England by his German employer. The family live in a house rented for them by the company. The children have settled at school very fast.

Suela herself was bored. She had liked the adrenaline rush of a busy emergency unit and did not want to be a housewife, even if they did not need her to be earning. English hospitals did not recognise her Nicaraguan qualifications and she had to take another year's course if she wanted to work in Britain. In the meantime she took a job as care worker at Rowan House, a home for people with dementia. In her first few weeks, many things surprised her but she was too busy trying to learn the new job to think. She got to know Teresa, a nurse from Nigeria, and they talked about why the English locked their old people away. Suela wanted to ask Teresa why all the service users were taken to the toilet at set times, whether they wanted to go or not, and why the doctor had not been called to look at Mrs Holden's large pressure sore. Suela thought it might be a grade 3 and Mrs Holden kept crying out as if she was in pain.

As Suela arrived for her shift one afternoon, Teresa was leaving in tears and said she had been sacked by matron who was in a foul mood. During that shift matron told Suela that she was to do the drugs round, although previously she had not been allowed to do it. When she questioned the matron about this she said: 'Well, you will just have to do it – there isn't any one else on shift who is a nurse, whatever mud hut they were taught in.' Suela gave service users their medication, recognising some of the brand names and pharmacological terms. She thought that people received far too many medicines, sometimes ones that should not be taken at the same time, and what seemed to be a double dose of sedatives.

The next day Suela met Teresa, who said that she had seen one of the English nurses hit a woman called Mrs Dean. She had been so upset that she had reported it. Matron's response was that Teresa had not seen anything of the sort in her nursing home, and that she was sacked. She also used threats to prevent Teresa telling anyone else.

However, Suela found out about the National Care Standards Commission (NCSC) and told them about the medication, the toilet times and the pressure sore. The next day the GP came and sent Mrs Holden to hospital in an ambulance. A week later the NCSC made an unannounced inspection. They found enough evidence to take action without giving Suela's name away. The matron was suspended and every service user's care plan and medication was reviewed. People started going out to day centres and taking part in activities. In the end, the home was sold to new owners and Teresa got her job back.

Suela was told that there had been an adult protection meeting and that the names of the matron and the nurse who had hit Mrs Dean would be put on the Department of Health's POVA (Protection of Vulnerable Adults) index when it was set up, and that they had been referred to the UKCC for consideration of their deregistration as nurses.

TAKING ACTION – TOWARDS *NO SECRETS*

People experiencing mental health distress do fall within the remit of *No Secrets*. This chapter illustrates that it is a framework which, when used well, can empower people to access safety. The following Good Practice Points can be taken by mental health service providers to implement *No Secrets* multi-agency adult protection work.

Good Practice Points

1. Engage with local adult protection structures – e.g. the Multi-Agency Adult Protection Committee – in the on-going development and implementation of adult protection work

2. Enable mental health service users to access any service user fora that are engaged in adult protection work

3. Promote the empowerment of service users as a central principle of adult protection work

4. Develop and make all staff aware of a clear internal structure (integrated with other clinical governance structures) for reporting and responding to concerns of abuse of service users. Expect and promote engagement with multi-agency partners to protect individuals, including the police

5. Enable staff to access training about recognising abuse and working with service users who are experiencing abuse

6. Include standards relating to human rights and the prevention of institutional abuse in all service audits and risk assessments

7. In all assessments and within the CPA (Care Programme Approach) process, include a consideration of any risk to the person's safety, including safety from abuse. Care plans should include a protection plan if appropriate

8. Provide accessible information, to service users in all settings, about the right to live life free from violence and abuse. This should include information about how to access victim support services, the police, independent advocates, how to make a complaint and how to access the adult protection process

9. Commission services that support people leaving violent situations and which are accessible to people experiencing mental health distress

REFERENCES

Adult Protection Coordinators Network (2003) Symposium organised by Pavilion Publishing and the University of Canterbury's Department of Applied Sociology, Telford, June.
Commission for Health Improvement (November 2000) *Investigation into The North Lakeland NHS Trust. Report to the Secretary of State*. London: Commission for Health Improvement.

CHI (Commission for Health Improvement) (2003) *Investigation into Learning Disability Services Provided by the Bedfordshire and Luton Community NHS Trust*. London: Commission for Health Improvement.

Department of the Environment (2001) *Supporting People: Policy into Practice*. 00HC1269. London: DETR.

DH (Department of Health) (2001) *Valuing People – A Strategy for Learning Disability for the Twenty-First Century*, cm 5086. London: The Stationery Office.

DH (Department of Health) (2002) *The NHS Plan*. London: DH.

DH (Department of Health) (2003) *Women's Mental Health: Into the Mainstream – Strategic Development of Mental Health Care for Women*. London: DH.

DH (Department of Health) and the Home Office (2000) *No Secrets – Guidance on the Developing and Implementing Multi-agency Policy and Procedures to Protect Vulnerable Adults from Abuse*. London: DH.

Herman, J.L. (1992) *Trauma and Recovery: From Political Terror to Domestic Violence*. London: Pandora.

Home Office (2000) *Achieving Best Evidence in Criminal Proceedings: Guidance for Vulnerable and Intimidated Witnesses Including Children*. London: Home Office Communication Directorate.

Kingston, P., Bond, P. and Palmer, J. (2003) 'Institutional indicators of elder abuse and neglect.' In J. Sanmartin (ed.) *Elder Abuse and Neglect*. Kluwer Academic/Plenum Publishers. Presented to the INPEA Conference, Spain, September.

POPANE (Prevention of Professional Abuse Network) (1999) *Annual Report 1998–9*.

Public Policy Working Committee of the Royal College of Psychiatrists (1996) *Sexual Abuse and Harassment in Psychiatric Settings*. CR52. London: Royal College of Psychiatrists.

Reid, J. and Baker, S. (1996) *Not Just Sticks and Stones: A Survey of the Stigma, Taboos and Discrimination Experienced by People with Mental Health Problems*. London: MIND.

ReSisters (2002) *Women Speak Out*. Leeds: Women and Mental Health Action Group.

Wassell, J. (2003) 'Blowing the whistle.' *Professional Social Work*, April, 16–17.

Williams, J. and Keating, F. (2000) 'Abuse in mental health settings: Some theoretical considerations.' *The Journal of Adult Protection* 2, 3, 32–9.

STATUTES

Care Standards Act (2000)
Family Law Act (1996), Part IV
Human Rights Act (1998)
Protection from Harassment Act (1997)
Youth Justice and Criminal Evidence Act (1999)

CHAPTER 18

MANAGING VIOLENCE

ROY BUTTERWORTH

INTRODUCTION

Violence in one form or another has become a familiar aspect of everyday human experience. Through the media violent events are indirectly witnessed when reading a newspaper, watching television or attending the cinema. People of all ages, particularly children, can 'enjoy' indirect participation in violence whilst playing specifically designed computer games.

Violence takes many forms, including war, homicide, suicide, rape and self-injury. Domestic violence is a particular issue for vulnerable people such as children or elders. Each form of violence involves a series of interpersonal events or dynamics that result in the physical or psychological violation of one or more individuals carried out either by themselves or others.

Within the context of good practice this chapter will explore the role of the practitioner in knowing, understanding and approaching difficult situations in order to pre-empt and avoid violent outcomes. The physical management of violence involving breakaway and control and restraint manoeuvres is beyond the remit of this chapter and requires specific education and psychomotor training in order to elevate knowledge, understanding and practice to competent levels.

VIOLENCE AND MENTAL ILLNESS – DISPELLING THE MYTHS

The management of violent behaviour requires a broad range of knowledge, understanding and skills in order to respond effectively to the needs of others and, where necessary, to the actions of a perpetrator in a safe and effective manner. Proactive avoidance of conflict and violence can be achieved through the effective instrumental use of interpersonal, social and communication skills.

Capable, confident practice in this area begins with an appreciation of the social perspectives and stereotypes often attributed to mental health service users. The words 'violent' and 'dangerous' have become intertwined in the public's perception of mental illness (Chin 1998). Media descriptions of the mentally ill provide the public with opportunities to identify and associate a negative perspective with personal anxieties and fears for individual safety.

Such generalised anxieties have previously had the capacity to shape government policy towards the mentally ill, in an effort to ensure that care is appropriately managed and public concerns are satisfied (DH 1990). However, when the statistics on extreme forms of violence are reviewed, for example suicide and homicide, it becomes clear that violence and dangerousness are not exclusive characteristics of the mentally ill (Appleby et al. 2001). For the practitioner working with mental health service users, personal self-awareness about one's own values and beliefs is essential in supporting a confident ability to interact effectively and instrumentally with others.

VIOLENCE IN HEALTH AND SOCIAL CARE

In an employment context 'aggressive' or 'violent' conduct towards care providers includes a broad spectrum of behaviours ranging from verbal abuse and threats to serious physical injury. Aggression and violence have been acknowledged as an everyday hazard for practitioners working with mental health service users to the extent that specific organisational policies and procedure are required in order to respond to the problems presented (HSE 1997).

Essential pre-requisites to safe and effective practice

Within all care situations the pre-requisites that will support safe practice require practitioner orientation to the environment; appropriate employment policy and the necessary systems in use that articulate relevant policies and procedures in practice.

Many practitioners work alone with service users in unfamiliar surroundings. The workplace environment often includes the service user's own home, the hospital ward, the office, or a wide range of hostel and community-living accommodation. Each of these present their own unique set of circumstances and all practitioners should therefore understand, as employees, the risks presented in their environment of work and how their organisation supports safe practice (HSE 1997; RCPCRU 1998; Wright *et al.* 2001). Case Study 18.1 provides an example.

CASE STUDY 18.1 COMMUNITY SETTING

Sharon, a mental health social worker, was out on her visits to clients receiving community care. One afternoon she made an unplanned visit to George, a man who is forty-five years of age and who has a history of paranoid schizophrenia. George had missed his recent clinic appointment. On opening his door to Sharon, George appeared unkempt; he grudgingly acknowledged Sharon and allowed her into his flat. On entering the flat Sharon observed that George had locked the front door behind them. During her enquiry as to why George had not attended his appointment he became irritable and began shouting at her.

Outcome

Sharon did manage to defuse this situation by distracting George from the focal issue of the appointment. He acknowledged that it was important to attend the clinic but on this occasion he had forgotten to do so and had been irritated about the need to be reminded. He agreed to attend a new appointment. Sharon reassured George with a view to reducing his irritability and suggested they discuss this on her next visit.

Questions for discussion

1. What are the overriding concerns regarding this incident and how could Sharon have approached it differently?

2. On leaving George's home what would you do next had you been the practitioner visiting George?

3. Given George's presentation and his missed appointment what concerns should Sharon raise with members of the clinical team?

As a lone worker Sharon has an obligation to let her colleagues know where she is and whom she is visiting at any one time. Making an unplanned visit such as this may have placed her in danger, particularly had the interaction with George exacerbated his irritability and anger to the point of aggression. Sharon had to rely upon her knowledge of George, his previous history and her skills as a practitioner to ensure that the situation was managed effectively.

In avoiding this situation Sharon should have followed specific locally agreed 'lone worker arrangements'. In addition, the environmental and clinical risk assessments and the care programme in place for George may have provided other important indicators as to the risks of visiting alone at this time. An event such as this constitutes an incident of unsafe practice and should be explored with the practitioner through post-incident review and clinical supervision.

A knowledge and understanding of risk assessment and management is crucially important in facilitating safe and effective choices and decision making (for example, see Alberg, Hatfield and Huxley 1996). On assessment the service user's history, the intent and severity of previous violence, whether that violence had been planned and evidence of current ideas regarding violence are important factors to take into consideration. Subsequent assessments can be conducted whenever a change to the treatment plan is considered or a violent incident has occurred.

PROMOTING COMPETENT RESPONSES TO CONFLICT

Conflict managed ineffectively will often escalate towards anger, aggression and, ultimately, violent behaviour. The confident management of conflict requires an appreciation of how one's own behaviour can contribute to the dynamics of respective situations and the likely responses one has to the challenges, resistance and difficult behaviours presented by others.

The manner in which we all conduct ourselves in social interaction is dependent upon effective social skills and emotional competencies. A person with low self-esteem, for example, may misinterpret the intentions of others because of personal feelings of negativity and worthlessness. Understanding emotional responses can allow reason to be considered before emotion in order to make sense of the world around us. Without emotional competence and the capacity to rationalise everyday stressors, 'fight or flight' responses prevail (Goleman 1996).

Experience, values and beliefs

Previous experience of conflict, aggression and violence influences and shapes our personal values, beliefs, attitudes, behaviour and general conduct. Revisiting past experiences can help us develop an understanding of the meaning of violence and aggression, its impact on our own behaviour and the styles of intervention we choose when confronted by new, difficult situations. Given the unique impact of individual experiences it is not surprising that we respond better to some service users and their conditions than to others (Farrell and Gray 1992).

Of particular importance is the practitioner's capacity to understand the role of values and beliefs and how these translate into prejudice and discriminatory attitudes and behaviour. Values, morals and everyday social skills also contribute to cultural differences. Each has the potential to create interpersonal communication problems (Fontana 1990) which, in turn, can result in misunderstanding and offence. Within care establishments an inconsistent application of values and beliefs can promote fragmented and uncoordinated care experiences for the service user. The importance of listening to service user perspectives is apparent in Case Study 18.2.

CASE STUDY 18.2 VALUES AND BELIEFS

John, a 24-year-old service user with a history of anxiety and depression, had been abused by his parents as a child. He has recently started to self-injure and the residential accommodation care team are individually at odds with how to manage his behaviour. Some practitioners are keen to deter John from physically injuring himself whilst others consider that he should be allowed to do so in a negotiated risk-managed way.

Outcome

The subject of self-injury provokes inconsistent responses within a team of practitioners. An inability to negotiate and agree team approaches to practice can lead to fragmented and uncoordinated care experiences. The teams of practitioners were brought together to share and understand individual perspectives and appreciate the current evidence base supporting person-centred care. Once the team had collectively reframed their perspective on care for John, his care coordinator was able to negotiate a flexible and responsive package of care with him that incorporated his perspectives.

Questions for discussion

1. What are the dilemmas for practitioners in this case study and how could these have been managed?

2. How can teams of practitioners effectively demonstrate a collaborative perspective of their values and beliefs?

3. To what extent do you as a practitioner believe that service users should be involved in determining their own approaches to care?

An anti-discriminatory perspective requires sensitivity to the individual perspectives of others and their rights to choice, dignity, respect and independence, regardless of their personal background and presentation (Thompson and Mathias 1994; Williams and Dale 2001).

Within the context of mental illness, choice and independence must be considered alongside any presenting risk factors. A sensitive balance between safety and effective care must be maintained within systematic risk assessments and negotiated plans for care (Hodgins and Muller-Isberner 2000). When safety and security are routinely prioritised over other important person-centred values, particularly within institutional care, practitioners can all too easily alienate themselves from service users. As a consequence, care practice may deteriorate towards routinised, task-orientated activities around the needs of the staff and the organisation, promoting a 'them and us' culture.

The opportunity to contribute to culture must, therefore, be extended to those who have personal experiences of and perspectives on receiving care. The traditional paternalistic/subservient roles of practitioner and service user can then be challenged, involving the latter as educator, guide and advisor to the practitioner, who acts as facilitator for positive mental and social well-being.

Attitudes and behaviour can directly contribute towards triggering anger and conflict. A lack of appreciation of personal beliefs and attitudes towards others can result in these leaking out into everyday behaviour through non-verbal communication (Farrell and Gray 1992). The potential impact on relationships may be inadvertently to offend, devalue and disregard others.

Knowledge for intervention

In order to respond confidently to service user need, the practitioner must build upon self-awareness, with appropriate social behaviour and therapeutic interventions. These three elements can be brought together to facilitate effective engagement and interaction.

Often a practitioner's initial awareness of potential conflict emerges from observing the behaviour of others. The essence of communication involves both verbal and non-verbal behaviours and interaction, often referred to as *social skill* (Wilkinson and Canter 1982). In order that the practitioner can effectively articulate observations and engagement concerning the main elements of social skill s/he must be able to identify the pertinent aspects of human behaviour. It is recommended that all practitioners further investigate these issues.

The practitioner's insights, knowledge and skills in this area support an active consideration of personal thoughts, feelings and social interaction. The 'internal' self, represented by thoughts and feelings, can have a direct or indirect effect on the 'external' self, represented by social behaviour (Holland, Orr and Soar 1992). As suggested earlier with values and beliefs, true feelings can also be inadvertently transmitted to the service user.

In order to develop understanding and insight effectively, it is useful to either engage in personal reflection about previous experiences of violence and aggression or role-play with colleagues. Reflection on thoughts and feelings evoked by previous experiences can be facilitated on paper within a 'reflective diary'. This offers personal, safe space within which the practitioner can learn (Schon 1983). It is important to consider positive aspects of the experience and others that might have been achieved differently. Using this information the practitioner will often be able to arrive at a new perspective, one that is informed and aware, supporting the potential for positive experiences in the future.

If experiences are potentially troubling, the practitioner should confide in a colleague within a professional clinical supervision relationship designed to offer support and promote learning. Discussions should remain confidential with the practitioner retaining autonomy regarding how much to disclose. Where an experience appears to be troubling to the extent that this is disruptive to work performance, the practitioner should be encouraged or directed to seek line manager supervision involving further structured support.

Role-play, particularly with the use of video equipment, offers an opportunity to acquire direct feedback about the effectiveness of one's behaviour in difficult circumstances. For some, role-play will be viewed as a risky learning strategy only to be entertained in a structured, supportive environment with appropriate supervision and confidentiality.

Difficult situations involving threatening, aggressive or violent antisocial behaviours naturally provoke 'fight or flight' responses (Sutherland and Cooper 1990). Goleman (1996) describes the outcome of these responses as an 'emotional hijacking'. The brain engages an emergency emotional response to threat before the time required to think about the emergency has occurred. With appropriate levels of self-awareness it is possible to remain conscious of one's emotions, think clearly about the options and take necessary action to defuse a situation before it gets out of control.

It is essential that the practitioner is aware of how service users interact with others and whether their general presentation relies upon aggressive, passive or assertive behaviours. The verbal and non-verbal behaviours employed provide important clues about how the service user is feeling and what s/he may be thinking about. It is essential in any consideration of a service user's behaviour that the impact of prescribed medication is taken into account (see Case Study 18.3).

CASE STUDY 18.3
AGITATION AND IRRITABILITY

James has been in hospital for the past week. He has a history of schizophrenia and is thirty-four years of age. Following admission James's behaviour has deteriorated despite being given regular anti-psychotic medication. On the evening in question James presented as irritable and unable to settle. He was pacing back and forth complaining of feeling anxious and agitated. On studying his care record and prescription card the nurse had recognised a trend of increased dosages of medication and additional administrations as necessary. The nurse decided to ask for a medical review.

Outcome

On review the doctor considered the nurse's observations and agreed that the medication was causing side-effects known as akathisia (see the glossary at the end of this book). This essentially left James experiencing an inner restlessness sometimes mistaken for agitation. The medication was reviewed and appropriate medicines were provided to counter the side-effects. James became more settled over the next few hours. He was provided with information about his medicines and was asked to inform the nurse if similar feelings returned.

Questions for discussion

1. How can the care team and the service user raise their awareness of medicines and their side-effects?

2. Describe the subjective and objective symptoms of akathisia and how these can be managed effectively.

3. What other side-effects of medications can contribute to misinterpretation and misunderstanding?

Wherever the service user is receiving care, appropriate information should also be provided about the expected outcomes and any potential concerns. All service users should be given relevant information about their medicines; for example, in order to facilitate concordance and an appreciation and understanding of the role of medication in their lives. The behaviour of a person experiencing inner restlessness can all too often be misunderstood as irritability and agitation. With appropriate knowledge the service user can proactively raise concerns with the practitioner.

Identifying aggressive behaviour is something that most people can manage to do instinctively. However, responding to the aggressive person may require a regime of interventions designed to raise the perpetrator's personal awareness as to how the respective behaviours impact on others.

A thorough assessment of the service user's social interaction with others and the impact of the environment will identify potential 'triggers' for emotional or aggressive behaviours (Farrell and Gray 1992). A history of previous episodes of aggression and careful listening to the service user's rationale for these provides invaluable insights into the circumstances surrounding such events. Opportunities to explore these issues with the service user should be approached with caution, avoiding provocation of further aggression. However, such opportunities are the source of assisting the service user to develop alternative strategies for behaviour and communication.

It is important to remain aware of subtle non-verbal communication as well as overtly aggressive verbal and physical behaviours. Facial expression incorporating intense staring, glaring or sarcastic sneers and smiles will telegraph the individual's underlying emotional state. Leaning over into another person's personal space or adopting a higher position than another can also be interpreted as threatening, as can the more obvious gestures such as finger-pointing, shaking fists and hand thumping (Lindenfield 1993).

Particular note should be taken of the service user's use of proximity, which normally allows for comfortable social contact at between four to twelve feet (DeVito 1996). Proximity is, however, dependent upon cultural differences.

An individual made to feel uncomfortable by the unwelcome close proximity of another may interpret the behaviour as aggressive. Vocal cues suggesting aggression include high emotional tone and pitch, loud volume, rapid speed and emphasis placed on key words within a sentence (Wilkinson and Canter 1982). These behaviours may indicate the need for the service user to consider involvement in social skills education and training programmes. Assessments related to the service user's emotional skills may indicate the need for anger management approaches and an exploration of the experiences that provoke anger. Typical trigger events for aggression will include the receipt of bad news or feelings of frustration, boredom, stress or threat. Each has the potential to provoke the response of anger and will require sensitive proactive intervention by the practitioner to avoid escalation.

EFFECTIVE INTERVENTIONS

Effective interventions by the practitioner are underpinned by capabilities in psychological and social skills. A key feature in any conflict situation is the practitioner's relationship with the service user. Intervening in potentially violent incidents can be a precarious endeavour and should never be attempted alone. The potential for defusing situations can be viewed within a cycle of events (McDonnell, McEvoy and Deardon 1994). Each event will often have been 'triggered' by a particular circumstance; for example, in Case Study 18.4 the trigger appears to be the manner in which Jack has been spoken to. Exploring previous episodes of violence with the service user may indicate patterns or trends related to the factors that trigger aggressive incidents or behaviour.

A common trigger feature can be any occasion where an act or intention by the service user is thwarted or frustrated by another person; such situations demand a sensitive respect for the service user, providing every opportunity for discussion and negotiation rather than an expectation of compliance. Where the service user has an acknowledged pattern of aggressive behaviours it is important that the management of the trigger phase is planned for. The practitioner will discuss, negotiate and agree a proactive approach, with the service user, to responding to and managing the trigger event. This will be articulated within an agreed contract or care plan document.

The avoidance of triggers, or encouragement of the service user to rethink the role of the particular trigger in creating aggressive responses, can be useful. More often than not the service user will need to practise new ways of thinking about the trigger in order to disentangle it from the previously habitual emotional response. This may also require education about emotions and how they take over one's behaviour when aroused. The escalation phase is where the incident could potentially get out of hand. Emotions begin to take hold and anger becomes a form of response to the trigger. *De-escalation* involves specific interventions designed to disrupt the escalating features of the service user's emotional presentation. An example of this might be distraction; some people can be easily distracted or diverted from the focus of their concern, allowing valuable time for their anger to dissipate until a more rational presentation allows them to look at the issues more objectively.

Again referring to the last case study, the GP distracts the attention of the two people in conflict from their behaviour by asking them both to attend the surgery. Similarly, Sharon in the first case study may have simply diverted George's attention from the issue of the missed appointment to another subject, therefore reducing the need for his anger.

A skilful practitioner can de-escalate a difficult situation by acknowledging the service user's perspective regarding the circumstances contributing to conflict. An expression of regret regarding the service user's

CASE STUDY 18.4 THE RECEPTION AREA

Jack has been receiving care in supported accommodation for several years. Whilst attending the general practice surgery with a new care team member he complains to the member of staff about the way he has been spoken to. The inexperienced staff member appears embarrassed and in need to demonstrate that he has everything under control. Squaring up to Jack, the practitioner engages him in a debate that quickly escalates into a shouting match. Jack resorts to finger-pointing and shaking his fists. As the shouting increases more people within the reception area gather around.

Discussion

This scenario suggests that Jack has been assertive in complaining about the way he has been spoken to. The practitioner's attitude is less than sensitive to Jack's concerns. The practitioner, embarrassed and lacking confidence, reacts with a confrontational stance. The fact that the situation has occurred in front of an audience drastically increases the potential for 'loss of face' and an improbable early resolution.

Outcome

Jack's GP, on hearing the noise, came into the reception area and called the two men to his surgery, advancing Jack's appointment. Both the distraction of being called and the removal of the audience offered a short time for both men to take stock of what had happened. The doctor informed the practitioner's supervisor who provided guidance and arranged for training in conflict management.

Questions for discussion

1.   What factors have contributed to this scenario and how could the care team have avoided the incident?

2.   As the practitioner's supervisor how would you now approach your next supervision session?

3.   Describe the skills development that the inexperienced practitioner might benefit from through education and training.

situation can go a long way towards entertaining a collaborative, shared and supportive stance aimed at seeking a solution. If the service user can see the practitioner as part of the solution and not part of the problem then the need for conflict can begin to dissipate. Working in collaboration with the service user the practitioner can employ understanding and empathy, both of which assist in identifying with elements promoting frustration and anger. Of vital importance to the service user will be that the practitioner is taking the expressed concerns seriously and affording the service user due validity and respect. The practitioner's rational rather than emotive perspective can therefore assist in creating a pathway towards resolution.

Inevitably, there will be those occasions where the potential for violence enters the latter phases of the 'cycle', requiring physical interventions such as 'breakaway techniques' and 'control and restraint' manoeuvres in order to maintain personal safety and the safety of the perpetrator.

DEVELOPING COMPETENCE, LEARNING FROM PRACTICE

The dynamics of many conflict situations are complex and often beyond a practitioner's immediate awareness. There may have been aspects of the individual conflict episode where the practitioner has not benefited from a conscious experience of instrumental intervention. However, these aspects may have, nevertheless, influenced the outcome of the situation. Greater awareness of the various dynamics involved can be facilitated through reflection both on and in practice.

Inevitably, there will be a phase of the post-conflict situation when the practitioner can set aside time to reflect on the effectiveness of the interventions adopted. The routine and obligatory use of post-incident review serves to promote confidence by systematically providing support and challenge to the practitioner in a manner that promotes further learning and insights.

Within the practice environment the right to adequate psychological support in the form of supervision and emotional first aid should be made available to all concerned. Post-incident review should therefore also involve the service user wherever possible. A sensitive consideration that the service user may be experiencing embarrassment, guilt and remorse for involvement in an incident of violence should be retained. It is important that the key practitioner and the service user should each revisit the episode in question and, where possible, explore the thoughts and feelings that were being experienced at the time. Particular sensitivity should be adopted when exploring and challenging the events that had led to the use of physical interventions. In addition, the potential for the service user to have experienced a re-traumatisation, concerning previous life experiences, during restraint should also be given serious consideration.

Other practitioners involved in the incident can offer to share their insights with the service user with a view to broadening an understanding of what had contributed to the violent outcome. The primary aim of such discussions should be to provide support to the service user, but they should also engage in an appraisal of the respective approaches to care with a view to avoiding future conflict.

Crucial to ongoing arrangements for care and risk management will be the relationship of the violence, its intensity and severity, with the service user's mental illness. The more extreme episodes of violence can involve service users who have entrenched ideas and perceptions of feeling threatened resulting in the perceived need to defend by attacking. Other presentations might involve emotionally impulsive behaviours where the inability to control anger spills over into rage.

In all events the service user needs to be fully engaged wherever possible in planning how to avoid and manage proactively future potential for violence and aggression. This will inevitably require the service user being motivated to be involved in the negotiated development of care plans designed to address proactively trigger situations and responses.

Within all arrangements for post-incident review, the essential values and beliefs of the service concerned, regarding degrees of tolerance for violence and aggression, should be considered against the need to report the incident to the police. Violence and aggression is an under-reported phenomenon within care situations and service users can and do build up long histories of dangerous behaviour that never come to the attention of the courts. Inevitably some service users will, for the safety of all concerned, gravitate towards care within environments that offer greater security.

EDUCATION AND TRAINING IN THE MANAGEMENT OF VIOLENCE AND AGGRESSION

The provision of education and training in the management of violence and aggression is in need of standardisation. Many practitioners simply receive training focused on the physical management of the violent individual. Such programmes are primarily designed to meet safety needs rather than develop an appropriate awareness and management of the care environment and proactive responses to conflict situations.

Figure 18.1 offers the practitioner a reference network to the many areas of skills development that should be addressed in order to demonstrate capability in the management of violence.

Figure 18.1 The Management of a violence skills network
Note: All aspects of the network contribute to the effective proactive management of violence and constitute am integrated map of practictioner capability issues. The interconnecting lines represent the roles of reflective practice and the interdependency of each part of the network with the whole.

CONCLUSION

The network of skills development should be considered by all practitioners working within potentially conflict-oriented or violent situations. Commencing with a good understanding of the dynamics related to the practice milieu, this essential information should be supplemented by a self-awareness regarding personal capability as a practitioner and the knowledge specifically required when intervening effectively in conflict situations. These three areas drawn together contribute to the emergence of safe and effective practice. The competent practitioner will be articulate in all areas of the framework and, most important, be capable of reflecting in practice, listening both visually and aurally to the respective conflict situation as it unfolds and responding according to the emerging events. Practice will always offer opportunities for learning and, regardless of the eventual outcome for each event, practitioners should entertain specific review and debriefing activities in order to refine and hone skills for the future.

REFERENCES

Alberg, C., Hatfield, B. and Huxley, P. (eds) (1996) *Learning Materials on Mental Health Risk Assessment*. Manchester: Department of Health, University of Manchester.

Appleby, L., Shaw, J., Sherratt, J., Amos, T., Robinson, J. and McDonnell, R. (2001) *Safety First. Report of the National Confidential Inquiry into Suicide and Homicide by People with Mental Illness*. London: The Stationery Office.

Chin, C.J. (1998) 'Dangerousness: Myth or clinical reality?' *Psychiatric Care 5*, 2, 66–71.

DeVito, J. (1996) *Essentials of Human Communication*. Second edition. New York: HarperCollins.

DH (Department of Health) (1990) *The Care Programme Approach Guidance on an Approach to Provide a Network of Care in the Community, for People with Severe Mental Illness, which would Minimise the Risk that they Lose Contact with Services*. Department of Health Circular HC(90)23. London: Department of Health.

Farrell, G.A. and Gray, C. (1992) *Aggression: A Nurses' Guide to Therapeutic Management*. London: Scutari Press.

Fontana, D. (1990) *Social Skills at Work*. London: The British Psychological Society in association with Routledge Ltd.

Goleman, D. (1996) *Emotional Intelligence: Why it can Matter More than IQ*. London: Bloomsbury Publishing.

Hodgins, S. and Muller-Isberner, R. (2000) 'Evidence based treatment for mentally disordered offenders.' In S. Hodgins and R. Muller-Isberner (eds) *Violence, Crime and Mentally Disordered Offenders: The Concepts and Methods for Effective Treatment and Prevention*. Chichester: John Wiley and Sons.

Holland, S., Orr, J. and Soar, C. (1992) *Managing Aggression*. London: Distance Learning Centre, Technopark, Polytechnic of the South Bank.

HSE (Health and Safety Executive) (1997) *Violence and Aggression to Staff in Health Services: Guidance on Assessment and Management*. Sudbury: HSE Books.

Lindenfield, G. (1993) *Managing Anger: Positive Strategies for Dealing with Difficult Emotions*. Glasgow: Thorsons.

McDonnell, A., McEvoy, J. and Deardon, R.L. (1994) 'Coping with violent situations in the caring environment.' In T. Wykes (ed.) *Violence and Health Care Professionals*. London: Chapman and Hall.

RCPCRU (Royal College of Psychiatrists College of Research Unit) (1998) *Management of Imminent Violence: Clinical Practice Guidelines to Support Mental Health Services*. RCPCRU Occasional Paper OP41. London: RCPCRU.

Schon, D.A. (1983) *The Reflective Practitioner: How Professionals Think in Action*. New York: Basic Books Inc.

Sutherland, V.J. and Cooper, C.L. (1990) *Understanding Stress: A Psychological Perspective for Health Professionals*. London: Chapman and Hall.

Thompson, T. and Mathias, P. (1994) 'Antidiscriminatory practice.' In T. Thompson and P. Mathias (eds) *Lyttle's Mental Health and Disorder*. Second edition. London: Baillière Tindall.

Wilkinson, J. and Canter, S. (1982) *Social Skills Training Manual Assessment, Programme Design and Management of Training*. Chichester: John Wiley and Sons.

Williams, P. and Dale, C. (2001) 'The application of values in working with service users in forensic mental health settings.' In C. Dale and T. Thompson, *Forensic Mental Health Issues in Practice*. London: Harcourt Publishers Ltd.

Wright, S., Gray, R., Parkes, J. and Gournay, K. (2001) *The Recognition, Prevention and Therapeutic Management of Violence in Mental Health Care*. London: United Kingdom Central Council for Nursing, Midwifery and Health Visiting.

FURTHER READING

Beadsmore, A., Moore, C., Muijen, M., Shepherd, G., Warren, J., Moore, W. and Wolf, J. (1998) *Acute Problems: A Survey of the Quality of Care in Acute Psychiatric Wards*. London: The Sainsbury Centre for Mental Health.

Bolt, E. and Powell, J. (1993) *Becoming Reflective*. London: Distance Learning Centre, South Bank University.

Department of Health (1989) *Homes are for Living In: A Model for Evaluating Quality of Care Provided, and Quality of Life Experienced, in Residential Care Homes for Elderly People*. London: HMSO.

Department of Health (1999) *Mental Health Nursing: 'Addressing Acute Concerns'*. Report of the Standing Nursing and Midwifery Advisory Committee. London: DH.

Department of Health (2000) *Withholding Treatment from Violent and Abusive Service Users in NHS Trusts*. Resource Guide, NHS Zero Tolerance. London: DH.

Lindenfield, G. (1995) *Self Esteem*. Glasgow: Thorsons Publishers.

Littlechild, B. (1997) *Dealing With Aggression: Practitioners Guide*. Birmingham: Venture Press.

Royal College of Nursing (1997) *The Management of Aggression and Violence in Places of Care*. A Royal College of Nursing positional statement. London: Royal College of Nursing.

Webster, C.D., Eaves, D., Douglas, K.S. and Wintrup, A. (1995) *The HCR-20 Scheme: The Assessment of Dangerousness and Risk*. Vancouver, BC: Mental Health Law and Policy Institute, and Forensic Psychiatric Services Commission of British Columbia.

ACKNOWLEDGEMENTS

I would like to thank Tony Ryan, Service Development Manager and Senior Research Fellow at the Health and Social Care Advisory Service for the support and guidance he has provided me during the development of this chapter. Also thanks are due to Mr Billy Watt, Personal Safety Coordinator and Nurse Manager at Lancashire Care NHS Trust, England, for assisting in the collation of relevant literature.

GLOSSARY

Affective disorders

Affective disorders are disorders of mood. The term is used for a group of conditions that relate to a person's mood including depression, anxiety and mania (extreme elation). Affective disorders can be observed in both psychotic (e.g. psychotic depression, manic depression and mania) and non-psychotic (e.g. anxiety and depression) forms.

Akathisia

Akathisia is a common, unpleasant side effect of many anti-psychotic medications. In its milder form, the person taking medicines may appear anxious, but severe forms can involve feelings of tension, panic, marked irritability and impatience. The service user experiencing akathisia may complain of restlessness accompanied by movements such as fidgeting of the legs, rocking from foot to foot, pacing, or an inability to sit or stand. The subjective experience of akathisia may be indistinguishable from the ongoing symptoms of illness. The associated severe anxiety can exacerbate a psychosis resulting in an increased risk of violence. Misdiagnosis, resulting in the treatment of anxiety with further medication, will further exacerbate the condition. Commonly, the medical management of akathisia will involve a reduction in dosage of the drug that is provoking the condition and the prescription of other medicines to counter the side effect. In extreme cases the offending medicine may have to be discontinued.

Alcohol and drug misuse

Alcohol is a tranquilliser and is addictive. Whilst taken in moderation it can have some health benefits, but it also causes significant physical and mental health problems when misused. Apart from nicotine, alcohol is the most misused drug in the West. It can cause depression and is implicated in a large number of deaths by suicide. Alcohol can also cause a wide range of physical health problems and is implicated in around 30,000 deaths each year in the UK. In extreme cases it can cause brain damage, one example being Korsakoff's syndrome which is caused by lack of thiamine (vitamin B1) and is characterised by short-term memory impairment. Other drugs result in fewer deaths by comparison to alcohol but do create significant social problems in respect of acquisitive crime associated with maintaining the addiction.

Drug misuse often refers to drugs other than alcohol, illicit and prescribed. Illicit drugs include opiates such as heroin, hallucinogens such as LSD and magic mushrooms, and stimulants such as cocaine, 'crack' cocaine, ecstasy and amphetamine sulphate (or 'speed'). Opiate-based analgesics (such as codeine and dihydrocodeine), sedatives and benzodiazepines are also popular drugs of abuse and all create dependency, whether this is physical, psychological or both. Solvents and a number of glues are also misused by some people.

In cases of alcohol or opiate dependency, detoxification may be necessary, either through a home-based programme or in a specialist facility or hospital unit. This involves substituting the alcohol or opiate for another drug and weaning the person off this. Unlike withdrawal from opiates, alcohol withdrawal has been fatal in a small number of cases. Withdrawal from both alcohol and opiates can cause seizures if not managed effectively. Ongoing support is best provided through talking therapies, and agencies such as Alcoholics Anonymous and Narcotics Anonymous have been shown to be effective. This may also need to be in conjunction with support for housing and other social issues.

It is also possible to substitute opiates with methadone and remain on a maintenance dose. This is particularly useful in cases of addiction where the person finds the psychological dependency too strong to cease taking the opiate but would prefer the safer lifestyle created by this approach. It can lead to subsequent 'weaning off' at a later stage through reducing the methadone gradually.

Alzheimer's disease and dementia
Dementias mainly affect older people, although not exclusively. One in five people over 80 experience some degree of dementia, although a small number of people experience dementias before the age of 65. Dementias can cause people to be forgetful, have difficulty in expressing themselves as they would like and reduce their cognitive functioning. Many other effects include anxiety and depression, personality changes, out-of-character behaviours and loss of the ability to look after oneself. Although the exact causes are not known there is evidence to suggest that the most common form of dementia, *Alzheimer's disease*, can run in families. Other causes include cardiovascular attacks (or strokes), infections (such as Creutzfeldt-Jakob syndrome or AIDS) and lack of vitamins (such as Korsakoff's syndrome caused by thiamine deficiency). Dementias are degenerative diseases that can develop and progress rapidly over a few months or

more slowly over several years. They are not reversible although in some cases their progress can be slowed through medication and use of strategies designed to manage everyday life, such as memory aids.

Anorexia nervosa and bulimia nervosa

Anorexia nervosa and bulimia nervosa are the two main eating disorders. Anorexia is characterised by an extreme loss of weight resulting from excessive dieting. The sufferer has a distorted body image and believes that s/he is fat and overweight. If untreated anorexia sufferers can die, although with treatment many will make a full recovery. Anorexia is much more common in young women, although occasionally young men are also known to experience this illness.

Bulimia nervosa is much more common than anorexia with sufferers concerned that they may gain weight. It is characterised by food craving and binge eating which is followed by the person making him-/herself sick or by overuse of laxatives to remove what s/he has eaten.

Psychotherapy and family therapy are often useful in helping the person to change his/her view of him-/herself and for those around him/her to provide support. In extreme cases people may need hospitalisation to manage weight loss. Cognitive behaviour therapy is often useful in helping the person to manage his/her self-image.

Anxiety disorders

It is normal to experience some level of anxiety and at times it can help to improve performance. However, when feelings of fear are overwhelming and are out of proportion to the situation or experience they can form a disorder. Anxiety is experienced as a combination of physical and psychological symptoms. The psychical symptoms can include shaking, sweating, raised pulse/heart rate, dry mouth, dizziness and breathlessness; while psychological symptoms can include feelings of dread and fear. Anxiety states are diagnosed more frequently in women than men and, as with depression, this may be the result of women being more likely to seek help than men. Anxiety states are one of the most common forms of mental illness and also easily evoke empathy as most people have experienced being anxious at some point in their lives. Treatment can involve talking therapies and anxiety management techniques such as relaxation and breathing exercises. Medication can also help but should be used only in the short term given that many anxiolytics are addictive if taken long term. Their effectiveness also decreases with excessive use. Anxiety disorders can include generalised anxiety, panic disorder, post-traumatic stress disorder and phobias.

Delusions

Delusions are falsely held beliefs that are strongly held by the person and inappropriate to the intelligence of the person, their culture or background. The belief will be fixed and intensely held. For example, the person may believe that s/he has supernatural powers or is being observed by beings from another planet. Sometimes the beliefs may be less outrageous but equally untrue.

Depression

As with anxiety disorders most people have experienced low moods where they feel 'blue' or 'down' and can therefore empathise to some degree with people who experience clinical depression. Along with anxiety disorders, depression is a common form of mental illness. Depression is often experienced through feelings of very low mood, poor sleep pattern, lethargy (or overactivity in the case of agitated depression), isolation, loss of appetite and loss of volition. Depression can have physical causes, such as infections or thyroid dysfunction, but is commonly triggered by life events such as bereavement. However, in some cases there may be no apparent cause. Various talking therapies are effective, particularly where the cause is known, and they can be provided in one-to-one settings or groups. Exercise is also known to be helpful. Medication may be useful but, as with anxiolytics, long-term use of anti-depressants should be avoided as they can create dependency and become less effective over time. In some cases electroconvulsive therapy may be needed. Although this may sound extreme it can be very effective, particularly in cases where responses to other treatments have been ineffective.

Electroconvulsive therapy (ECT)

Originally developed as a treatment for schizophrenia, ECT is now given for severe depressive illnesses that prove resistive to drug treatments. It is a controversial treatment but has been shown to be far more effective than anti-depressant drugs and placebos. It induces a seizure by passing electric currents bilaterally (at each temple) or unilaterally (to a single temple) and is administered under general anaesthetic with a muscle relaxant. Treatment is given in a course, usually twice a week with two days between treatments, unless signs of the depression lifting are observed. Courses of treatment may vary in number from six or eight up to twenty in extreme cases. Some people experience short-term memory loss, although there have been reports of long-lasting memory impairment.

Manic depression/bipolar disorder

People with this condition may experience wide fluctuations in mood, or either severe 'highs' or severe 'lows' by themselves. Features of the manic or high phase may include grandiose delusions, hyperactivity, pressure of speech or pressure of thought (where they cannot process thoughts or words as fast as they would like because they are continuous), restlessness and poor sleep patterns. Sufferers are extremely vulnerable as they do not have any insight into their condition and often will do things that are out of character and that they later regret, such as being promiscuous or financially irresponsible. There is some evidence that manic depression runs in families and is caused by physiology rather than other factors, hence it is very receptive to being controlled by medicines such as lithium carbonate. The depressed phase is very similar to other forms of depression and requires similar interventions. However, periods of depression may be greater for people with a bipolar disorder and they may also experience violent fluctuations in mood, particularly if they cease taking medications. This condition is as common in men as it is in women.

Obsessive-compulsive disorder (OCD)

Obsessions can be described as thoughts that a person experiences that seem trivial or unpleasant and which s/he does not feel s/he has control over. Compulsions are things that people feel they need to do and feel powerless to prevent themselves for doing even if they do not want to. OCD can affect people of all ages and exists where both these features are present. Cognitive behaviour therapy and other talking treatments are the most effective methods of dealing with this condition, although in some cases medication may be required, particularly if the person is experiencing anxiety or depression as a result of the OCD.

Personality disorders

There are a wide range of conditions and behaviour patterns that form personality disorders. They are often first observed in childhood or adolescence and, while they may coexist with other mental illnesses, are most frequently found as a single diagnosis. They are long-term maladaptive conditions that can be characterised by distorted perceptions, mood disturbances, lack of control over impulses and high levels of expressed emotions and anxiety. There is some dispute about the usefulness of interventions, although talking and behavioural treatments appear to have some efficacy. Personality disorders are mental disorders but not mental illnesses. In a small number of cases people with a personality disorder may be dangerous, although in most cases they present a greater danger to themselves through suicide and self-injury.

Postnatal mental illnesses

Sometimes referred to as 'puerperal psychoses' this condition usually develops shortly after a woman has given birth and is thought to be related to hormonal changes at the end of the pregnancy and after the birth of the child. It is very rare, although a woman who has experienced it once is likely to be at increased risk in the future. It can manifest in three main forms: mania, depression and schizophrenia. In some cases combinations of these forms of illness can be found. Puerperal psychosis responds extremely well to interventions, particularly if treatment is commenced quickly. There is rarely any wilful danger to the child, although neglect may occur. Treatment is usually best provided in an inpatient setting and medications are almost always necessary, such as anti-depressants or anti-psychotics. Education afterwards is essential in order that the mother may consider the costs and benefits to having further children.

Psychosis

A psychosis may feature disorders of thought, perception, speech, mood and behaviour. Thought disorders may include delusions (where the person has a fixed belief about something that is not correct), incoherence, ideas of reference (where the person believes that events have a special meaning or relate particularly to them when in reality it has no relation to them) or paranoid beliefs. Disorder of perceptions may include hallucinations (commonly seeing or hearing things that others do not, although hallucinations relating to other senses can be experienced). Speech disorders may include rambling, flight of ideas (where the person moves quickly from one subject to another) or pressure of speech (characterised by excessive speed or content or both). Mood disorders may range from being emotionless through to euphoria. Behaviour disorders may include agitation, hyperactivity, retardation and impulsivity.

Schizophrenia

Schizophrenia usually affects the way a person feels, thinks and behaves and can be experienced as a one-off short-term episode or a life-long condition. It is characterised by a wide range of symptoms including hallucinations (sensory experiences that are real only to the person, such as hearing voices or seeing people that no one else hears or sees), delusions (fixed beliefs that are irrational to others, such as being an important historical figure or being under the control of the secret services), mood disorders (flattening of affect through to elation), apathy and lack of insight. People with schizophrenia are significantly more likely to harm themselves than anyone else and are often extremely vulnerable, particularly if not treated effectively. Schizophrenia affects men more than women and is probably the most stigmatised of all of the mental disorders, due in part to the way that the media erroneously depicts this condition. Treatments can involve a combination of medications, talking treatments, psychoeducation and various forms of social support. During acute phases people may require hospitalisation, although many people are now supported effectively in the community without ever being admitted to hospital.

There are a wide range of theories about the cause of schizophrenia including genetics, social deprivation, stress and changes in brain chemistry or structure. It is probably true that each of these may be related to the development of schizophrenia, either as individual causes or in combinations.

Severe and enduring mental illness

Any mental illness that is extremely disabling through its symptoms or its consequences which is long-lasting may be referred to as a severe and enduring mental illness. Many people, although not all, who experience schizophrenia may experience the condition as a life-long illness from the period of onset. Other conditions such as depression, anxiety disorders and bipolar disorders may also be experienced as a disabling and long-term condition.

LIST OF CONTRIBUTORS

Lynn Agnew has over twenty years' experience in the mental health field. After qualifying as a social worker she practised in adult and then adolescent services, undertaking further training in counselling and systemic family therapy. She became an Approved Social Worker in 1984. Moving into training, she developed courses for mental health and social care staff, service users and carers in the statutory and voluntary sectors. In 1995 she became the manager of an integrated community mental health team. Two years ago she left to become the manager of the planning and performance team of a social services department.

Piers Allott is from a social work, management and health-planning background and has experience in the design and delivery of community-based mental health services in the UK and overseas. He is committed to the development of self-management approaches to recovery, recovery-oriented personal supports and services and services run by 'experts by experience'. He is Senior Service Development Fellow at the University of Wolverhampton and the NIMHE (National Institute for Mental Health in England) Fellow for Recovery.

Carey Bamber has worked in mental health services for the past twelve years and is also a user of services. Over this time she has worked in advocacy and user-involvement work programmes across the range of services in the north-west region, and has also served as a Mental Health Act Commissioner since 1995. She is currently Service Development Manager with the National Institute for Mental Health England (NIMHE), based with the North West Regional Development Centre, where she takes a lead on service user, carer and voluntary sector work programmes. Carey is an avid scuba diver, and mother to two-year-old Marcie.

Roy Butterworth (MBA (Distinction), BA(Hons) Health Studies, DMS, RMN) has extensive experience in the evaluation and development of mental health care practice and is currently employed within secure mental health services in Preston. He is particularly interested in the facilitation of effective care provision through the development of mental health practitioners and the organisational environments within which they engage with service users.

Jane Gilbert has extensive clinical and managerial experience within NHS mental health services, both at primary and secondary care levels, most recently as Acting Director of Psychological Services, Dumfries and Galloway Primary Care Trust. She has an excellent understanding of managing change, and is able to provide sensitive negotiation and facilitation skills. Jane is now freelance and has carried out independent consultancy in mental health, both in the UK and Africa. She has designed and delivered workshops to staff in various settings and is able to facilitate the development of creative solutions to complex problems.

Sandra Griffiths manages The Mellow Campaign, a partnership programme that targets young African and Caribbean men with mental health difficulties in East London and that is well respected locally and nationally. The campaign is known for its cutting edge and creative solutions in addressing the over-representation of young black men in the mental health system. Sandra's work over the last twelve years reflects her commitment to promoting healthier outcomes for black and minority ethnic communities. She has played an active role in setting up both services and campaigns around both physical and mental health services.

Barbara Hatfield is Lecturer in Psychiatric Social Work and Director of the Mental Health Social Work Research Unit in the Department of Psychiatry at the University of Manchester. She has a background in local authority social work, both mental health and child care practice. She is involved in the training of mental health social workers and Approved Social Workers, and researches and publishes widely in the field of mental health law and services. Barbara is also an approved assessor for the GSCC mental health award.

Rick Henderson is currently Director of Advocacy Across London, the resource and support agency for London's advocacy sector. Rick is an Associate Fellow of the School of Health and Social Studies and has over fifteen years' experience of managing and developing advocacy services. His publications include *A Right Result? Advocacy, Justice and Empowerment* (2001, Policy Press) and *Protocol for PALS and Independent Advocacy Working Together* (2002, NHS London Regional Office).

David Hewitt is a solicitor and a partner with Hempsons, one of the country's pre-eminent health care law firms. He has been involved in many human rights cases, on behalf of patients and service users, NHS bodies and statutory authorities. David has been a member of the Mental Health Act Commission since 1995 and sits on the editorial board of the *Journal of Mental Health Law*. He is a frequent contributor to the *New Law Journal* and has lectured to professional and academic audiences throughout England and overseas. He contributed a chapter on mental health law to Christopher Baker (ed.), *The Human Rights Act 1998: A Practitioner's Guide* (1999, Sweet and Maxwell).

Mark Holland has worked with the severely mentally ill in a range of settings for twenty years. The prevalence of drug and alcohol misuse in inner-city Manchester is such that the majority of service users at some time in their lives are affected by it. Mark leads a managed practitioner network across the city to meet dual diagnosis needs. He has visited services in North America, Australia and at home in the UK helping inform local and national developments in the field. He is currently a member of the national forum of nurse consultants in dual diagnosis which act as an advisory group and is a strong supporter of the mainstreaming of substance misuse interventions in psychiatry.

Ruth Ingram is possibly the only person in the country to date to have held the post of adult protection coordinator in two different local authorities. She currently works in Bradford. Amongst other occupations, she has worked for Leeds Inter-agency Project (Women and Violence), developing practice in health and social services in relation to domestic violence (including in mental health services), and worked with young women fleeing sexual abuse in their families. She was a founder member of Re*Sisters* – Leeds Women and Mental Health Action Group. She has worked with youth arts and social housing projects, run a tour company, been a gardener, a play worker and a residential care worker.

Vall Midson has worked as a CPN for the past twenty-two years. After training at Prestwich Hospital in Greater Manchester she spent six years nursing in North Wales. Since returning to Manchester she has worked in the north of the city. Over the past fifteen years she has worked with homeless people including setting up joint working partnerships with local statutory and voluntary agencies, which received national awards and recognition. Currently working as a CPN in a mental health team, Vall has a special interest in dual diagnosis. As a trainer and supervisor, primarily in this field of dual diagnosis, she plays a key role in developing the city's dual diagnosis initiative.

Karen Newbigging is currently Director of Mental Health for the Health and Social Care Advisory Service. She originally trained and worked as a clinical psychologist for sixteen years. She worked as a lead commissioner for mental health services before joining the Centre for Mental Health Services Development in 1999 to establish a regional development centre. She has worked extensively with community mental health teams: as a member, as a commissioner and latterly providing development support through evaluation, team development and service development. Karen has a broad range of interests in mental health including health inequalities, primary care, implementing evidence-based approaches and whole system development.

Debbie Nixon is Programme Coordinator for Primary Care for NIMHE North West Development Centre. She is also the NIMHE Link for the Cheshire and Merseyside Strategic Health Authority (SHA) area. Debbie has worked in the NHS in the north-west for the past twenty years in a variety of clinical, managerial and commissioning roles. She became involved in the development of mental health services in the mid-1990s when she implemented a primary care mental health service model within two GP fundholding practices. This service was identified as a first-wave NHS beacon site for primary care and mental health. She was appointed as mental health commissioning lead for Chester City PCT and expanded the service to enable full population coverage, improving equity and access to a range of interventions for service users in primary care.

Alison Pearsall is an experienced mental health practitioner who has worked in a variety of hospital and community settings, ranging from acute inpatient, forensic, substance misuse and the community, since 1983. Alison now manages a prison in-reach service in several Lancashire prisons. She also works as an associate consultant for the Health and Social Care Advisory Service, and has been involved with the coordination of the North West Suicide Prevention Network, a national project aiming to improve access for people with learning disabilities to mental health care and the reviewing of out-of-district placements for people with serious mental illness in the north-west.

Rob Poole trained at St George's Hospital, London, and in Oxford. Since 1988 he was a consultant psychiatrist in Liverpool until he moved to North Wales in 2004. He is a community psychiatrist whose primary interest is in the mental health of deprived and marginalised populations. He has been closely involved in developing new ways of working; for example, establishing a homelessness outreach team in Liverpool. He has previously written on a range of subjects including 'drug-induced psychosis', parental psychiatric disorder, and long-term psychiatric care in the private sector. He is a musician and has written about psychiatry and music.

Simon Rippon qualified as a psychiatric nurse in 1987 and has worked in a variety of mental health settings, more recently as a nurse consultant. His clinical and practice training has included postgraduate programmes related to cognitive behavioural therapy for those experiencing psychosis and psychosocial interventions for serious mental health problems. Simon has more recently been involved in a number of national health policy guidance developments and has provided consultancy to a range of national mental health development agencies. He has experience of training and practice development in both health and social care organisations. Currently Simon is a programme coordinator with the NIMHE North West Development Centre, where he leads on work related to leadership and team effectiveness and service redesign.

Tim Saunders has been a full-time GP in Chester since 1988 and has been actively involved in change management and service development during the 1990s. Tim is involved in undergraduate education with students from the University of Liverpool. His interest in mental health has contributed to the development of an NHS beacon site for primary care mental health services in Chester. He has presented this work with colleagues at national and local conferences around the UK. He has also published articles on mental health issues in primary care. Tim has also worked as an independent consultant for the National Institute for Mental Health England (North West) Regional Development Centre, the Health Advisory and Social Care Advisory Service and the Sainsbury Centre for Mental Health.

Jacquie White has been a mental health nurse for seventeen years. She became interested in the discrepancy between the medication management people receive in clinical trials as opposed to clinical practice when working as a research nurse. In 1999 she conducted a study into the role of the nurse in medication management on the acute unit which was supported by a Band Trust Research Scholarship from the Florence Nightingale Foundation. Dissemination of the results led to funding for a local medication management practice development project. In July 2001 she completed the first 'Train the Trainers' course in medication management at the Institute of Psychiatry. Jacquie now works as a lecturer in clinical nursing at the University of Hull and facilitates the Hull and East Riding Medication Management Network.

Rhian Williams acquired an honours degree in humanities in 1979 having specialised in philosophy and social anthropology. Following this she did a postgraduate nursing course and, having then spent a period of time travelling, consolidated her nursing experience in Sheffield. She trained as a health visitor in London in 1985 and started her health-visiting career in Tower Hamlets. She has worked in a variety of settings since. Rhian's ongoing interest and involvement in social exclusion led to her current post as a health worker for refugees and asylum seekers in Wandsworth Primary Care Trust. This three-year Health Improvement Project has been successfully developed over the past two years and will become an established post in the trust next year. Rhian currently lives with her son in South London.

Linda Williamson trained as both a general nurse and a health visitor and developed an interest in socially excluded groups. She is currently employed by Wandsworth Primary Care Trust as a specialist nurse for homeless people. Linda is working to expand the existing health team for homeless refugees and asylum seekers. She is current Joint Chair of the London Standing Conference for Nurses – Homeless Group, and a member of the CPVHA Special Interest Group for homeless refugees and asylum seekers. She has, in addition, contributed to family policies for the Bed and Breakfast Unit.

Melba Wilson is Chair of Wandsworth Primary Care Trust. She has also recently been appointed as Black and Minority Ethnic Mental Health Service Improvement Leader. This is a joint post between the London Mental Health Development Centre and the Greater London Authority. Melba is a former journalist.

Lillian Yates is a carer and the Patient Advice and Liaison Officer for Pennine Care NHS Trust with responsibility for the five boroughs covered by this specialist mental health trust. Although she feels that it is important that carers are given support together with information about illness and medication, it is vital that they are given hope. She is a BACP counsellor in training and hopes to offer counselling to carers when she qualifies. She is particularly interested in early-onset psychosis and the part that family intervention can play in recovery and the prevention of relapse.

Subject Index

340

AUTHOR INDEX